First World War
and Army of Occupation
War Diary
France, Belgium and Germany

50 DIVISION
Divisional Troops
252 Brigade Royal Field Artillery
5 August 1914 - 31 August 1915

WO95/2817/4

The Naval & Military Press Ltd
www.nmarchive.com
Published in association with The National Archives

Published by

The Naval & Military Press Ltd

Unit 10 Ridgewood Industrial Park,

Uckfield, East Sussex,

TN22 5QE England

Tel: +44 (0) 1825 749494

www.naval-military-press.com

www.nmarchive.com

This diary has been reprinted in facsimile from the original. Any imperfections are inevitably reproduced and the quality may fall short of modern type and cartographic standards.

© Crown Copyright
Images reproduced by permission of The National Archives, London, England, 2015.

Contents

Document type	Place/Title	Date From	Date To
Heading	WO95/2817-4		
Miscellaneous	50th Division 3rd Northumbrian Bde Became 252nd Bde RFA Apr 1915-Jan 1917 & 1-1st Durham Battery Jun-Sep 1915		
Heading	50th Division 3rd Northumbrian Bde RFA Vol I 17.4-30.5.15		
War Diary	NW Castle on Tyne	17/04/1915	17/04/1915
War Diary	Southampton	18/04/1915	18/04/1915
War Diary	Havre	19/04/1915	19/04/1915
War Diary	Hazebrouck	20/04/1915	20/04/1915
War Diary	Rouge Croix	21/04/1915	23/04/1915
War Diary	Beethen	24/04/1915	24/04/1915
War Diary	Rouge Croix	24/04/1915	25/04/1915
War Diary	Rattekot Imn	25/04/1915	26/04/1915
War Diary	St Laurent	26/04/1915	25/05/1915
War Diary	Ypres	26/05/1915	30/05/1915
Miscellaneous	A Form Messages And Signals.		
Operation(al) Order(s)	Operation Order No. D.M.37 By Lieut Col G.T Pearson R.F.A. commanding 3rd Northumbrian Brigade R.F.A.	18/05/1915	18/05/1915
Heading	50th Division 3rd North Bn. Bde RFA Vol II 30.5-29.6.15		
War Diary		30/05/1915	09/06/1915
War Diary	Ypres	09/06/1915	22/06/1915
War Diary	Neuve Eglise	23/06/1915	29/06/1915
Miscellaneous	A Form Messages And Signals		
Miscellaneous	O.C.3rd Inf. Bde. R.F.A.	31/05/1915	31/05/1915
Miscellaneous	A Form Messages And Signals		
Operation(al) Order(s)	50th Division Operation Order No. 3	05/06/1915	05/06/1915
Operation(al) Order(s)	50th Division Operation Order No. 4	10/06/1915	10/06/1915
Operation(al) Order(s)	50th Division Operation Order No. 6	15/06/1915	15/06/1915
Miscellaneous	50th Divisional Artillery Operation Order	15/06/1915	15/06/1915
Miscellaneous	O.C. 3rd Northumbrian Brigade R.F.A.	18/06/1915	18/06/1915
Operation(al) Order(s)	50th Division Operation Order No. 7	18/06/1915	18/06/1915
Operation(al) Order(s)	50th Division Operation Order No. 8	19/06/1915	19/06/1915
Miscellaneous	Table Of Moves And Reliefs-50th. Divisional Artillery		
Miscellaneous	March Table	19/06/1915	19/06/1915
Miscellaneous	3rd Northumbrian Brigade R.F.A.	20/06/1915	20/06/1915
Miscellaneous	Moves And Reliefs Of Units 50th Divisional Artillery		
Operation(al) Order(s)	50th Division Operation Order No. 9	24/06/1915	24/06/1915
Miscellaneous	3rd Northumbrian Brigade R.F.A.	28/06/1915	28/06/1915
Heading	50th Division 3rd Northumbrian Bde R.F.A. (addition To) Vol II 14.6.15		
War Diary	Ypres	14/06/1915	14/06/1915
Heading	50th Division 1/3rd North Bn Bde R.F.A. Vol III 1-31-15		
War Diary	Neuve Eglise	30/06/1915	18/07/1915
War Diary	Pont De Nieppe	19/07/1915	19/07/1915
War Diary	Armentieres	20/07/1915	31/07/1915
Operation(al) Order(s)	50th Division Operation Order No. 10	11/07/1915	11/07/1915
Miscellaneous	War Diary Copy	11/07/1915	11/07/1915

Type	Description	Date From	Date To
Miscellaneous	3rd Northumbrian Brigade R.F.A.	11/07/1915	11/07/1915
Operation(al) Order(s)	50th Division Operation Order No. 11	13/07/1915	13/07/1915
Operation(al) Order(s)	50th Division Operation Order No. 12	15/07/1915	15/07/1915
Miscellaneous	March Table		
Miscellaneous	Addition To Operation Order No. 12	15/07/1915	15/07/1915
Operation(al) Order(s)	50th Divisional Artillery Operation Order No. 8	16/07/1915	16/07/1915
Miscellaneous	3rd Northumbrian Brigade R.F.A.	16/07/1915	16/07/1915
Miscellaneous	Operation Orders By Lieut col. G.T Pearson. R.F.A. (T)	17/07/1915	17/07/1915
Heading	50th Division 3rd North'bn Bde R.F.A. Vol IV From 1st To 28th August 1915		
War Diary	Armentieres	01/08/1915	28/08/1915
Operation(al) Order(s)	50th Divisional Operation Order No. 3	14/08/1915	14/08/1915
Miscellaneous	Operation Order No by Lt Col G.T Pearson Comdg 3rd Northumbrian Bde RFA.	15/08/1915	15/08/1915
Operation(al) Order(s)	Operation Order No. 13 by Brigadier General J.S.M. Shea C.B D.S.O. Commanding 151st Infantry Brigade	18/08/1915	18/08/1915
Heading	50th Division 3rd Northumbrian Bde RFA Vol V (aug &) Sept1.15		
War Diary	Armentieres	29/08/1915	30/09/1915
Miscellaneous	B Form Messages And Signals.		
Operation(al) Order(s)	Operation Orders No.17 By Brigadier General J.S.M Shea C.B D.S.O. Commanding 151st Infantry Brigade	11/09/1915	11/09/1915
Operation(al) Order(s)	Operation Orders No.18 By Brigadier General J.S.M Shea C.B D.S.O. Commanding 151st Infantry Brigade	17/09/1915	17/09/1915
Miscellaneous	3rd Northumbrian Brigade R.F.A.	17/09/1915	17/09/1915
Operation(al) Order(s)	Operation Orders No.19 By Brigadier General J.S.M Shea C.B D.S.O. Commanding 151st Infantry Brigade	22/09/1915	22/09/1915
Operation(al) Order(s)	50th Division Operation Order No. 13	24/09/1915	24/09/1915
Miscellaneous	Special Instructions To C.R.A. Infantry Brigade Commanding	24/09/1915	24/09/1915
Operation(al) Order(s)	50th Divisional Artillery Operation Order No. 4	24/09/1915	24/09/1915
Miscellaneous	3rd Northumbrian Brigade R.F.A.	24/09/1915	24/09/1915
Miscellaneous	50th Divisional Artillery. Artillery Programme	25/09/1915	25/09/1915
Miscellaneous	50th Divisional Artillery Operations	25/09/1915	25/09/1915
Miscellaneous	3rd Northumbrian Brigade R.F.A.	24/09/1915	24/09/1915
Miscellaneous	50th Divisional Artillery Operations	25/09/1915	25/09/1915
Miscellaneous	Headquarters 50th Division	24/09/1915	24/09/1915
Operation(al) Order(s)	50th Division Operation Order No. 14	26/09/1915	26/09/1915
Operation(al) Order(s)	50th Division Operation Order No. 15	27/09/1915	27/09/1915
Heading	50th Divn 3rd Northumbrian Bde RFA Vol VI Oct 15		
War Diary	Armentieres	01/10/1915	31/10/1915
Miscellaneous	3rd Northbn Bde R.F.A.	04/10/1915	04/10/1915
Miscellaneous	3rd Northbn Bde R.F.A.	11/10/1915	11/10/1915
Miscellaneous	Operation Orders	13/10/1915	13/10/1915
Miscellaneous	3rd Northbn Bde RFA	12/10/1915	12/10/1915
Miscellaneous	2nd Corps G.8.	11/10/1915	11/10/1915
Miscellaneous	Reference Sheet 36. N.W.		
Miscellaneous	50th. Divn. G.S.64	13/10/1915	13/10/1915
Miscellaneous	B.H./612/5.	14/10/1915	14/10/1915
Miscellaneous	Reference Sheet 36. N.W.		
Miscellaneous	Operation Orders By Lieut Col.G.T. Pearson R.F.A. For 21st October 1915	21/10/1915	21/10/1915
Miscellaneous	3rd North Bde R.F.A.	21/10/1915	21/10/1915
Miscellaneous	Operation Orders By Lieut col G.T Pearson R.F.A. (T) Commanding 3rd Northumbrian Brigade R.F.A. for Saturday Oct 23rd And Sunday 24th Oct 1915	22/10/1915	22/10/1915

Miscellaneous	O.C. 3rd Nth. Bde. R.F.A.	14/10/1915	14/10/1915
Miscellaneous	Arrangements For Demonstration On Our Front:-	11/10/1915	11/10/1915
Miscellaneous	50th Division		
Heading	50th Div 3rd Northumbrian Bde RFA Dec Vol VIII		
Heading	3rd Northumbrian Brigade R.F.A. (T) 50th Division November 1915 Vol VII		
War Diary	Noote Boom	01/11/1915	13/12/1915
War Diary	Hondeghem	17/12/1915	20/12/1915
War Diary	Kruisstraat	21/12/1915	31/12/1915
Miscellaneous	Operation Orders By Orders By Lieut Colonel G.T. Pearson R.F.A. (T) Commanding 3rd Northumbrian Brigade R.F.A.	03/12/1915	03/12/1915
Miscellaneous	Operation Orders By Orders By Lieut Colonel G.T. Pearson R.F.A. (T) Commanding 3rd Northumbrian Brigade R.F.A.	15/12/1915	15/12/1915
Miscellaneous	March Table		
Operation(al) Order(s)	50th Divisional Artillery Operation Order No. 8	16/12/1915	16/12/1915
Miscellaneous	Operation Orders By Orders By Lieut Colonel G.T. Pearson R.F.A. (T) Commanding 3rd Northumbrian Brigade R.F.A.	19/12/1915	19/12/1915
Heading	1/3rd Northbn Bde R.F.A. Jan Vol IX		
War Diary	Kruisstraat Sheet 28.H.2.4.a.6.8	01/01/1916	31/01/1916
War Diary	Sheet 28 H24.a.68	13/02/1916	29/02/1916
War Diary	Kruisstraat Sheet 28 H24.a.68	01/02/1916	12/02/1916
War Diary	Sheet 28 H.23.B.5.9	01/03/1916	31/03/1916
Miscellaneous	Officer Commanding Left Group 50th D.A.	07/03/1916	07/03/1916
Operation(al) Order(s)	Operation Order No. 2 by Major F.L. Pickersgill R.F.A. (T) Commanding Left Group 50th D.A.	07/03/1916	07/03/1916
War Diary	Sheet 28 H 23 B 5 9	01/04/1916	05/04/1916
War Diary	Steenvoorde	06/04/1916	06/04/1916
War Diary	Nr La Clytte	07/04/1916	30/04/1916
War Diary	La Clytte	01/05/1916	01/05/1916
War Diary	Ecke	02/05/1916	29/05/1916
War Diary	La Clytte	30/05/1916	31/05/1916
Miscellaneous	Operation Orders No By Lieut Col F.L. Pickersgill R.F.A. (T) Commanding 3rd Northumbrian Brigade R.F.A.	03/03/1916	03/03/1916
Miscellaneous	Operation Orders No By Lieut Col F.L. Pickersgill R.F.A. (T) Commanding 3rd Northumbrian Brigade R.F.A.		
Miscellaneous	Operation Orders No By Lieut Col F.L. Pickersgill R.F.A. (T) Commanding 3rd Northumbrian Brigade R.F.A.	27/05/1916	27/05/1916
War Diary	La Clytte	01/06/1916	30/06/1916
Operation(al) Order(s)	Operation Orders No.4 A No By Lieut Col F.L. Pickersgill R.F.A. (T) Commanding 252nd Northumbrian Brigade R.F.A.	03/06/1916	03/06/1916
Operation(al) Order(s)	Operation Order No 5 A By Lieut Col F.L. Pickersgill R.F.A. (T) Commanding 252nd Northumbrian Brigade R.F.A.		
Operation(al) Order(s)	Operation Order No 6 A By Lieut Col F.L. Pickersgill R.F.A. Commanding 252nd Northumbrian Brigade R.F.A.		
War Diary	La Clytte	01/07/1916	31/07/1916
Operation(al) Order(s)	Operation Order No 7A By Lieut Col F.L. Pickersgill Commanding 252nd Northumbrian Brigade R.F.A.	11/07/1916	11/07/1916

Type	Description	Start	End
Operation(al) Order(s)	Operation Order No 10A By Lieut Col F.L. Pickersgill R.F.A. Commanding 252nd Northumbrian Brigade R.F.A.	29/07/1916	29/07/1916
War Diary	Dranoutre	01/08/1916	09/08/1916
War Diary	Ecke	10/08/1916	12/08/1916
War Diary	Le Meillard	13/08/1916	15/08/1916
War Diary	Behencourt	16/08/1916	18/08/1916
War Diary	Albert	19/08/1916	31/08/1916
Operation(al) Order(s)	Operation Order No 13A By Lieut Col F.L. Pickersgill R.F.A. Commanding 252nd Northumbrian Brigade R.F.A.	07/08/1916	07/08/1916
Operation(al) Order(s)	Operation Order No 12 A 252 (Nor) R.F.A.	04/08/1916	04/08/1916
Operation(al) Order(s)	Operation Order No 11 A By Lieut Col F.L. PickersGill R.F.A. (T) Commanding 252nd (Northumbrian) Brigade R.F.A.	00/08/1916	00/08/1916
Operation(al) Order(s)	Operation Order No 14 A By Lieut Col F.L. Pickersgill R.F.A. Commanding 252nd Northumbrian Brigade R.F.A.	14/08/1916	14/08/1916
Operation(al) Order(s)	Operation Order No 16 A 252 R.F.A. Brigade	17/08/1916	17/08/1916
Operation(al) Order(s)	Operation Order No 15 A By Lieut Col F.L. Pickersgill R.F.A. Comdg 252 Northumbrian Bde R.F.A.	15/08/1916	15/08/1916
Heading	50th Divisional Artillery 252nd Brigade R.F.A. 50th Divisional Artillery September 1916		
War Diary	Albert	01/09/1916	30/09/1916
Operation(al) Order(s)	Operation Order No 18A		
Operation(al) Order(s)	Operation Order No 17A	02/09/1916	02/09/1916
Miscellaneous	Alterations And Additions To Operation Orders No.17 A	02/09/1916	02/09/1916
Miscellaneous	252 RFA O.O. No.20 A	09/09/1916	09/09/1916
Miscellaneous	O.O. No.19 A	09/09/1916	09/09/1916
Operation(al) Order(s)	Operation Order No. 18 A 252 R.F.A. Brigade	03/09/1916	03/09/1916
War Diary	Albert	01/10/1916	17/10/1916
War Diary	Frechencourt	18/10/1916	31/10/1916
Operation(al) Order(s)	Operation Order No. 23 A By Lieut Col F.L. Pickersgill R.F.A. (T) Commanding 252nd (Northumbrian) Bde. R.F.A.		
Operation(al) Order(s)	Operation Order No. 24 A By Lieut Col F.L. Pickersgill Commanding 252nd (Northumbrian) Brigade R.F.A.	16/10/1916	16/10/1916
Operation(al) Order(s)	252 (North'bn) Brigade RFA. Operation Order No. 21 A	30/09/1916	30/09/1916
Miscellaneous	Programme Of Bombardment		
Map	Map		
Miscellaneous	Addendum To Operation No 21 A 252nd Brigade R.F.A.	01/10/1916	01/10/1916
Operation(al) Order(s)	Operation Order No 22 A By Lieut Col F.L. Pickersgill Commanding 252nd (Northumbrian) Brigade R.F.A.	07/10/1916	07/10/1916
Miscellaneous	Programme Of Bombardment	07/10/1916	07/10/1916
War Diary	Frechencourt	01/11/1916	15/11/1916
War Diary	Moulliens Au Bois	16/11/1916	21/11/1916
War Diary	Montauban	22/11/1916	22/11/1916
War Diary	Flers	23/11/1916	12/12/1916
Miscellaneous	Programme Of Bombardment For Le-PDRS 252nd (Northumbrian) Brigade R.F.A.		
War Diary	Behencourt	27/12/1916	30/12/1916

Type	Description	Start	End
Operation(al) Order(s)	Operation Order No. 27a By Major L.A Common. R.F.A. (T). Commanding 252nd (North'bn) Brigade R.F.A.	08/12/1916	08/12/1916
Operation(al) Order(s)	Operation Order No. 28A By Lieut Col H.E. Hanson D.S.O. Commanding 252nd (Northumbrian) Brigade R.F.A.	28/12/1916	28/12/1916
Miscellaneous	Relief Of Batteries Of 50th D.A.		
War Diary	Behencourt	01/01/1917	11/01/1917
War Diary	Longueval	12/01/1917	20/01/1917
War Diary	Fricourt	21/01/1917	31/01/1917
Operation(al) Order(s)	Operation Order No. 29a By Lieut Col H.E. Hanson D.S.O. Commanding 252nd (Northbn) Brigade R.F.A.	13/01/1917	13/01/1917
Operation(al) Order(s)	Operation Order No. 30a By Lieut Col H.E. Hanson D.S.O. Comdg 252nd Brigade R.F.A.	17/01/1917	17/01/1917
Heading	50th Division 1st Durham Battery R.F.A. Jun-Sep 1915		
Heading	50th Division 1st Durham Batty (3rd North Bn Bde) R.F.A. Vol I 5.8.14-23.6.15		
War Diary	Durham	05/08/1914	14/08/1914
War Diary	Newcastle	20/08/1914	20/08/1914
War Diary	Ravensworth	15/11/1914	15/11/1914
War Diary	Low Fell	17/11/1914	17/11/1914
War Diary	Sunderland	18/11/1914	29/12/1914
War Diary	Low Fell	30/12/1914	17/04/1915
War Diary	Southampton	18/04/1915	18/04/1915
War Diary	Havre	19/04/1915	20/04/1915
War Diary	Hazebrouck	20/04/1915	20/04/1915
War Diary	Rouge Croix	20/04/1915	23/04/1915
War Diary	Berthen	24/04/1915	24/04/1915
War Diary	Rouge Croix	24/04/1915	25/04/1915
War Diary	Rattekot	25/04/1915	26/04/1915
War Diary	St Laurent	26/04/1915	27/04/1915
War Diary	Le Temple	27/04/1915	04/05/1915
War Diary	Winnezeele	04/05/1915	10/05/1915
War Diary	Watou	10/05/1915	25/05/1915
War Diary	Brandhoek	25/05/1915	25/05/1915
War Diary	Kruisstraat	26/05/1915	26/05/1915
War Diary	Belgium	26/05/1915	26/05/1915
War Diary	Ypres	31/05/1915	01/06/1915
War Diary	Abeele	02/06/1915	05/06/1915
War Diary	Ypres	05/06/1915	23/06/1915
War Diary	Wulverghem	24/06/1915	18/07/1915
War Diary	Armentieres	19/07/1915	19/07/1915
Heading	50th Division 1st Durham Batty (3 North'bn Bde) RFA Vol III From 1st To 30th August 1915		
War Diary	Armentieres	01/08/1915	06/08/1915
War Diary	Pont De Nieppe	07/08/1915	16/08/1915
War Diary	Houplines	18/08/1915	30/08/1915
Heading	50th Division 1/1st Durham Batty R.F.A. Vol II 24-6-19-7-15		
Heading	50th Division 1/1 Durham Batty R.F.A. Vol IV Sept 15		
War Diary	Houplines	04/09/1915	27/09/1915
Heading	50th Division 2nd Durham Battery R.F.A. Jun-Sep 1915		
Heading	50th Division 2nd Durham Battery R.F.A. Vol I 4-30.6.15		
War Diary	Abeele	04/06/1915	04/06/1915

War Diary	Poperinghe	05/06/1915	06/06/1915
War Diary	Zillebeck Pond	07/06/1915	08/06/1915
War Diary	Ypres	08/06/1915	09/06/1915
War Diary	Salient	09/06/1915	22/06/1915
War Diary	Ypres	22/06/1915	22/06/1915
War Diary	Vlamertinghe	23/06/1915	23/06/1915
War Diary	Neuve-Eglise	24/06/1915	30/06/1915
Heading	50th Division 2nd Durham Batty (3rd Northbn Bde) R.F.A. Vol II 10-7-4-8-15		
War Diary	Neuve Eglise	10/07/1915	18/07/1915
War Diary	Pont De Nieppe	19/07/1915	04/08/1915
Heading	50th Division 3rd Durham Batty (3rd Northbn Bde) RFA From 5th To 31.8.15		
War Diary	Armentieres	05/08/1915	05/08/1915
War Diary	Pont De Nieppe	07/08/1915	15/08/1915
War Diary	Houplines	16/08/1915	31/08/1915
Heading	50th Division 3rd Durham Batty RFA (1/3 Northbn Bde RFA) Vol IV Sept.15		
War Diary	Houplines	01/09/1915	30/09/1915
Heading	50th Division 3rd Durham Battery R.F.A. May-Aug 1915		
Heading	50th Division 3rd Durham Batty RFA (3rd Northbn Bde RFA) Vol 9-31.5.15		
War Diary	Dequerker	09/05/1915	09/05/1915
War Diary	Watou	09/05/1915	09/05/1915
War Diary	Vlamertinghe	19/05/1915	19/05/1915
War Diary	Ypres	19/05/1915	23/05/1915
War Diary	Vlamertinghe	24/05/1915	29/05/1915
War Diary	Ypres	30/05/1915	31/05/1915
Heading	50th Division 3rd Durham Batty (3rd Northbn Bde) RFA Vol II 1-30.6.15		
War Diary	Ypres	01/06/1915	21/06/1915
War Diary	Locre	22/06/1915	22/06/1915
War Diary	Neuve Eglise	23/06/1915	30/06/1915
Heading	50th Division 3rd Durham Batty (3 North'bn Bde) RFA From 1st To 31st July 1915		
War Diary	Neuve Eglise	01/07/1915	18/07/1915
War Diary	Pont De Nieppe	19/07/1915	31/07/1915
Heading	50th Division No 3 Durham Batty R.F.A. Vol IV August 15		
War Diary	Pont De Nieppe	01/08/1915	14/08/1915
War Diary	Armentieres	15/08/1915	28/08/1915
War Diary	Chapelle	28/08/1915	28/08/1915
War Diary	D'Armentieres	28/08/1915	31/08/1915

w 95/287 (a)

w 55/217 (a)

50TH DIVISION

3RD NORTHUMBRIAN BDE
BECAME 252ND BDE RFA
APR 1915-JAN 1917
&
1-1ST DURHAM BATTERY
JUN-SEP 1915
2ND DURHAM BATTERY
JUN-SEP 1915
3RD DURHAM BATTERY
MAY-AUG 1915

BDE BROKEN UP
1917 JAN

121/5444

50th Division

3rd Northumbrian Bde R.F.A.

Vol I. 17.4 — 30.5.15

Army Form C. 2118.
N° 1.
1

WAR DIARY of 3rd Northumbrian Brigade R.F.A. T

INTELLIGENCE SUMMARY. From 17 April 1915.

(Erase heading not required.)

Instructions regarding War Diaries and Intelligence
Summaries are contained in F.S. Regs., Part II.
and the Staff Manual respectively. Title pages
will be prepared in manuscript.

Hour, Date, Place	Summary of Events and Information	Remarks and references to Appendices
1.15 p.m. 17/4/15. Newcastle on Tyne	Entrained for Embarkation	
2.0 a.m. 18 Apl. S. Hampton	Arrived 2 a.m. embarkation commenced 3 a.m. sailed 5.15 p.m	A.710
11.0 a.m. 19 apl. Havre	Disembarked at Quai de Ville 11 a.m. Transhipped equipment for 710 to train at Gare maritime. Train departs 11/5 pm.	fol 710
7.0 pm 20 Apl Hazebrouck	Arrived by train 7 p.m. via Abbeville, Blois, & St Omer. Detrained, marched by Road to Rouge Croix. Arriving 10.30 pm Headquarters of Brigade at Esteminet Vieille Croix - Rouge Croix. 3 Batteries and Amm. Column billets in farms on Road Rouge	fol 710
21 Apl Rouge Croix	Croix - Caester. Brigade completing equipment & resting.	fol 710
7 am 22 Apl "	German aeroplane passes overhead	1/11
6 a.m. 23 Apl "	Stop 6 am. 7 am.	1/11
2 pm 24 Apl BEETHEN	Brigade ordered to march to BOESCHEPE - marched via LE TRE. found roads patches	
3 pm	arrived at BEETHEN. Bivouaced over night	
10 pm	Orders to return to ROUGE CROIX	
12 Noon "	(marched)	
2 pm " ROUGE CROIX	arrived ROUGE CROIX. Billeted	
4 pm "	Ordered to move to arras 1 mile South of PTE INN Brigade in	1/11
7 pm "		

WAR DIARY
or
INTELLIGENCE SUMMARY.
(Erase heading not required.)

3rd Northumbrian Brigade R.F.A. Army Form C. 2118.
1/7th Northumbrian Division No 2.

Instructions regarding War Diaries and Intelligence Summaries are contained in F.S. Regs., Part II. and the Staff Manual respectively. Title pages will be prepared in manuscript.

Hour, Date, Place	Summary of Events and Information	Remarks and references to Appendices
2.30 a.m. 25 April 15. ROUGE CROIX.	Brigade marched to RATTE KOT INN via FLETRE and GODEWAERSVELDE.	
5.0 a.m. — RATTE KOT INN	Arrival & Billets. NDA Headquarters RATTS KOT INN. Brigade Headquarters TRAPPIST MONASTERY. Position of area. 2.38"E x 50.51' North.	p.70
12.0 Noon 26 April	Received orders to move to area of ST LAURENT.	
3.30 pm " "	Marched via WATOU. Arrived at ST LAURENT. 5 pm.	p.72
3.45 " "	Received orders from NDA. Small arm Section Am: Column to be prepared to advance, possibly to East of POPERINGHE.	
6.30 " "	Received orders to attach S.A. Section Am: Column to report to 28 Divisional H.Q. near POPERINGHE.	p.72
7.0 " "	S.A. Section under Capt. Albert & 2nd Lt Milburn marched as ordered.	
12.0 Noon 27 April	O.C. "B" Battery reported Bombs dropped at his Billets — also at RATTEKOT INN shortly after midnight. Bombs also reported falling on supposed GHQ at ST LAURENT during the previous night. Battery had no casualties.	p.70
2.0 pm " "	Received orders from NDA to march to LE TEMPLE Area. About 2 miles South of West of STEENVOORDE QUATRE CHEMIN Eslaminet Road & 5/4m	p.70
4.0 pm " "	Brigade marched to LE TEMPLE Area. NDA Headquarters S.A. at WORMEZEELE	p.70
28 April	Billets LE TEMPLE area West of STEENVOORDE ROAD.	p.70
29 "	do	
30 "	do	
1 May	do. S.O.C. Division expects Batteries in Billets to be prepared to move to ARNEKE on following day.	p.71
7 pm 2 "	N.D.A. orders to be prepared to move.	p.71
11 pm 2 "	N.D.A. cancelled orders for move.	p.71
2.30 pm 3 "	N.D.A. orders Brigade to move to area on West side of LE TEMPLE — STEENVOORDE ROAD. Between LE TEMPLE & WINNEZEELE.	p.71
8.30 pm 4 "	Ammunition Column relieved from VLAMERTINGHE. No casualties.	p.71

Army Form C. 2118.

[The 2nd Northumbrian Brigade R.F.A.(T)]

WAR-DIARY
or
INTELLIGENCE SUMMARY
(Erase heading not required.)

Instructions regarding War Diaries and Intelligence Summaries are contained in F.S. Regs., Part II. and the Staff Manual respectively. Title pages will be prepared in manuscript.

Hour, Date, Place	Summary of Events and Information	Remarks and references to Appendices
1915 May		
4th	Brigade in Billets near LE TEMPLE –	
5th	do	
6th	do – 1 – Brigade attached to General Reserve	
7th	do	
8th	do	
19	Brigade moved to Huits WATOU area	
	Brigade moved to Reinf. C.R.A. 3rd Durham Div. YPRES	Ammunition gun
	C.R.A. 27th Div ordered 1 Battery to take up position in action Pet. Sheet 28 NW 1.15.B.7 remaining Batteries to rejoin	B/g.g. & forces received p.77
	Verlorenhoek Station WATOU Battn. C. Blaney C. Passloor Vlamertinghe C. Rich'ds Junction Brielen	
20 K	3rd Div Battery took up position. Brigade H.Q. at Lousboom	
29 K	Battery opened fire against German Salient 3 a.m. on zone	
	Zone Menin Road – Stirling Castle – entrance of Sanctuary & alley going to shoot camps opens fire on our waggon lines at night, one wounded line and when Germans advanced following to high ground who now taken and of action to return to high p.m.	
	Almost exhausted ammunition for 29th L.R. & 11th Hy. S. eng. Evacuation Mounted Cape 30th L.R. & 11th Hy. H.Trant Brigade at mo gun line 18 of 20 of Bgdes R.F.A.	
25 K	Received orders to retire to YPRES –	
25 – 10 p.m.	Montonne Jones. Battery occupied positions Montmy B/gdue 1" m. Battery sending my information at of Brigade under orders of orig. commander G gunnery of light remaining Battery	27th Dec & 8 November Operation when returning p.77

WAR DIARY
or
INTELLIGENCE SUMMARY
(Erase heading not required.)

Army Form C. 2118.

3rd Northumbrian Bde R.F.A.

Hour, Date, Place	Summary of Events and Information	Remarks and references to Appendices
10 am 26 May 1915 YPRES	3 Casualties (names) on H.Q. Staff. Zone allotted to 3rd Northumbrian Bde – A18, 59, 6 & 11, 12. Wilkinson on J 24.D.r. J.30.B. 27 Div Artillery ordered and ordered 7 August Reinforf.	A/1
12.30 p.m – 30 May 1915 YPRES		/3

To Officer in Charge of
Asst-General's Office
at Base

W. T. Knowles Lt Col
Comdg 3rd Northumbrian Bde R.F.A.

Ypres
30th May 1915

"A" Form.
MESSAGES AND SIGNALS.
Army Form C. 2121.
No. of Message _____

| Prefix ____ Code ____ m. | Words. | Charge. | This message is on a/c of: | Rec'd. at ____ m. |
| Office of Origin and Service Instructions. | Sent At ____ m. To ____ By ____ | | ____ Service. (Signature of "Franking Officer.") | Date ____ From ____ By ____ |

TO { 3rd Nottinghamshire Brigade R.H.A.

| Sender's Number | Day of Month | In reply to Number | **AAA** |
| S.C. 266 | 25th | | |

Your brigade will move into action tonight in relief of 20th Brigade R.H.A.
(2) Immediately on receipt of this order your batteries and brigade HQ are to move off at a trot and walk as under
(a) Brigade HQ and 1 battery via VLAMERTINGHE – DEN GROENEN JAGER CABARET – N of CHATEAU in H.23 b to road junction at H.24 a 9.10 where a guide will meet them.
(b) Two batteries via VLAMERTINGHE – DEN GROENEN JAGER CABARET (H 16 d 1.1) to KRUISSTRAATHOEK (H 30 d 3.1) where two guides will meet these batteries
(c) Yourself and one officer per battery will proceed at once to H.Q. 20th

From
Place
Time

The above may be forwarded as now corrected. (Z)

Censor. | Signature of Addressee or person authorised to telegraph in his name
* This line should be erased if not required.

"A" Form. Army Form C. 2121.

MESSAGES AND SIGNALS.

Bde R.H.A. at H 24 a 9.10 where full instructions for the relief will be given. You and the one officer per battery should therefore get to this spot as early as you possibly can.
(d) For the present your Bde ammn column will remain in its present situation

W. Orr Capt.
for Bde Major R.A.

From 25/5/15
Time 8.45 pm
27th Div.

"A" Form. Army Form C. 2121.
MESSAGES AND SIGNALS.

Prefix	Code	m.	Words	Charge	This message is on a/c of:	Recd. at _____ m.
Office of Origin and Service Instructions.			Sent At _____ m. To _____ By _____		_____ Service. (Signature of "Franking Officer.")	Date _____ From _____ By _____

TO | B m 1st Bde

Sender's Number.	Day of Month	In reply to Number	
AX 222	24		A A A

Enemy attacked about 3 am and sent gas down the ROULERS Railway. 3rd Durham Battery opened fire on their zone 3 rounds gun fire every 2½ minutes about 4 am a great number of 21st Lancers and 15th Hussars came past Railway Bridge I.16.a.5.8 as they could not stand the gas in the trenches about 4.45 am they returned to their trenches. 4 of them are at this Bridge gassed. 3rd Battery casualties nil

From OC 3rd Durham Battery
Place
Time 5. a m

Army Form C. 398.

To:-

DESPATCH.	RECEIPT.
Sender's No....................	Date................hour............m.
Date..............hour..........m.	Signature :—

URGENT or ORDINARY.

"A" Form.
Army Form C. 2121.
MESSAGES AND SIGNALS. No. of Message _____

TO: Officer Commanding

Sender's Number: DM 39 Day of Month: 22 In reply to Number: AAA

The Brigade will move into action tonight in relief of the 20th Brigade RFA. Immediately on receipt of this order OC 1st Battery will march at a trot & walk from wagon lines on VLAMERTINGHE-POPERINGHE road via VLAMERTINGHE DEN GROENEN JAGER CABERET north of CHATEAU in H.23.6 to road junction at H.24.a.9.10 facing east where they will be met by Headquarters Staff and a guide. OCs 2nd & 3rd Batteries will march via VLAMERTINGHE - DEN GROENEN JAGER CABERET. H.16.d.1.1 to KRUISSTRAATHOEK H.30.d.3.1 where two guides will meet their Batteries AAA. The OC Brigade and Battery Commander from each Battery will report to HQ 20th Brigade RFA at H.24.a.9.10 where full instructions for the relief will be given. Battery Commanders will report in person.

From Place: H.24.a.9.10
Time:

"A" Form.
MESSAGES AND SIGNALS.
Army Form C. 2121.

No. of Message _____

Prefix ● Code ____ m.	Words	Charge	This message is on a/c of:	Recd. at ____ m.
Office of Origin and Service Instructions.	Sent			Date ____
	At ____ m.		Service.	From ____
	To			
	By		(Signature of "Franking Officer.")	By

TO: to my H.Q at KRUISSTRAAT. H.18d 6.4 when I will accompany them to HQ 20ᵗʰ Brigade AAA Ammunition

| Sender's Number | Day of Month | In reply to Number | AAA |

Column will remain in its present situation

WJ Pearson? Lieut Col.
Comdg 3rd? Howitzer? Bde RFA

Remainder of HQ Staff at wagon lines on VLAMERTINGHE ROAD will rejoin HQ at KRUISSTRAAT immediately

From ____
Place ____
Time 9-45 p.m.

The above may be forwarded as now corrected. (Z)

Censor. Signature of Addresser or person authorized to telegraph in his name

* This line should be erased if not required.

Reference BELGIUM - HAZEBROUCK 5a.

OPERATION ORDER No D.M.37 by LIEUT.COL.G.T.Pearson.R.F.A.(T)
Commanding 3rd Northumbrian Brigade R.F.A.(T).

WATOU.
18th May,15.

1. The following will parade at Brigade Headquarters ready to move off by 6am. 19th May,15. :-
    Officer Commanding 1st Battery & 1 Horse Holder
    Officer Commanding 2nd Battery & 1 Horse Holder
    Officer Commanding 3rd Battery & 1 Horse Holder
    3rd By Reconnoitring party.
    Colonels 2nd Horse with groom & Trumpeter
    Adjutants 2nd Horse with groom
    Regimental Sergeant Major
    Telephone Wagon with ~~attachments~~ detachment
    2 Orderlies

2. Remainder of Brigade Headquarters,3rd Battery and Ammunition Column will march in the order named as far as the cross roads ¼ of an inch north of the second K in DICKEBUSCHBK XXXXXX on the POPERINGHE - YPRES road. The head of the column to be halted there by 8pm.

3. The head of the column named in 2 will pass the starting point the Cross roads ¼ of an inch North West of the W in WARANDEBECK XXXXXXXXXX at 3pm on the 19th inst.

4. The Ammunition Column will park in the position selected by the Officer Commanding. and the Brigade Headquarters will be notified by Orderly who will remain at the cross roads ¼ of an inch north of the second K in DICKEBUSCHBK XXXXXXXXXXXX till picked up by part of the Brigade Headquarters.

5. Further orders will be issued to the 1st and 2nd Batteries later. These 2 Batteries will be ready to move off at the usual 2 hours notice

6. No shell will be fuzed.

7. Baggage Wagons will march with their Units.

8. Dismounted parties will march under Unit arrangements.

9. Men undergoing Field Punishment will be handed over to the 2nd Battery.

10. The meeting point for supplies will be the cross roads sheet 27.E.39 (c). Guide will be sent by all Units

Issued in writing at 9.15pm 18th May,1915.

Adjutant

~~Commanding~~ 3rd Northumbrian Brigade R.F.A1(T)

50A. Kinnear

3rd notes for Bels R+H.

Vol II   30.5 — 29.6.15

181/594

92
0/6

Army Form C. 2118.

WAR DIARY
or
INTELLIGENCE SUMMARY.
(Erase heading not required.)

Instructions regarding War Diaries and Intelligence Summaries are contained in F.S. Regs., Part II. and the Staff Manual respectively. Title pages will be prepared in manuscript.

Hour, Date, Place	Summary of Events and Information	Remarks and references to Appendices
30th May 1915.	27th Bn'l inoc'd — On 27th Sep'r Enemy Tomorrow will be offr taking and attacks of 3rd tomorrow adminis Turkey.	
31st May 1915. 9.30 pm	3rd Northumb: Brigade relieved h.q. dets from each Battery of 42nd Brigade R.F.A. (not fielders)	A.1
1st June 1915 9.30 pm	Remainder of Brigade relieved by 42 Brig'de R.F.A.	
2nd 3rd 4th June	Batt'n Brigade withdrawn to ABEELE area. B.M. notes 31/5/15 strength – trades	A.2
5th June 9.30 pm	A section from Left Battery of 3rd North'n Lin'n Brigade relieved a section of Left Battery of 42nd Brigade	
6th June 9.30 pm	Remaining section relieved 42nd Brigade O.C. 3rd Brigade took over from O.C. 42nd Brigade	A.3
7th June 9.30 pm	3rd Battery dug new position 1. 27.A.8.10. South side of ZILLEBEKE LAKE.	
8th June 9.30 pm	3rd Battery occupied one section of new position	
9th June 9.30 pm	3rd Battery occupied remaining section of new position	

Army Form C. 2118.

3rd Northumbrian Brigade R.F.A.
50th Division R.F.A.   No 6

WAR DIARY
or
INTELLIGENCE SUMMARY.
(Erase heading not required.)

Hour, Date, Place	Summary of Events and Information	Remarks and references to Appendices
YPRES 9th June 1915	Lieut Guy Johnson 3rd Battery wounded in Shrapnel by a stray Rifle bullet	½M
10th June 12 noon	O.C. 3rd Northumbrian Brigade R.F.A. Lt Col H.C.T Pearson took over formg. command of 3rd Northumbrian Bde R.F.A. and a section of 5th Durham Howitzer Section. Division order No 6. herewith.	½M
15th June	Operation order No. 6 - attached - also subsequent order	— marked A.4. A.5.
18th June	Operation order No. 7. attached.	½M marked A.6.
19th June 22nd June	Operation order No. 8. attached. The Brigade moved from YPRES to NEUVE EGLISE. Instructions on moving Actions on arriving on the march of 22nd. Meaning out to 50th Lancs. Power R.F.A. of 23rd inst. Issued out to 50th Lancs. Power Brigade R.F.A.	marked A.7. ½M ½M marked A.8.
NEUVE EGLISE. 23rd June	Operation order No 9. instead herewith. Relieving Sections marched from YPRES to NEUVE EGLISE relieving the 1st North Midland Brigade - 3rd Northumbrian Brigade taking over.	moved to Supports to Division in Change.
24th June	All Batteries registered on zones. E.5.c.1.3 Zone Trenches C.1.b.3.4. rebroke subsidiary trench T.35.c.2.1. to N.36.c.7.4. supporting 149th Infantry Brigade under 18th Durham Fielding.	Sept Generals Office at Base.
29th June	Line allotted to 4 High Brigade now extends from Trench D1 to C Ikhorine. D6 R.A. order attached - marked.	29th June 1915 ½M Pearson Lt Col o/c 3rd Northumbrian Bde R.F.A. A.9

"A" Form.   Army Form C. 2121.

MESSAGES AND SIGNALS.

A.1
3 Aug

TO: Officer Commanding

				AAA
The	42nd	Brigade	R.F.A	will
relieve	this	Brigade	in	the
following	order.			
After	dusk	tonight	one	section
will	occupy	the	position	of
the	forward	section	of	the
2nd	Battery. One	section	will	
occupy	a	section	of	the
3rd	Battery. One	section	will	
occupy	a	section	of	the
1st	Battery			
The	sections	relieved	from	each
Battery	will	retire	to	the
Bivouac	lines	on	VLAMERTINGHE - POPER-
INGHE	Road	and	bivouac	there
until	tomorrow			
The	Reply	Officer	Lieut	Place

From
Place
Time

"A" Form.   MESSAGES AND SIGNALS.   Army Form C. 2121.

Prefix	Code	m.	Words	Charge		This message is on a/c of:		Recd. at	m.
Office of Origin and Service Instructions.			Sent					Date	
			At	m.		Service.		From	
			To					By	
			By		(Signature of "Franking Officer.")				

TO {

Sender's Number	Day of Month	In reply to Number	**AAA**

and	the	sender	Identifier	will
report	to	headquarters	50 d	Division
Artillery	by	10 a.m.	tomorrow	June 1st
for	the	purpose	of	selecting
billets	in	squares	L 21 c	and e
and	L 27 a	and b	sheet	27
South	of	ABELLE	POPERINGHE	Road
As	soon	as	the	
billets	are	arranged	the	Orderly
Officer	will	guide	the	retired
Sections	and	their	component	wagons
to	the	new	billets.	
		When	the	remaining	sections
are	relieved	by	the	42nd
Brigade	RFA	the	Majors	of
each	Battery	will	retire	their
Sections	as	detailed	above	except

From
Place
Time

The above may be forwarded as now corrected.   (Z)

"A" Form.   Army Form C. 2121.

MESSAGES AND SIGNALS.

that they will pick it
the equipment wagons and meets
direct to the next billeting
the Ammunition column will remain
in it present position until
all guns are withdrawn when
it will retire to the
next billeting area XE Battery
from 12 noon tomorrow
the Headquarters of the 50th
Divisional Artillery will be
at a farm in
L 21 a 4.7.
H.Q. Staff will move to new Billets

from Lt Comdg 3rd Nbn Bde RFA(T)

War Diary

O.C. 3rd Lbn: Bde: R.F.A.

A.2   2 sheets   1

With reference to the attached copy of a telegram received from H.Q. 50th Division, would you please make arrangements for all the sections that may be withdrawn to-night to bivouac near your wagon-lines.

We are moving into a new billetting area to-morrow, (June 1st), and these sections will enter it to-morrow morning.

Please, therefore, send on an officer in advance with your interpreter and sheet 27 to be at these H.Q. by 10.0. a.m. on June 1st. He will then be shown his billetting area and can then make all the arrangements necessary for the accommodation of the troops.

Your area is roughly in the Squares L.21.(c) +(d). and L.27. (a) +(b). Sheet 27. South of the ABEELE — POPERINGHE Road.

If found necessary, more ground will be allotted to you.

H.Q.
50th D.A.
St Jean-ter-Biezen.
31=5=15.

A. auger Captain.
S.C. 50th D.A.

"A" Form.   Form C. 2121.
                    MESSAGES AND SIGNALS.   No. of Message _____

Prefix ____ Code ____ m. | Words | Charge | | Recd. at ____ m.
Office of Origin and Service Instructions. | Sent | | This message is on a/c of: | Date ____
_____ | At ____ m. | Service. | From ____
_____ | To ____ | |
_____ | By ____ | (Signature of "Franking Officer.") | By ____

TO { Officer Commanding _____
     _____

Sender's Number | Day of Month | In reply to Number | AAA
    DM 22 | 5 June 1915 | |

Ammunition Orders

OC 1 Battery a section of
your battery will occupy a section
of the position evacuated by 42nd
Brigade in I.26.c.5.9. the position
you were in before
OC 2nd Battery a section of your
battery will relieve a section of the
42nd Brigade in H.24.b.2.7
OC 3rd Battery a section of your
Battery will relieve a section of the
42nd Brigade in I.13.d.3.5
The sections of each Battery
to be under the charge of a subaltern
officer & will report to HQ 42 Bde
at H.24.c.9.10 between 8.30 - 9.30 pm today

From _____
Place _____
Time _____

The above may be forwarded as now corrected.   (Z)
                                    Censor.   Signature of Addressor or person authorized to telegraph in his name
              * This line should be erased if not required.
58 S. B. Ltd. Wt. W5673/619—50,000. 10/14. Forms C2121/10.

"A" Form. Army Form C. 2121.

MESSAGES AND SIGNALS.

No. of Message ______

Prefix ...... Code ...... Office of Origin and Service Instructions.	Words / Charge — Sent: At ...... m. To ...... By	*This message is on a/c of:* ...... *Service.* (Signature of "Franking Officer.")	Recd. at ...... m. Date ...... From ...... By ......

TO

Sender's Number.	Day of Month	In reply to Number	AAA
*			

Headqrs of the Brigade from 6 pm [illegible] will be at H 24.c.9.6.10 the Headqrs Staff will occupy the same billets as before. [illegible] date

W. Thomson [illegible] Lieut Col

Cmdg [illegible] RFA

From
Place
Time

The above may be forwarded as now corrected.

...... Censor.

(Z) ...... Signature of Addressor or person authorised to telegraph in his name.

* This line should be erased if not required.

(C32) —McC. & Co. Ltd., London.— W 11400/2045. 100,000 2/15. Forms C 2121/10.

Wt. W1154/2240. 7/11. 7,500,000. Sch. 4a.   "A" Form.   Army Form C. 2121.

MESSAGES AND SIGNALS.

No. of Message _____

| Prefix Code m. | Words 26 | Charge | This message is on a/c of: | Recd. at 9-5 a.m. |
| Office of Origin and Service Instructions. Yeh WN. | Sent At 7.40 m. To By 9-0am | | _____Service. (Signature of "Franking Officer.") | Date 29-5-15 From By |

TO | Div R A | | |

| Sender's Number. Y G 351 | Day of Month 29th | In reply to Number | A A A |

A brigade R F A of 3rd
Div will relieve third
Northbn Bde by sections
commencing night of 31st

From 50th Div
Place
Time 8-40 am

The above may be forwarded as now corrected.   (Z)

.... Censor.   Signature of Addresser or person authorised to telegraph in his name.

* This line should be erased if not required.

MESSAGES AND SIGNALS.

"A" Form.   Army Form C. 2121.

The remaining sections of Batteries will relieve 42nd Brigade at the same hour tomorrow 6th inst at the same positions under OC that Battery will relieve in Section in T.15.d.8.8 as before. Wagon lines — A suitable farm for wagon lines is situated in H.21.b.3.3. East of the cross roads this farm was not occupied this afternoon. Batteries will make their own arrangements in the neighbourhood if other suitable farms are available. Amm. Col. will take up billets by 8-30 pm tomorrow 6th in square G.24.a.4.3. This farm was not occupied by troops this afternoon. Early partial occupation is advised.

A3.

Copy No 10

2 Sheets

5pth. Division Operation Order No. 3.

Ref: Sheet 28 N.W.
$\frac{1}{20000}$

5 - 6 - 15.

1. On night of 6th./7th. June 150th. Infantry Bde. will relieve 9th. Infantry Bde. of 3rd. Division in the line from right of 5th. Corps in I. 30. c. 8.8. to about I. 24. d. 9.9..
Details of relief to be arranged between G. O.s C. Brigades concerned.

G. O. C. 50th. Division will assume command of the front at 12 midnight on 6th/7th. or on completion of reliefs if they are not concluded at that hour.

After relief H. Q. 150th. Infantry Brigade will be ECOLE DE BIENFAISANCE I. 9. c..

2. 3rd. Northumbrian Bde. R. F. A. will relieve 42nd. Bde. R. F. A. of 3rd. Division, now supporting 9th. Infantry Bde., advanced sections relieving on night 5th./6th. remainder on night 6th/7th. June.

Relieving Brigade will be under command of 3rd. Division till command of this section of front is transferred to 50th. Division.

3. Progress and completion/ of reliefs to be reported to 50th. Division.

4. From hour of transfer of command from 3rd. to 50th. Division the boundaries of 50th. Division Area for purposes of defence will be:-

Southern - From present right of 5th. Corps in I. 30. c. to where the ZILLEBEKE Switch on G. H. Q. 2nd. Line crosses the ZWARTELEEN - ZILLEBEKE Road, thence to south east corner of ZILLEBEKE Pond, thence by North bank of Pond to north west corner, thence to road junction I. 20. a. 5.6. and thence to where canal line of defence crosses canal in I. 19. d..

Northern. - From point of junction between 50th. and 3rd. Divisions to road junction in I. 24. a. 2.5 thence westward including farms in I. 23. b. and I. 23. a. central to road junction in I. 16. d. 7.2. to crossing of ZILLEBEKE Switch over road in I. 16. d. central (road inclusive to 50th. Division), thence to farm in I. 13. c. inclusive, thence to railway I. 14. b. 10,0, thence south of railway and road to south of bridge 13 in I. 13. a. 7.3,.

2.

The Division will be responsible for all defensive works south of this line, with the exception of the canal line.

5. The Division will be responsible for the protection, maintenance, and repair of bridges 14 to 19 both inclusive.

6. Programme of reliefs between Infantry Brigades will be issued separately.

7. Divisional H. Q. at G. 21. c. 6.6..

G.V. Hordern.
Lt.-Col.
General Staff,
50th. Division.

Issued at 2 p.m.

A4

Copy No. 10

50th. Division Operation Order No. 4.

10 - 6 - 15.

1. On nights 10/11th. and 11/12th. June 149th. Infantry Brigade will relieve 7th. Infantry Brigade of 3rd. Division in the line from left of 150th. Infantry Brigade to a point about I. 18. c. 3.8.

    Details of relief to be arranged between Brigades concerned.

    Progress and completion of relief to be reported to Divisional Headquarters.

2. On completion of relief, G. O. C. 50th. Division will assume command of front now occupied by 7th. Infantry Bde.

3. (a) Northern boundary of 50th. Division area for purposes of defence will then be - From point about I. 18. c. 3.8 to road junction I. 17. d. 5.7 thence westwards along road to road junction I. 17. c. 8.7, thence to point where road from East crosses ZILLEBEKE Switch in I. 16. b. 4.5 (road to 3rd. Division) thence south of road junction I. 16. b. 2.4 to present dividing line in I. 14. b. 10.0.

    (b) Dividing line between Brigades of the Division will be the original northern boundary of 50th. Division area, (see operation order No. 3, para. 4.)

4. A Field troop of 1st. Indian Field Squadron is placed at disposal of the Division.

5. The detachment 175th. Tunnelling Company now with 3rd. Division will, on completion of relief of 7th. Infantry Brigade, be transferred to the Division.

6. Detailed arrangements for Artillery support will be communicated separately.

7. From 9-0 p.m. 11th. June the dug-outs in H. 23. a. and b. will be occupied by 2 Battalions of the 151st. Infantry Brigade.

Lt.-Col.
General Staff,
50th. Division.

Issued at 5-15 p.m.

22 - 6 - 15.

The following alterations are made to Operation Order No. 8 of 19 - 6 - 15 :-

Para. 2. (e)
　　Divisional H. Q. will move at 10 a.m. 24/6/15 to M. 31. b. central.

Para. 3. (d).
　　150th. Infantry Bde. will be relieved by 139th. Infantry Bde. on night 23rd/24th. June.

Para. 4 (b).
　　The change of command will take place at 12 noon on 24th. June.

Appendix B.
　　Last paragraph.
　　150th. Infantry Bde., 2nd. Northbn. Field Coy. R.E., No. 3 Coy. Divisional Train, will march on 25th. June.

　　　　　　　　　　　　　　　　　　P.W. Hordern.
　　　　　　　　　　　　　　　　　　　Lt.-Col.
　　　　　　　　　　　　　　　　　General Staff,
　　　　　　　　　　　　　　　　　50th. Division.

Issued at 6-0 p.m.

Ref: Map 1/10000
ZILLEBEKE Sheet
showing German
trenches numbered.

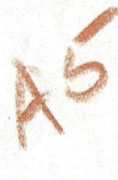

Copy No. 9

50th. Division Operation Order No. 6.

15 - 6 - 15.

1. 5th. Corps is to attack on 16th. June and seize the BELLEWARDE FME ridge.

   3rd. Division is to seize and hold the line Y. 21 - Y. 19 - Y. 18 - Y. 7 - its first objective being the enemy's trenches between Y. 16 and N. E. corner of RAILWAY Wood.

   An Artillery bombardment will begin at 2-50 a.m. and will continue till 4-15 a.m. - with pauses at 3-10 a.m. - 3-40 a.m. and 4-0 p.m.

   3rd. Division assaults at 4-15 a.m..

2. 50th. Division will co-operate in the attack of 3rd. Division by rifle and machine gun fire along the whole front.

3. 149th. Infantry Brigade will seize any opportunity of taking the offensive and improving its position about HOOGE and will especially assist the attack of 3rd. Division against point Y. 21.

4. Divisional Collecting Station and Advanced Dressing Station as at present - Wounded able to walk to be directed to KRUISTRAAT - H. 18. d. 10.5.

5. Captured prisoners to be sent to DICKEBUSCH GATE I. 13. a. 7.3.

6. Advanced Divisional H. Q. will be established at H. 18. d. 6.4 from 11-30 p.m. tonight. From this hour all messages in connection with operations will be addressed "Advanced 50th. Division".

G. V. Hordern.
Lt.-Col.
General Staff,
50th. Division.

Issued at 12-15 p.m.

SECRET.　　　　　　　　　　　　　　COPY No. 3.

50th Divisional Artillery OPERATION ORDER

(on O.O. No. 6, 50th Division).

Ref: Special Map 1/10,000 and Sheet 28 N.W., 1/20,000

15th June, 1915.

1. The Batteries of the 3rd Northumbrian Brigade R.F.A., the 2nd E. R. Battery, 2nd Northumbrian Brigade R.F.A., the one Battery of the 23rd Brigade R.F.A. left to the 50th Division and the Section 5th Durham Howitzer Battery are not to open fire unless they receive an order to do so from me.

    In the event of an urgent request being made to them to open fire, reference should be made to me, if possible.

    If the situation does not permit of this being done, batteries or sections will act on their own initiative, reporting to me as soon as possible what action they have taken.

2. The O.C., 3rd Northumbrian Brigade R.F.A. will detail an Officer to be with the H.Q., 150th Infantry Brigade at the "ECOLE DE BIENFAISANCE".

3. Any observations or impressions gained by the artillery of what is going on in their front will be passed back as quickly as possible to Divisional Artillery Headquarters.

4. If called upon to fire, Battery and Section Commanders must make certain that the expenditure of ammunition is no more than is absolutely required by the tactical situation existing at the moment.

5. D.A. H.Q. will be with 50th Division H.Q. at H. 18. d, 6. 4. from 10.30 p.m. to-night. All messages for me must be addressed "Advanced 50th Division".

　　　　　　　　　　　　　　　　　　　L.G. Thomson,
　　　　　　　　　　　　　　　　　　　Major, R.A.,
　　　　　　　　　　　　　　　Brigade Major, 50th D.A.

Copy No. 2 to 2nd Northumbrian Brigade R.F.A. (for O.C. 2nd E.R. Bty. R.F.A.
Copy No. 3 to 3rd Northumbrian Brigade R.F.A.
Copy No. 4 to 23rd Brigade R.F.A.
Copy No. 5 to O.C. Section 5th Durham Howitzer Battery.

SECRET

O.C.,
~~2nd~~ Northumbrian Brigade R.F.A.
~~A.6~~

Herewith Copy No. 10 of 50th Division Operation Order No. 7 dated 18/6/15.

Please acknowledge receipt.

R.G. Thomson
Major R.A.
Brigade Major, 50th D.A.

Hq. 50th D.A.
18. 6. 15.

Correction. In para: 1.(b). line 2. for I.18.a.5.7.
read I.24.d.9.9. R.G.T.

Copy No. 10

50th. Division Operation Order No. 7.

18 - 6 - 15.

1. (a) On night 18th./19th. June 7th. Infantry Bde. of 3rd. Division will take over the front from present left of 50th. Division to east end of HOOGE Village about I. 18. b. 7.4 from 149th. Infantry Bde.

   (b) On night 19th./20th. June remainder of front held by 149th. Infantry Bde. viz to about I. 18. a. h4d99 5.7 will be taken over by 7th. Infantry Bde.

   Command of front relieved will pass to G. O. C. relieving Division on completion of each relief.

   Details of relief will be arranged between Infantry Bdes. concerned.

   Progress and completion of reliefs to be reported to Divisional H. Q..

2. (a) On completion of reliefs night 18th./19th. June:- 23rd. Bde. R.F.A. will return to the Command of 3rd. Division from 50th. Division, but it will continue to support that part of the front of 50th. Division which is included in its zone.
   One section 23rd. Trench How. Battery from 50th. Division will, as a temporary measure, be transferred to 3rd. Division.

   (b) 4th. Northumbrian How. Brigade (less 1 section) remains under command of 3rd. Division, but will be available to support troops of other Divisions within the zones they cover, on application to C. R. A., 3rd. Division.

3. From the hour of completion of reliefs dividing lines between 3rd. and 50th. Divisions for purposes of defence and for responsibility for all defensive works except the Canal line, will be :-

   (1) On completion of relief on night 18th./19th. June:- Same as at present (see para. 3 (a) 50th. Division Operation Order No. 4).

   (2) On completion of reliefs on night 19th./20th.:- From point of junction in front line (I.24.d.9.9.) to road junction I.24.a.2.5., thence westwards North of Farms in I.23.b. and a. central to road junction I.16.d.7.2, thence to South of point where the ZILLEBEKE SWITCH line crosses the road in I.16.d.3.4, thence South of that road and of farms to I.15.d.8.5, thence to railway in I.15.c.0.10, and westwards South of railway to South of Bridge 13 about I.13.a.8.3..

P.T.O.

4. The responsibility for protection, maintenance and repair of bridges 14 to 19 remains with the 50th. Division.

5. From the hour of completion of reliefs on night 18th./19th. Detachment 175th. Tunnelling Company Company R.E. will be transferred to 3rd. Division.

G.V. Horden
Lt.-Col.
General Staff,
50th. Division.

Issued at 1-0 p.m.

A.7.

Copy No. 10

50th. Division Operation Order No. 8.

Ref: Map 1/40000
Sheet 28

19 - 6 - 15.

1. The Division will be transferred temporarily to II Corps in relief of 46th. Division.

2. MOVES.

    (a) Moves and reliefs of Divisional Artillery, (including 23rd. Trench Howitzer Battery), will be carried out as shown in table, Appendix A.

    (b) R.E., Infantry and 1st. & 2nd. Field Ambulances and Train will move to new area as shown in March Table, Appendix B.

    3rd. North'n Field Ambulance will move under orders of A.D.M.S. Move to be completed on 24th. June.

    H. Q. and No. 1 Company of the Train will move as required under orders of O. C. Train to vicinity of BAILLEUL.

    (c) "A" Squadron, Yorks. Hussars and Cyclist Coy. to be clear of billets and bivouacs by 2 a.m. 23rd. June and march to neighbourhood of ST. JANS CAPPEL at an hour to be arranged by O.s C. concerned.

    (d) Sanitary Section and Mobile Veterinery Section to march under orders of A.D.M.S. and A.D.V.S. respectively.

    (e) Divisional H.Q. will move at 10 a.m. 23rd. June to M. 31. b. central.

3. RELIEFS.

    (a) Details of Artillery reliefs will be arranged by C. R. A., 50th. Division.

    (b) On night 21st/22nd. June 151st. Inf. Bde. will relieve 138th. Inf. Bde.
    Officers to go into trenches morning of 21st. June.

    (c) On night 22nd/23rd. June 149th. Inf. Bde. will relieve 137th. Inf. Bde.

    Officers to go into trenches morning of 22nd. June.

    (d) On night 22nd/23rd. June 150th. Inf. Bde. will be relieved by 139th. Inf. Bde.

    (Officers of 139th. Inf. Bde. go into trenches on night of 21st/22nd. June).

    (e) Reports of progress of reliefs to be sent to Div. H.Q. by 7 a.m. daily.

P.T.O.

4. COMMAND.

(a) Brigadiers will retain command of the Trench line until relieved.

(b) G. O. C. 50th. Division will take over command of the right Section of 2nd. Corps line at 12 noon on 23rd. June.

G. O. C. 46th. Division assumes command of 50th. Division area and troops contained in it at same hour.

5. The Section 23rd. Trench Howitzer Battery now attached to 3rd. Division will return to 50th. Division night of 22nd/23rd. June.

6. The Detachment 171st. Tunnelling Coy. R. E. will be attached to 46th. Division on arrival of that Division.

7. From 20th. June Field Cos. R. E. will be affiliated to Infantry Bdes, as follows:-

1st. Northumbrian Field Co. R.E. to 149th. Inf. Bde.

2nd.   "   "   "   "   " 150th.   "   "

7th. Field Coy. R. E.   " 151st.   "   "

Issued at 10.45 pm.

G. V. Horden
Lt.-Col.
General Staff,
50th. Division.

APPENDIX. A.

TABLE OF MOVES AND RELIEFS - 50th. DIVISIONAL ARTILLERY.

DATE.	UNITS	FROM	TO	REMARKS.
20.3.15.	2nd Northumbrian Bde. complete.	Billets	Trenches in 2nd Corps area to relieve 3rd. North Midland Bde. R.F.A.	Head of the Brigade to be at the road junction M.23.c.4.2., at 10.0 a.m. A guide will meet it there. Ref: Sheet 28 S.W.
21.3.15.	1st. Northumbrian Bde. RFA complete.	Billets	Trenches in 2nd Corps area to relieve 2nd North Midland Bde. R.F.A.	Head of the Brigade to be at the road junction M.23.c.4.2. at 10 a.m. A guide will meet it there. Ref: sheet 28, S.W.
22.3.15.	3rd. Northbn. Bde. 1 section per Batt'y 2 sub-sections from each section of the Bde. Amm.Col. with 2/3rd Trench How. Battery.	Emplacements.	To trenches in 2nd Corps area, to relieve 1st. North Midland Bde R.F.A.	Rear of the column to be clear of the road junction in G.30.c.5.9. by 8-0 a.m. Reference Sheet 28 N.W. Head of the Brigade to be at the road junction M.25.c.4.2. at 10.0 a.m. A guide will meet it there. Ref: Sheet 28 S.W.
23.3.15	H.Q.,3rd Northbn.Bde R.F.A., 1 Section per Battery & remainder of Amm. Col.	Emplacements.	Trenches in 2nd Corps area to relieve 1st. North Midland Bde. R.F.A.	Rear of the column to be clear of the road junction in G.30. c.5.9. by 8-0 a.m., Reference Sheet 28 N.W. Head of the Brigade to be at the road junction M.23. c.4.2. at 10-0 a.m. A guide will meet it there. Ref: Sheet 28 S.W.
-do-	4th Northbn (How) Brigade R.F.A.	Billets	Trenches in 2nd. Corps area to relieve 4th North Midland Brigade R.F.A.	Rear of the column to be clear of the road junction in G.30. c.5.9. by 7-0 a.m. Ref: Sheet 28 N.W. Head of the Brigade to be at the road junction M.23.c.4.2. at 9-0 a.m. A guide will meet it there. Ref. sheet 28 S.W.
-do-	50th. Div. Amm. Column.	Billets	To relieve North Midland Divisional Amm. Col.	Head of the Column to be at the road junction M.23.c.4.2. at 12 noon. A guide will meet it there. Ref. Sheet 28, S.W.

Brigades will march into the 2nd. Corps area as a whole and will then relieve the Batteries they are taking over from, by sections at a time.

APPENDIX B.

Issued with
Operation Order
No. 8

MARCH TABLE   50th. Division.   Date 19 - VI - 15.

DATE.	UNIT.	STARTING POINT.	TIME.	ROUTE.	REMARKS.
20th. June.	Headquarters 151st. Inf. Bde. 6th/8th. Durham L.I. 6th. Bn. Durham L.I. 5th. Bn. North'd. Fusiliers. 5th. Bn. Border Regt. 7th. Field Coy. R.E. No. 4 Co. Divisional Train.	Road junction OUDERDOM G.30.c.4/8.	9-0 a.m.	ZEVECOTEN LOCRE to DRANOUTRE.	
	2nd. North'n Field Ambce.	Their billets at G.26.c.		WESTOUTRE – cross road M.17.c.6/5 – LOCRE to DRANOUTRE.	Will follow in rear of 151st. Inf. Bde. at cross road M.17.c.6/5 at 10-15 a.m. Time of starting to be fixed by C.O.. A portion will move to ST JANS CAPPEL under orders of C.O.
21st. June.	Headquarters 149th. Inf. Bde. 4th. Bn. North'd. Fusiliers. 5th. " " " " 7th. " " " " 7th. " Durham L.I. 1st. Northbn. Field Coy. R.E. No. 2 Coy. Divisional Train.	Road junction OUDERDOM G.30.c.4/8.	9-0 a.m.	ZEVECOTEN LOCRE – DRANOUTRE W. of NEUVE EGLISE.	The Brigade will be met at DRANOUTRE and conducted to billets West of NEUVE EGLISE. 7th. Durham L.I. will leave the column at DRAN- OUTRE and rejoin 151st. Infantry Bde.

P. T. O.

APPENDIX B.

Issued with
Operation Order   M A R C H   T A B L E.   2.   50th. Division.   Date 19 - VI - 15.   No.
No. 8.

DATE.	UNIT.	STARTING POINT.	TIME.	ROUTE.	REMARKS.
21st. June.(Cont)	1st. Northbn. Field Ambce.	WIPPENHOEK.	9-0 a.m.	WESTOUTRE Cross roads M.17.c.6/5 LOCRE - NEUVE EGLISE.	Will follow 149th. Inf. Bde. from Cross Roads M.17.c.5/5 reaching that place at 10-15 a.m. The portion forming Rest station at BAILLEUL will march under orders of C. O.
22nd. June.	5th. Loyal N.Lancs. Regt.	Road junction OUDERDOM G.30.c.4/8	9-0 a.m.	ZEVECOTEN - LOCRE - to DRANOUTRE.	Under orders of Officer Commanding.
24th. June.	150th. Infantry Bde. 2nd.Northbn.Field Co. R.E. No. 3 Coy.Divisional Train.	Road junction OUDERDOM G.30.c.4/8.	9-0 a.m.	ZEVECOTEN to LOCRE.	The A.D.M.S. will arrange for two Horse Ambulances to accompany the Brigade joining the Column at cross roads M. 17. c. 6/5 at 10-15 a.m.

Commander
G.O.C. 150th.
Infantry Bde.

BM/S6

O.C.,
3rd Northumbrian Brigade R.F.A.

When marching from your emplacements on the 22nd and 23rd June into the 2nd Corps area, please note that on each day of movement, all Artillery units moving South are to be clear of OUDERDOM by 8.0 am.

They will enter the area by way of ZEVECOTEN and LOCRE.

R.G. Thomson.
Major, R.A.,
Brigade Major, 50th D.A.

Hq. 50th D.A.
20. 6. 15.

O.C.,
3rd Northumbrian Brigade R.F.A.

B.M/S6

With reference to my B.M./S.6 sent you this morning, and the table headed "Moves and reliefs of Units -50th D.A.", in the column of remarks, for "Head of Brigade to be at the "road junction M. 23 c. 4.2. at 10.0 a.m.", read "Head of the "Brigade to be at the Road Junction M/23 c. 4.2 at 9.0 a.m."

Herewith new table.

L.G. Thomson.

Major, R.A.,
Brigade Major, 50th D.A.

Hq. 50th D.A.
20. 6. 15.

MOVES AND RELIEFS OF UNITS.   50TH DIVISIONAL ARTILLERY.

DATE.	UNITS.	From	To	REMARKS.
20.6.15.	2nd Northumbrian Bde.RFA. complete.	Billets.	Trenches in 2nd Corps area to relieve 3rd North Midland Brigade R.F.A.	Head of the Brigade to be at the road junction M.23 c.4.2 at 10.0 a.m. A guide will meet it there. Ref. Sheet 28 S.W.
21.6.15.	1st Northumbrian Brigade R.F.A. complete.	Billets	Trenches in 2nd Corps area to relieve 2nd North Midland Brigade R.F.A.	Head of the Brigade to be at the road junction M.23 c. 4.2 at 9.0 am. A guide will meet it there. Ref: Sheet 28 S.W.
22.6.15	3rd Northumbrian Bde: 1 Section per Batty, 2 Sub-sections from each Section of the Bde. Ammn. Col, with 23rd Trench Howitzer Battery.*	Emplace- ments.	To trenches in 2nd Corps area, to relieve 1st North midland Brigade.R.F.A.	Rear of the column to be clear of the road junction in G. 30 c. 5.9. by 8.0 am. Ref. Sheet 28 N.W. Head of the Brigade to be at the road junction M. 23 c.4.2 at 9.0 am. A guide will meet it there. Ref. Sheet 28, S.W.
23.6.15	H.Q., 3rd Northbn. Bde R.F.A., 1 Section per Emplace- Battery and remainder ments. of Ammunition Column.		Trenches in 2nd Corps area to relieve 1st North Mid- land Bde R.F.A.	Rear of the Column to be clear of the road junction in G. 30 c. 5.9. by 8.0 am. Ref. Sheet 28 N.W. Head of the 3rd Brigade to be at the road junct- ion M. 23 c. 4.2. at 9.0 am. A guide will meet it there. Ref. Sheet 28 S.W.
23.6.15	4th Northbn. (How) Brigade R.F.A.	Billets	Trenches in 2nd Corps area to relieve 4th North Mid- land Brigade.	Rear of the column to be clear of the road junction in G. 30 c.N.W. 5.9. by 7.0 a.m. Ref: Sheet 28 N.W. Head of the Brigade to be at road junction in M. 23 c.4.2. at 8.0 a.m. A guide will meet it there. Ref. Sheet 28 S.W.
24.6.15	50th Divnl. Ammn. Col.	Billets	To relieve North Midland Divisional Ammn. Col.	50th Dvl. Ammn.Col. will march into its new area. starting at 2.30 am.

* The 23rd Trench Howitzer Battery, at present attached to 3rd Northbn. Bde. Ammn. Col. requires to 3-ton lorries to carry as ammunition and guns. It has no transport of any sort. Brigades will march into the 2nd Corps area as a hole and will then relieve the Batteries they are taking over from, by sections at a time.

Copy No. 10

50th. Division Operation Order No. 9.

A8

24 - 6 - 15.

1. The line held by the Division will be adjusted as follows :-

   (a) Night 24th./25th. June portion of H. Sector trenches at present held by 151st. Infantry Brigade will be taken over by 83rd. Infantry Brigade of 28th. Division.

   (b) Night 28th./29th. June 150th. Infantry Brigade will take over from right of trench D. 3 to left of trench 15 from 149th. Infantry Brigade, and from latter point to left of trench E. 6 from 151st. Infantry Brigade.

   Officers of 150th. Infantry Bde. to go into trenches on morning of 28th. June.

   G. O. C. 150th. Infantry Brigade will assume command of the line from right of trench D. 3 to left of trench E. 6 on completion of reliefs.

   Details of reliefs to be arranged between Brigades concerned.

   Completion of reliefs to be reported to Divisional H. Q..

2. On completion of reliefs Boundary lines for purposes of defence will be :-

   (a) <u>Between 50th. Divn. and 3rd. Corps.</u>

   Front Line - Trench 7 (U. 1. a. 8.4) inclusive to 3rd. Corps.

   WULVERGHEM SWITCH. - Bridge over STUIVERBEEK on WULVERGHEM - MESSINES road (inclusive to 50th.Div).

   G.H.Q. 2nd. Line - WULVERGHEM - NEUVE EGLISE road in T. 10. c. (inclusive to 50th. Div.).

   (b) <u>Between 149th. and 150th. Infantry Brigades.</u>

   From junction of trenches D.2 and D.3 thence to R.E. Farm (inclusive to 150th. Infantry Bde), thence to BUS Farm (inclusive to 149th. Infantry Brigade.)

   (c) <u>Between 150th. and 151st. Infantry Brigades.</u>

   From right of trench E.2 to N.35.a.10.10 (Piccadilly to 150th. Infantry Bde.) thence due west along dividing line between N. 28 and N. 34.

2.

(d) <u>Between 50th. Division and 28th. Division.</u>

Front Line — Trench H. 1 (inclusive to 28th. Divn.

VIERSTRAAT
SUBSIDIARY
LINE — Road South of Wood in N. 22. a.
(inclusive to 28th. Division).

G.H.Q. 2nd.
Line — KEMMEL — LACLYTTE road (inclusive to 28th. Division).

3. Infantry Brigades will be responsible for the maintenance and improvement of the G. H. Q. 2nd. Line and all defences in front of it within their areas.

G V Horden
Lt.-Col.
General Staff,
50th. Division.

Issued at 2 p.m.

SECRET

B.M./S.b./.

O.C., 3rd Northumbrian Brigade R.F.A.

A.9.

The line allotted to the 149th Infantry Brigade is from Trench D.2. to Trench C.1. (both inclusive).

Please make arrangements at once to cover this zone and re-allot, (if necessary), the zones for your Batteries.

Please inform the G.O.C., 149th Infantry Brigade of the action you have taken and let him know the exact hour to-morrow at which your batteries will be ready to support him and the zones allotted to each.

Please acknowledge receipt.

R.G. Thomson.

Major, R.A.
B.M., 50th D.A.

Hq. 50th D.A.
28. 6. 15.

50th Division.

151/6015

8th Northumbrian Bde: R.F.A.

(addition to) Vol II   14.6.15

a²/a96

Army Form C. 2118.

3rd Northumbrian Brigade R.F.A.
No 6.A.

WAR DIARY
or
INTELLIGENCE SUMMARY.
(Erase heading not required.)

Hour, Date, Place	Summary of Events and Information	Remarks and references to Appendices
14 June 1915. YPRES.	Organisation in War Diary 1 Battery of 2nd East Riding Brigade attached to 2nd L.S.D. G.T. Reserve Group Command. Group Command consists of:- 3rd Northumbrian Brigade R.F.A. 1 Battery of 2nd East Riding Brigade R.F.A. 1 Trench Mortar Battery R.G.A. 1 Section 5th Durham Howitzer Battery R.F.A.	Forwarded per Haworth [signature] Officer in charge Adj Generals Office at Base 14 July 1915.

50th Division

21/6272

H/3rd North'n Inf Bde BEF.

Vol III

1-31-7-15

WAR DIARY
or
INTELLIGENCE SUMMARY.

(Erase heading not required.)

Army Form C. 2118.

3rd North Humbrian Brigade R.F.A. (T.)

No. 7.

Hour, Date, Place	Summary of Events and Information	Remarks and references to Appendices
NEUVE EGLISE - June 30 - 1915.	Trenches allotted to this Brigade from line to Douve to 29 June shown head - German Trenches C.1. C.2. C.3. C.4 D.1. and D.2. inclusive.	
July 1. -	Progress Nil. Hostile gun fire over Batteries	
2. -	Progress Nil. Hostile gun fire on NEUVE EGLISE	
3. -	Progress Nil. Suspected Reconnoitred position for an advanced gun section in T.S.O. near WULVERGHEM.	
4. -	C.R.A. ordered a section of a Battery to occupy position on Hill 63 near PLOEGSTEERT. To enfilade German Trenches.	
5. -	Made Reconnaissance of hill 63 & selected gun positions, also prepared same ready for occupation - the man killed in 1st Battery by hostile artillery fire. Orders for occupation on Hill 63 cancelled by C.R.A.	
6. -		
8. -	Called on Brig Genl Clifford, commdg 149th Infantry Brigade with my Adjutant.	
9. -	Made a tour of Infantry Trenches in my Brigade Zone.	

1/OT Pennson 15/Jul/

Army Form C. 2118.

3rd Northumbrian Brigade R.F.A.

No 8.

WAR DIARY
or
INTELLIGENCE SUMMARY.
(Erase heading not required.)

Instructions regarding War Diaries and Intelligence Summaries are contained in F.S. Regs., Part II. and the Staff Manual respectively. Title pages will be prepared in manuscript.

Hour, Date, Place	Summary of Events and Information	Remarks and references to Appendices
NEUVE EGLISE		
July 10. 1915	Hostile Artillery fire on NEUVE EGLISE.	
11 "	Operation order No 10 attacks marked B.O.	
- 12. -	Reconnoitre positions for 2nd line Battery sun & wagon line positions in case of retirement – positions are as marked on attached sheet dated 11 July 1915 – marked B.1.	
- 13. -	Preparing second line positions – Hostile fire on NEUVE EGLISE	
- 14. -	Brigade notified that 50th Division will move to neighbourhood of ARMENTIÈRES. Order to move will be issued later. Operation order No 11. marked B.2 attached –	
15. -	Hostile fire on NEUVE EGLISE – Church shelled and Burnt down	
16 -	Operation order No 12. marked B.3 Kenwith attacks.	
16 "	50th Divisional Artillery Operation order No 92 marked B.4. attacks	
16 "	50 DIV RA subsequent order BM/S/10. marked B.5. attacks	
16 "	50 Div RA subsequent order BM/S/10. marked B.6. attacks	
16 "	O.C. 3rd Northumbrian Brigade R.J.A. Operation order marked B.7	
(11am – 17h –)		

Army Form C. 2118.

WAR DIARY
or
INTELLIGENCE SUMMARY.

(Erase heading not required.)

3rd Northumbrian Brigade R.F.A.
50th Divisional Artillery
No 9

Instructions regarding War Diaries and Intelligence Summaries are contained in F.S. Regs., Part II. and the Staff Manual respectively. Title pages will be prepared in manuscript.

Hour, Date, Place	Summary of Events and Information	Remarks and references to Appendices
NEUVE EGLISE July 16th 1915	One Section of a Battery of 146th Brigade R.F.A. relieved a section of 1st Durham Battery. 2nd Durham Battery vacated its position and withdrew to its wagon lines.	Omission from entry for July 16 of forms sheet No 8.
July 18th 1915 9.30 p.m.	Brigade marched from NEUVE EGLISE to PONT DE NIEPPE.	
PONT DE NIEPPE. July 19th 1915.	Brigade placed in reserve, and is engaged entrenching ground. The zone allotted to 50th Division is :— Front Line , from WEZ MACQUART — ARMENTIERES ROAD inclusive in I.16.C.7.10. to BRUN RUE — HOUPLINES Road inclusive in C.29.A.1.1 Ref ½ 20,000 "B" Series Sheet 36. N.W. Subsidiary Line. Between the above named roads inclusive in I.9.C.7.4 to C.22.C.8.1 G.H.Q 2nd Line. ARMENTIERES — BAILLEUL Railway- to COURTE RUE inclusive. G.H.Q 3rd Line. ARMENTIERES-BAILLEUL Railway to ARMENTIERES — BAILLEUL Road inclusive.	Ref ½ 20,000 "B" Series Sheet 36. N.W. photocopy list.

Army Form C. 2118.

3RD Northumbrian Brigade R.F.A.
No. 10.

WAR DIARY
or
INTELLIGENCE SUMMARY.
(Erase heading not required.)

Instructions regarding War Diaries and Intelligence Summaries are contained in F. S. Regs., Part II. and the Staff Manual respectively. Title pages will be prepared in manuscript.

Hour, Date, Place	Summary of Events and Information	Remarks and references to Appendices
ARMENTIERES		
July 20. 1915	Brigade H.Q. in ARMENTIERES. Brigade in reserve at PONT DE NIEPPE.	
" 21 "	ditto	
" 22 "	ditto	
" 23 "	ditto	
" 24 "	ditto	
" 25 "	ditto	
" 26 "	ditto	
" 27 "	ditto	
" 28 "	ditto	
" 29 "	ditto	
" 30 "	ditto	
" 31 "	ditto	

Jn. Pearson Lt.Col.
cdg 3 Northumbrian Brigade R.F.A.

Copy No.

50th. Division Operation Order No. 10.

11 - 7 - 1915.

1. On night 12th/13th. July the portion of front from KEMMEL - WYTSCHAETE road inclusive to present left of 151st. Infantry Brigade will be taken over by 83rd. Infantry Brigade of 28th. Division.

Details of relief to be arranged between Brigades concerned.

Completion of relief to be reported to Divl. H. Q..

On completion of relief the G. O. C. 28th. Division will assume command of the above-mentioned front.

2. 2nd. Northumbrian Brigade R.F.A. will continue to cover its present zone after the Infantry reliefs have taken place.

3. As regards rear lines, points of junction between 50th. and 28th. Divisions will remain as at present.

Lt.-Col,
General Staff,
50th. Division.

Issued at 2-0 p.m.

SECRET. War Diary Copy

B.1.

To.
    B.H.
    50th D.A.

Rear positions have been selected as follows :-

(1) For WULVERGHEM Switch Line.

	Guns.	Waggon Line.
Brigade H.Q.	S.12.b.6.8	
1st Durham Battery.	T.1.d.9.2	S.12.d.5.5
2nd Durham Battery.	T.14.a.9.0	T.13.c.8.8
3rd Durham Battery.	T.1.c.8.1	T.13.a.3.6

Brigade Ammunition Column remains in its present position.

(2) For G.H.Q. 2nd Line.

	Guns.	Waggon Lines.
Brigade H.Q.	S.12.b.0.8	
1st Durham Battery.	S.12.d.6.5	S.17.b.9.0
2nd Durham Battery.	T.13.d.4.5	S.24.b.0.8
3rd Durham Battery.	T.13.a.3.6	S.18.c.1.8
Bde Ammunition Column.	S.0.b.0.6	

    Sgd H.C. Stapylton
        Capt., R.F.A.
Adjutant. 3rd Northumbrian Brigade., R.F.A.

11th July, 1915.

SECRET.

O.C.,
        3rd Northumbrian Brigade R.F.A.

(a). In the event of the occupation by the Infantry of the WULVERGHEM SWITCH and subsidiary line, the positions of your Batteries will be as follows :-

    1st Durham Battery,   T.1.d.9.2.
    2nd Durham Battery,   T.14.a.9.9.
    3rd Durham Battery,   T.1.c.2.1.

Your wagon-lines will go to :-

    S.12.d.5.5. for the 1st Durham Battery.
    T.13.c.8.8. for the 2nd Durham Battery.
    T.13.a.3.6. for the 3rd Durham Battery.

Your Brigade Ammn. Col. will remain in its present position. Your Brigade Headquarters will move to S. 12.b.0.8.

(b) In the event of the occupation by the Infantry of the G.H.Q., 2nd Line, which runs from the WULVERGHEM - NEUVE EGLISE road, (T. 10.c.2.10) - COB FARM - LINDENHOEK - Road Junction N. 20.b.9.5., your Batteries will stay in the positions detailed above. A position should, however, be prepared in T. 13.d.4.5. for the 2nd Durham Battery in case of necessity. Your wagon-lines and Ammunition Column will stay where they are. *The 2nd Durham's Battery Wagon Lines will, if the Battery moves, be shifted to S. 24. b. 0. 8.*

Your zones will be allotted to you later, but, speaking roughly, in (a) your zone will be from the Bridge over the STUIVERBEEK ‡ - N.33.d.9.9., and in (b) from T.10.c.2.10 on WULVERGHEM - NEUVE EGLISE road - N. 33.d.9.9.

The positions mentioned are to be prepared as soon as possible.

                              R.G. Thomson.
                              Major, R.A.,
Hq. 50th D.A.   B.M., 50th D.A.
11. 7. 15.

‡ *add "on the WULVERGHEM - MESSINES ROAD"*

War Diary

Copy No. _____

B.2

50th. Division Operation Order No. 11.

15 - 7 - 15.

1. The Division is to move to the neighbourhood of ARMENTIERES and will be relieved in its present line as follows:-

   Night 14/15th. July.
   (a) 1st. Brigade, Canadian Division, will take over from Right of 149th. Infantry Brigade to Trench C. 4 inclusive.

   Command of this portion of front will pass to the G. O. C. Canadian Division on completion of relief.

   (b) 150th. Infantry Brigade will take over Trenches D. 1 and D. 2 and S. P. 5. from 149th. Infantry Brigade.

   Night 15th/16th. July.
   84th. Infantry Brigade of 28th. Division will take over the line at present held by 151st. Infantry Brigade.

   Night 16th/17th. July.
   85th. Infantry Brigade of 28th. Division will take over from Trench E. 6 inclusive to Trench D. 1 inclusive from 150th. Infantry Brigade.

   Command of the portions of front relieved by 28th Div. will pass to G. O. C. 28th. Division on completion of each relief.

   Details of reliefs will be arranged between Infantry Brigades concerned.

   Completion of reliefs to be reported to Divl. H.Q..

2. Orders regarding relief of Artillery will be issued later.

3. G.O.sC. Infantry Brigades will arrange for the accommodation in their own areas of relieved Battalions.

4. All cable and trench stores will be left in position and taken over by relieving units.

5. Orders for the move of the Division to its new area will be issued later.

Issued at 6-0 p.m.

G V Hordern Lt.-Col.
General Staff, 50th. Divn.

War Diary — B.3

Copy No. 10

50th. Division Operation Order No. 12.

15 - 7 - 15.

Reference 50th. Divn. Operation Order No. 11 :-

1. The Division will march to its new area as shown in attached march table and will take over a portion of the front held by 27th. Division as follows:-

   (i) Infantry.

   (a) Night 16th/17th. 149th. Infantry Bde. will take over from the right of Trench 74 (I. 5. c. 3.1) to left of Trench 79 (C. 29. c. 2.8) from 80th. Infantry Brigade.

   (b) Night 17th/18th. 151st. Infantry Bde. will take over from the right of Trench 67 on the ARMENTIERES - WEZ MACQUART road to left of TRENCH 73 (I. 5. c. 3.1) from 81st. and 80th. Infantry Brigades.

   Details of reliefs to be arranged between Infantry Brigades concerned.

   (ii) Artillery.

   (a) Artillery of 28th. Division will begin relief of that of 50th. Division on night 16th/17th. and complete by daylight 18th..

   (b) Artillery of 50th. Division will begin relief of that of 27th. Division on night 16th/17th. and complete by daylight 20th..

   The C. R. A. will arrange details of reliefs direct with C.R.A.s 28th. and 27th. Divisions.

   Existing cables are not to be moved if required by in-coming brigades.

2. Progress and completion of reliefs to be reported to Divisional H.Q..

3. At midnight 17th/18th. G. O. C. 50th. Division will assume command of new front.

P. T. O.

4. Boundaries for purposes of defence and allotment of billeting areas will be communicated separately.

5. Divisional H. Q. will remain in present position until further notice.

G. V. Horden
Lt.-Col.
General Staff,
50th. Division.

Issued at 2 p.m.

Issued with
Operation Order
No. 12

MARCH TABLE.   50th. Division.   15th. July.   No _____

DATE.	UNIT	COMMANDER.	STARTING POINT.	TIME.	ROUTE	DESTIN- ATION.	REMARKS.
16th. July.	149th. Inf. Bde. 1st. Northbn. Field Co. R.E. 2nd. Coy Div. Train. 3rd. Northbn. Field Amb.(less 1 section)	))) G.O.C) 149th.) Infantry) Brigade.)	BULFORD CAMP.	8-0 pm.	Road junction B.1 central – ARMENTIERES.	Trenches & billets in ARMENTIERES.	Head of 2nd. Coy. Divl. Train to be at road junc. B.1 central at 8-45 pm and follow in rear of column.
16th. July.	151st. Inf. Bde. 7th. Field Coy. R.E. 3rd. Coy. Divl. Train. 2nd. Northbn. Field Amb.(less 1 section)	))) G.O.C) 151st.) Infantry) Brigade.	DRANOUTRE.	8-15 pm.	NEUVE EGLISE – road junction B.1 central – ARMENTIERES road.	Billets abt. PONT DE NIEPPE.	Head of 3rd. Coy. Divl. Train to be at road junc. B.1 central at 10 pm and follow in rear of column.
17th. July.	150th. Inf. Bde. 2nd. Northbn. Field Co. R.E. 4th. Coy. Divl. Train 1 section 2nd. Field Ambulance. 1 section 3rd. Field Ambulance.	))) G.O.C) 150th.) Infantry) Brigade.	DRANOUTRE.	8-15 pm.	NEUVE EGLISE – road junction B.1 central – ARMENTIERES road.	Billets abt. PONT DE NIEPPE.	Head of 4th. Coy. Divl. Train to be at road junc. B.1 central at 10 p.m. and follow in rear of Column.

Divl. Artillery will march under orders of C. R. A. – but will not pass DRANOUTRE before 9-30 p.m. on 16th. or 17th. JULY.

Orders for move of Divl. Mounted Troops and other Divisional Units will be issued later.

G.V.K.
Lt.-Col.
General Staff,
50th. Division.

Addition to Operation Order No. 12 of 15/7/15.

On night 18th/19th July 149th Inf. Bde. will take over trench 80 from 56th Inf. Bde. of 12th Division.

Details of relief to be arranged between Inf. Bdes. concerned.

J. V. Horder
———————— Lt.Col.,
General Staff,
50th Division.

17/7/15.

War Diary (B-4)

50th Divisional Artillery Operation Order No. 2. Copy No. 7

1. The first sections of the 1st and 2nd Northumbrian Brigades RFA will be relieved to-night, 16/17 July, by the Advanced Sections of the 160th and 31st Brigades RFA respectively, of the 29th Division, and will march to the positions allotted to them near ARMENTIÈRES, going into action before daylight on 17th July.
   Two S.A. Wagons for Small Arm Ammunition from each of these Brigades' Ammunition Columns will march as follows:—
   From the 1st Northumbrian Bde. RFA, with the 151st Infantry Bde.
   From the 2nd Northumbrian Bde. RFA, with the 149th Infantry Bde.
   (See March Table attached to 50th Division Operation Order No. 12, dated 16.7.15).

   Two sub-sections of the Am Sections of these Brigades' Ammunition Columns, together with the remaining wagons S.A., and carts for small arm ammunition, will march with their own Brigades' advanced sections.

2. The head of the 1st Northumbrian Brigade RFA must reach the road junction in S.14.c.8.2. at 10.45p.m. on 16th July.
   The head of the 2nd Northumbrian Brigade RFA must be at the same road junction at 11.15p.m. on 16.7.15.

3. All existing wire now laid down is to be handed over to the incoming batteries.
   The Officers Commanding the 1st and 2nd Northumbrian Brigades RFA, will hand over all Secret Maps, Sheets 36 S.E., Maps Scale 1/10,000, all Panoramas, and any other information gleaned re the enemy positions, to the Officers Commanding the Brigades relieving them.

4. Those portions of the Brigade Ammunition Columns marching on night of 16/17th will go to their Brigades' Ammunition Column lines in the new area.

5. All communications and commands will be handed over to the incoming Commanding Officers at 6.0p.m. on 17.7.15.

6. The remaining sections of batteries belonging to the 1st and 2nd Northumbrian Brigades RFA, and the remainder of those Brigades' Ammunition Columns will be relieved on night of 17/18 July, and will march to their positions in the new area under the same arrangements as laid down for the advanced sections.

7. Incoming batteries will be met by guides under arrangements made between Officers Commanding the Brigades concerned.

8. Orders regarding relief of the 3rd and 4th Northumbrian Brigades R.F.A., 50th Divisional Ammunition Column, and 33rd French Howitzer Battery will be issued later.

9. All reliefs will be reported to this office when complete.

L.C. Thomson.

16. 7. 1915.

Issued at 12.20pm
Copies to :-
50th Division.
C.R.A., 29th Division.
C.R.A., 27th Division.

Major, R.A.,
Brigade Major, 50th Div. Arty.

O.C., 1st Northumbrian Brigade RFA.
O.C., 2nd Northumbrian Brigade RFA.
O.C., 3rd Northumbrian Brigade RFA.
O.C., 4th Northumbrian Brigade RFA.
O.C., 50th Divisional Amm. Col.
O.C., 33rd French Howitzer Battery.

B.M./S.10.

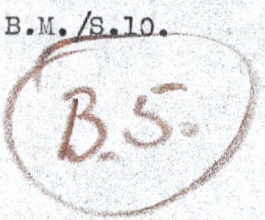

O.C.,

    3rd Northumbrian Brigade R.F.A.

    One section of the 1st Durham Battery, and the whole of the 2nd Durham Battery of the Brigade under your command will be withdrawn to-night at 9.0p.m., and will move to their respective wagon-lines.

    The 3rd Durham Battery will remain in position until to-morrow evening (night 17/18th July), when it, too, can be withdrawn.

    The wire laid down by the 1st Durham Battery R.F.A. is **not** to be reeled in; as the positions of the other batteries are not being occupied, their battery wires can also be reeled in when the relief is complete.

R.G. Thomson.

Major, RA.,
B.M., 50th D.A.

Hq. 50th D.A.
  16. 7. 15.

SECRET. *War Diary* B.M./S.10.

(B.6.)

O.C.,
3rd Northumbrian Brigade R.F.A.
———————————

In continuance of my B.M./S.10 sent you to-day, herewith further instructions :-

The remaining section of the 1st Durham Battery and the whole of the 3rd Durham Battery of the Brigade under your command will be withdrawn at 9.0p.m. on 17.7.15, and will move to their respective wagon-lines.

The whole of your Brigade will march into the new area on the night 18/19th July, and will proceed to the wagon-lines and Brigade Ammunition Column lines, of which you know the location.

It will march via NEUVE EGLISE - Road Junction on the BAILLEUL - ARMENTIERES road, (1600 yards N.E. of STEENWERCK STATION), - NIEPPE.

Starting point will be the 13th Milestone, 1300 yards S. of the 'E' in NEUVE EGLISE. Head of the Column to be at the starting point at 9.30pm on 18.7.15.

Reference Sheet 5A, 1/100,000, "HAZEBROUCK".

Please acknowledge receipt.

R.G. Thomson.

Hq. 50th D.A.
16. 7. 15.

Major, R.A.,
B.M., 50th D.A.

SECRET.

War Diary.

OPERATION ORDERS BY

LIEUT COL. G.T. PEARSON., R.F.A.(T).

COMMANDING 3RD NORTHUMBRIAN BRIGADE., R.F.A.(T).

1. The remaining section of the 1st Durham Battery and the whole of the 3rd Durham Battery will be withdrawn at 9 p.m. to-day, 17:7:15, and will move to their respective Waggon Lines.

2. Maps, sketches and all other useful information will be handed to the Battery taking over, by the O.C. 1st Battery. All other maps in possession of Battery Commanders will be handed into the Brigade Office for the benefit of the incoming Brigade.

3. Telephone Lines. O.C's 2nd and 3rd Durham Batteries will reel in their telephone lines after vacating their positions.

4. The Brigade will march into the new area on the night 18-19 July. It will march via NEUVE EGLISE Road junction on the BAILLEUL-ARMENTIERES Road (1,600 yards North East of STEENWERCK Railway Station NIEPPE).

5. The Starting Point will be the thirteenth mile stone 1,300 yards South of the last E in NEUVE EGLISE near 2nd Battery Waggon Lines.

6. Head of the Column to be at the Starting Point at 9.30 p.m., 18:7:15, where O.C's Units will report their readiness to move off.

7. Order of March.
   Brigade Headquarters.
   3rd Durham Battery.
   1st Durham Battery.
   2nd Durham Battery.
   Ammunition Column.
   Trench Mortar Battery.

8. The 2nd Battery will join the march when the tail of the 1st Battery has passed the thirteenth milestone. The Ammunition Column will be ready to join the march at the BAILLEUL-ARMENTIERES AND NEUVE EGLISE Road Junction, immediately the tail of the 2nd Battery passes that point. The Trench Mortar Battery will accompany the Ammunition Column.

9. Reference Sheet 5A, 1/100000 HAZEBROUCK.

            Lieut.Col.
Commanding 3rd Northumbrian Brigade., R.F.A.(T).

Issued at 11 a.m. to Brigade Headquarters.
            1st Durham Battery.
            2nd Durham Battery.
            3rd Durham Battery.
            Ammunition Column.
            Trench Mortar Battery.

17th July, 1915.

12/
6529

QRC

50th Division

2nd Lothian's Bde R.F.A.

Vol IV

From 1st to 8th August 1915

Army Form C. 2118.

WAR DIARY
or
INTELLIGENCE SUMMARY.
(Erase heading not required.)

3RD NORTHUMBRIAN BRIGADE R.F.A. No. 11

Instructions regarding War Diaries and Intelligence Summaries are contained in F.S. Regs., Part II. and the Staff Manual respectively. Title pages will be prepared in manuscript.

Hour, Date, Place	Summary of Events and Information	Remarks and references to Appendices
ARMENTIERES. August 1st 1915.	Brigade H.Q. in ARMENTIERES. Batteries in reserve at PONT DE NIEPPE	
2nd	ditto	
3rd	Brigade engaged digging dugout positions to cover any retirement on ARMENTIERES.	
5th–12th	Captain Abbott to England to stand off the strength owing to 25/7/15. 2nd Lieut Birkbeck reports for duty with the Brigade and is attached to 6 2nd Durham Battery.	
15th	3rd Northumbrian Brigade relieves 2nd Northumbrian Brigade by sections on 15th & 16th inst. O.C. 3rd Bde will take over command on completion of relief – 50 Divisional R.A. operation order No. 3. Received. (Marked C.I.) The Brigade in action supports 151st Infantry Brigade.	
15th (11.a.m)	1st 1st Infy Brigade Q.C. 3rd Northumbrian Bde R.F.A. reports to Lieut Genl T. Pearson - Brigadier Gl Shea 151st Infy Brigade - Brigadier Gl Shea 3rd Northumbrian Bde R.F.A. Operation order of 14th inst attached. (Marked C.2.)	
16th 8/pm	Relief completed – O.C. 3rd Northumbrian Brigade takes over from O.C. 2nd Northumbrian Bde R.F.A.	
17th 5pm	3rd Battery position subjected to heavy hostile fire.	
18th	151st Brigade relieved by 149th Brigade of Infantry operation order No 13. Marked C.3. Received.	

Commdg. 3rd Nbn. Bde. R.F.A.
Lieut. Col. R.F.A.

Army Form C. 2118.

WAR DIARY
INTELLIGENCE SUMMARY.
(Erase heading not required.)

3RD NORTHUMBRIAN BRIGADE R.F.A.
Sheet No 12

Hour, Date, Place	Summary of Events and Information	Remarks and references to Appendices
ARMENTIERES		
11.30 a.m. 19 Aug 1915	3rd Durham Battery heavily shelled.	
9.a.m. 20 Aug 1915.	O.C. 3rd Northumbrian Bde R.F.A reports to Brig. Genl. Clifford Commanding 149th Infantry Brigade.	Between 15th & 30th August the Batteries in my Brigade were firing daily, at the request of the Infantry covered on, hostile working Parties. Retaliation to hostile Artillery fire- and against enemies trenches.
6.30 pm 26th Aug	3rd Durham Battery position being subjected to heavy hostile fire – takes up a new position.	
6.30 p.m 28th Aug	Heavy shelling near Brigade H.Q. in ARMENTIÈRES - One man on H.Q. Staff wounded.	

ARMENTIERES
August 31. 1915

Jo. T. Pearson
Lieut. Col.
Commdg, 3rd. Nbn. Bde, R.F.A.

SECRET.   Copy No. 2.

50th DIVISIONAL OPERATION ORDER NO. 3.

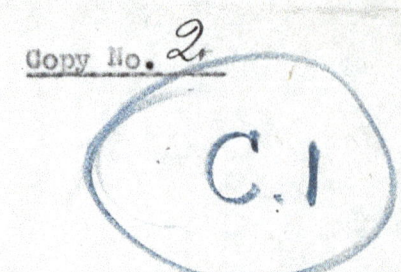

1. The 2nd Northumbrian Brigade R.F.A. will be relieved by the 3rd Northumbrian Brigade R.F.A. on the nights of the 15th and 16th, a section of each battery being relieved each night. Details will be arranged by O.s. C. Brigades.

2. On the completion of the relief the O.C., 3rd Northumbrian Brigade will take over command.

3. The O.C., 3rd Northumbrian Brigade will report himself to the G.O.C., 151st Infantry Brigade to-morrow.

4. After 8.0p.m. on the 16th, the Brigade Ammunition Column, 3rd Northumbrian Brigade will supply the Infantry Brigade occupying the Northern sector of the 50th Division, with S.A.A.

Hq. 50th D.A.
14th August, 1915.

Issued at 6. 30 p.m.

Captain, R.F.A.,
for Brigade Major, 50th Div. Arty.

Copies to :-

   2nd Northumbrian Brigade R.F.A.
   3rd Northumbrian Brigade R.F.A.
   G.O.C., 151stvInfantry Brigade.

Operation Order No
by Lt Col G.T. PEARSON Comdg 3rd Northumbrian Bde

15.8.15.

1. The brigade will relieve the 2nd Northumbrian Bde RFA on the nights of the 15th & 16th, a section per battery being relieved each night. Batteries will relieve those of the corresponding number of the 2nd Bde.

2. The relief will not take place before 8.15 p.m., but battery commanders will arrange the details. The actual guns are not to be changed, but they should arrange as far as possible to change waggons, gun stores &c. No wire need be handed over.

3. The guns of this brigade will be left in the waggon lines ready for handing over to the 2nd Bde.

4. After 8 p.m. on 16th, the Brigade Ammunition Column will supply the Infantry Brigade occupying the Northern sector of the 50th Divn. The OC Ammunition Column will place himself in touch with that brigade, at present the 151st.

5. Brigade headquarters will be at I 1.a.8.7 from 6 p.m. on 16th.

Issued at 8.30 am.
Copies to 1st 2nd 3rd batteries
& B.A.C.

JM Crafy
Capt & Adjt 3rd Nbn Bde RFA

Copy No. 7

C.3.

OPERATION ORDERS NO. 13

by

Brigadier General J.S.M. Shea, C.B., D.S.O.,

Commanding 151st Infantry Brigade.

Reference
Trench
Map.

18th August, 1915.

1. The Brigade will be relieved by the 149th Brigade on the night of the 19/20th.

2. Guides will be provided by Battalions as under, to be at Level Crossing C.27.a.2.2 at the times stated below:-

At 8.15 p.m. for the 7th Bn. Northumberland Fusiliers.

From 6th Bn. Durham L.I.

1 Guide for 74.
1 Guide for 74 S.
2 Guides each for two machine gun emplacements.

From 7th Bn. Durham L.I.

1 Guide for right half of trench 75.
1 Guide for 75 S.
1 Guide for 76 S.

At 8.30 p.m. for the 4th Bn. Northumberland Fusiliers.

From 7th Bn. Durham L.I.

1 Guide for each of 4 machine gun emplacements.
1 Guide for the left half of 75.
1 Guide for 76.
1 Guide for 77.
1 Guide for 77 S.
1 Guide for Battalion Headquarters.

At 8.45 p.m. for the 5th Bn. Northumberland Fusiliers.

From the 9th Bn. Durham L.I.

1 Guide for 78.
1 Guide for 78 S.
1 Guide for 79.
1 Guide for each of 2 machine gun emplacements.

From the 6th Bn. Durham L.I.

1 Guide for S.P. Y.
1 Guide for S.P. Z.

O.O. 13.   Sheet 2.

At 9 p.m. for the 6th Bn. Northumberland Fusiliers.

From the 9th Bn. Durham L.I.

    1 Guide for trench 80.
    1 Guide for 80 S.
    1 Guide for CANADA ROW.
    1 Guide for 79 S.
    1 Guide for left machine gun emplacement.
    1 Guide for Battalion Headquarters.

3.   Battalions on relief will proceed to billets in ARMENTIERES.

4.   The 5th Loyal North Lancs. Regt. and the 8th Bn. Durham L.I. will move, not before 8.30 p.m. to new billets which will be indicated to them in ARMENTIERES.

5.   Brigade Headquarters on completion of relief will move to 3, Rue Bayard.

6.   Completion of reliefs to be reported to this office.

                                      E.R. Clayton, Captain,
                                          Brigade Major,
                                  151st Infantry Brigade.

Copy No. 1 filed.
"   No. 2 to 6th Bn. Durham L.I.
"   No. 3 to 7th Bn. Durham L.I.
"   No. 4 to 8th Bn. Durham L.I.
"   No. 5 to 9th Bn. Durham L.I.
"   No. 6 to 5th Loyal N. Lancs. Regt.
"   No. 7 to 3rd Northumbrian Bde. R.F.A.
"   No. 8 to 1st Field Coy. R.E.

121/0918

50th Division

3rd Wellington Rifle Bde RFA.

Vol V

(Aug & Sep 15)

WAR DIARY
3RD Northumbrian Brigade R.F.A (T.)
INTELLIGENCE SUMMARY. 50 Division

Army Form C. 2118.

No. 13.

Hour, Date, Place	Summary of Events and Information	Remarks and references to Appendices
ARMENTIERES		
29 August 1915	11 Rounds fired in Retaliation to hostile fire.	The hostile fire was mainly directed against our infantry Trenches.
30 "	29 " " " " " "	
31 "	26 " " " " " "	
1 September	29 " " " " " "	Our Retaliation was on several known positions behind the enemy's line, and against their front line Trenches.
2	13 " " " " " "	
3	20 " " " " " "	
4	41 " " " " " "	
5	34 " " " " " "	
6	31 " " " " " "	
7	43 " " " " " "	
8	46 " " " " " "	
9	24 " " " " " "	
10	67 " " " " " "	
11	65 " " " " " "	

W.T. Pearson
Lieut. Col.
Commdg. 3rd. Nbn. Bde. R.F.A.

WAR DIARY 3rd Northumbrian Brigade R.F.A.
or
INTELLIGENCE SUMMARY. 50th Division.

Army Form C. 2118.

No. 14.

Hour, Date, Place	Summary of Events and Information	Remarks and references to Appendices
ARMENTIERES. 12 September 1915.	150th Infy Brigade covering will be relieved by 151st Infy Bde. 6 rounds 14. Rounds fired in Retaliation to hostile fire.	Operation orders marked D.1. herewith.
13th do.	14 — — —	
14th do.	Called on Brigade 151st Infy Brigade	
15th do.	38. Rounds fired in Retaliation to hostile fire	
16th do.	62 — — —	
17th do.	22 — — —	
18th do.	74 — — —	
19th do.	84 — — —	
	101 — — —	
	Relief in Battalions of 151st Infy Brigade.	Operation orders marked D.2. herewith.
20 do 4 p.m.	Our Divisional Artillery bombard German trenches on front as per operation orders marked D.3. 196 rounds were fired by this Brigade.	D.3. herewith.
21. do 7 a.m.	Heavy hostile bombardment on our trenches. Fired 67 rounds in retaliation.	

J W Peart
Lieut. Col.
Commdg. 3rd Nbn. Bde. R.F.A.

WAR DIARY or INTELLIGENCE SUMMARY.

3rd Northumbrian Brigade R.F.A Army Form C. 2118.
50th Division

No 15.

Hour, Date, Place	Summary of Events and Information	Remarks and references to Appendices
ARMENTIERES Sepr 22, 1915.	Heavy hostile fire directed against Trenches 75. 76 - 1st & 2nd Batteries retaliated - 199 rounds expended	
23. "	149th Infy Brigade relieved 151st Infy Brigade 125 rounds ammⁿ expended in retaliation to hostile fire.	Operation order herewith marked D.4.
24. "	21 rounds fired	50th Div Operation order herewith marked D.5
25. "	The Brigade took part in the Divisional demonstration under C.R.A in support of the Offensive by 1st & 3rd Armies. 50th Divisional Artillery programme herewith - 298. rounds ammⁿ expended. Casualties 1 man wounded - 12 horses killed 7 horses wounded. Telegraph to H.Q. Staff.	50th Div R.A. Ntks. D.6. - programme D.7.
26. "	151st Infy Brigade take over from 12th Division 136th Infy Brigade 25. Rounds fired. - 2 guns of 2nd Brigade at Romarin & Chapelle d'Armentieres respectively groups in ag^t commands.	Operation order herewith marked D.8.
27. "	ARMENTIERES Headquarters shelled by hostile fire. - 47 Rounds fired in retaliation. 151st Infantry Brigade take over trenches from 37th Infy Bde of 12th Division	Operation order D.9. herewith

fr Pearson Lieut. Col.
Commdg. 3rd. Nbn. Bde. R.F.A.

3RD Northumbrian Brigade
R.F.A. Army Form C. 2118.

No. 16.

WAR DIARY
or
INTELLIGENCE SUMMARY.
(Erase heading not required.)

Instructions regarding War Diaries and Intelligence Summaries are contained in F.S. Regs., Part II. and the Staff Manual respectively. Title pages will be prepared in manuscript.

Hour, Date, Place	Summary of Events and Information	Remarks and references to Appendices
ARMENTIERES		
Sep. 28. 1915	39 Rounds do fired in retaliation to hostile fire.	
" 29. 1915	8 Rounds fired in retaliation to hostile fire.	
" 30. 1915	12 Rounds fired " "	

Jos. [signature]
Lieut. Col.
Commdg. 3rd. Nbn. Bde. R.F.A.

Appendix 2

(1390) Wt. W 9044-1104. 12/14. 40,000 Pads. S. B. Ltd.
"B" Form.   Army Form C 2122

MESSAGES AND SIGNALS.   No. of Message

Prefix	Code	m.	Received	Sent	Office Stamp
Office of Origin and Service Instructions.	Words.	At ___ m.	At ___ m.	
		From	To	
		By	By	

TO — No 19 C.C.S.

| Sender's Number | Day of Month | In reply to Number | AAA |

Please send 3 NCOs & 20 men to report to OC South Midland Clearing Station for temporary duty. Rations for the day to be taken. OC South Midland CC Station to ration for monday. A lorry to be obtained on loan to convey party to AMIENS and return. Written orders to be given to NCO in charge. OC South Midland CC Station to return party on evening

From
Place
Time

* This line should be erased if not required.

(1380) Wt. W 9044-1194 12/14. 40,000 Pads. S.B. Ltd.
"B" Form.   Army Form C 2122
MESSAGES AND SIGNALS.   No. of Message_____

Prefix____Code____m.	Received	Sent	Office Stamp.
Office of Origin and Service Instructions. Words.	At____m.	At____m.	
	From	To	
	By	By	

TO {

| * Sender's Number | Day of Month | In reply to Number | AAA |

of Monday 6th in one of his own lorries. The party should leave Beauval not later than 9am tomorrow

From DM G.S. Army
Place
Time 11.5 pm

* This line should be erased if not required.

3RD NORTHUMBRIAN BDE R.F.A

WAR DIARY

Copy No. 8.

OPERATION ORDERS NO. 17
by
Brigadier General J.S.M. Shea, C.B., D.S.O.,
Commanding 151st Infantry Brigade.

D.I.

11th Sept. 1915.

Reference Trench Map.

2 Sheets

1. The Brigade will relieve the 150th Brigade on the night of Sept. 12/13th.

   The 8th Bn. Durham L.I. will take over trench 74 and 6 bays of trench 75 from the 5th Bn. Durham L.I.

   The 7th Bn. Durham L.I. will take over trench 75 (less 6 bays) from the 5th Bn. Durham L.I. Trench 76, 77 and 6 bays of trench 78 from the 5th Yorks. Regt.

   The 9th Bn. Durham L.I. will take over trench 78 (less 6 bays) from the 5th Yorks. Regt. Trench 79 and trench 80 from the 4th Yorks. Regt.

   The 6th Bn. Durham L.I. will take over S.P. Y and S.P. Z from the 4th East Yorks. Regt. These two supporting points will be under the orders of the O.C. 9th Bn. Durham L.I.

2. Battalions moving in relief will pass the level crossing C.27.a.2.2 at the following hours:-

   8th Bn. Durham L.I.   7.30 p.m.
   7th Bn. Durham L.I.   7.50 p.m.
   9th Bn. Durham L.I.   8.10 p.m.
   6th Bn. Durham L.I.   8.30 p.m.

3. Machine guns will be allotted to sectors as under:-

   9th Bn. Durham L.I., 5 guns, including one from
                                 the 8th Bn. Durham L.I.
   7th Bn. Durham L.I., 4 guns.
   8th Bn. Durham L.I., 3 guns.
   One gun from the 6th Bn. Durham L.I. will be placed
       in each of the two supporting points Y and Z.
   Two guns from the 5th L.N. Lancs. Regt. will be placed
       in the subsidiary line under the orders of the
       Brigade Machine Gun Officer.

4. Guides for machine guns will be at the level crossing C.27.a.2.2 at the following hours:-

   For the 8th Bn. Durham L.I. at 7.30 p.m.
       3 Guides for emplacements in 74, 74 S. and 75 from
           the 5th Bn. Durham L.I.
   For the 7th Bn. Durham L.I. at 7.50 p.m.
       1 Guide for an emplacement in trench 75 from
           the 5th Bn. Durham L.I.
       3 Guides for emplacements about trenches 76 and 77
           from the 5th Yorks. Regt.

1.

O.O.17.   Sheet 2.

D.1 continued

    For the 9th Bn. Durham L.I. at 8.10 p.m.
        4 Guides for emplacements in 79, 80 and 80 S.
           from the 4th Yorks. Regt.
        1 Guide for an emplacement in 78 from the
           5th Yorks. Regt.
    For the 6th Bn. Durham L.I. at 8.30 p.m.
        2 Guides for emplacements in supporting points
           from the 4th East. Yorks. Regt.

5. Artillery support is provided as under by the 3rd Northumbrian Brigade R.F.A:-

    1st Battery, C.27.b.2.2 support trenches 74.75.76.
    2nd Battery, C.27.d.2.8   "   "   77.78.
    3rd Battery, I.8.a.8.10   "   "   79.80.

6. The 5th L.N. Lancs. Regt. will move into billets as indicated by Staff Captain. This move is not to take place before 6.30 p.m.

7. Brigade H.Q. will take over the present Headquarters of the 150th Brigade - I.1.d.4.8, 55 RUE DE LILLE, at 10 p.m.

8. Communication trenches are allotted as under:-

    PLANE AVENUE will be used and kept in repair by the 8th Bn. Durham L.I. and will also be used by the 7th Bn. Durham L.I.
    AUSTRALIA AVENUE and JAPAN ROAD will be kept in repair by the 7th Bn. Durham L.I.
    That part of AUSTRALIA AVENUE which runs from S.P. Z to trench 78 will be used and kept in repair by the 9th Bn. Durham L.I.
    SPAIN AVENUE is allotted to the 9th Bn. Durham L.I.

9. The completion of reliefs to be reported to this office.

                                        E.R. Clayton, Major,
                                            Brigade Major,
                                      151st Infantry Brigade.

Copy No. 1 filed.
Copy No. 2 to 6th Bn. Durham L.I.
Copy No. 3 to 7th Bn. Durham L.I.
Copy No. 4 to 8th Bn. Durham L.I.
Copy No. 5 to 9th Bn. Durham L.I.
Copy No. 6 to 5th L.N. Lancs. Regt.
Copy No. 7 to 1st Field Coy. R.E.
Copy No. 8 to 3rd Nbn. Brigade R.F.A.
Copy No. 9 to 150th Inf. Brigade.

Copy No. 8

OPERATION ORDERS NO.18
by
Brigadier General J.S.M. Shea, C.B., D.S.O.,
Commanding 151st Infantry Brigade.

Reference
Trench
Map.

17th Sept. 1915.

1. Reliefs will take place within the Brigade on the night of Sept. 18/19th.

2. The 6th Bn. D.L.I. will take over trench 74 and the first 6 bays of 75 from the 8th Bn. D.L.I.

   The 5th L.N. Lancs. will take over trench 75 (less 6 bays) trenches 76, 77 and 6 bays of 78 from the 7th Bn. D.L.I.

3. Battalions will pass the level crossing C.27.a.2.2 at the following hours:-

   6th Bn. D.L.I. at 7.15 p.m.
   5th L.N. Lancs. at 7.35 p.m.

4. Supporting points Y and Z will come under the orders of the O.C. 6th Bn. Durham L.I.

5. The two machine guns of the 6th Bn. D.L.I. in S.P. Y and S.P. Z will be relieved by two machine guns of the 7th Bn. D.L.I. and will rejoin their Battalion in trench 74.

   One machine gun from the 8th Bn. D.L.I. and one from the 5th L.N. Lancs. will be posted in the Subsidiary Line in relief of the guns already there.

6. The 7th Bn. D.L.I. and 8th Bn. D.L.I. on relief will move into billets at places indicated by the Staff Captain.

7. Communication trenches are allotted as under:-

   PLANK AVENUE will be used and kept in repair by the 6th Bn. D.L.I. and will also be used by the 5th L.N. Lancs. Regt.

   AUSTRALIA AVENUE and JAPAN ROAD will be kept in repair by the 5th L.N. Lancs.

   That part of AUSTRALIA AVENUE which runs from S.P. Z to trench 78 will be used and kept in repair by the 9th Bn. D.L.I.

   PLANK AVENUE is allotted to the 9th Bn. D.L.I.

8. Completion of reliefs to be reported to this office.

E.R. Clayton, Major,
Brigade Major,
151st Infantry Brigade.

Copy No. 1 is filed.
Copy No. 2 to 6th Bn. D.L.I.
Copy No. 3 to 7th Bn. D.L.I.
Copy No. 4 to 8th Bn. D.L.I.
Copy No. 5 to 9th Bn. D.L.I.
Copy No. 6 to 5th L.N. Lancs.
Copy No. 7 to 1st Field Coy. R.E.
Copy No. 8 to 1st Nbn. Bde. R.F.A.

SECRET.   B.M. 532

O.C.,

3rd Northumbrian Brigade, R.F.A.

D.3.

3 sheets

1. At 4 P.M. on Monday, 20th. September, it is proposed to bombard a portion of the German trenches where, according to recent reports, there is much activity and a considerable amount of material has been brought up.

2. The Position selected for bombardment is from I.11.a.7½.9¾. to I.5.c.7½.1½., and the object is to surprise the enemy's working parties and destroy as much material as possible.

3/4. The Batteries taking part will be :-

    2nd. & 3rd. Northumberland Batteries,
        1st. Northumbrian Brigade, R.F.A.

    1st. Durham Battery,
        3rd. Northumbrian Brigade, R.F.A

    5th. Durham (Howitzer) Battery, R.F.A.

    2 Guns of 4th. Durham (Howitzer) Battery, R.F.A

    1 Gun of No. 2 Mountain Battery, R.G.A. (I.10.d.3.7.)

    3 Guns of 23rd. Trench Mortar Battery.

The fire of these Howitzers, 15 pdr. Guns, (with the exception of the 3rd. Northumberland Battery), Mountain Gun and Trench Mortars will be concentrated on this position; at the same time it will be enfiladed with machine guns.

The 3rd. Northumberland Battery will fire on "SPARROW'S NEST", (I.5.d.1.1.)

4. The following procedure will be carried out:-

FROM 3.30 P.M. TO 4.0 P.M. No guns will fire and no firing will take place in the trenches unless absolutely necessary.

3.55 P.M. Everyone taking part will "stand by" ready to open fire.

4.0 P.M. The 5th. Durham (Howitzer) Battery, R.F.A., will open fire and fire four rounds as rapidly as possible.

This will be the signal for the Bombardment to begin, and for every gun engaged to fire with the exception of the 2 guns of the 4th. Durham (Howitzer) Battery, R.F.A

The O.C., 4th. Durham (Howitzer) Battery, R.F.A.; will not open fire with his 2 guns until his F.O.O., reports that the 5th. Durham (Howitzer) Battery has fired its first four rounds. On this report being telephoned in, the 2 guns of the 4th. Durham (Howitzer) Battery, R.F.A. will each fire one round as quickly as possible and then fire at such a rate as will best spread the ammunition allotted them over the time of firing.

The 15 pdr. Batteries will each fire two rounds of "Gun fire" and then go to "Battery fire" at such a rate as will best spread the ammunition allotted them over the time of the firing.

The 1 gun of No. 2 Mountain Battery, R.G.A., will fire five rounds as quickly as possible and then five more during the period allotted to it.

The Trench Mortars will fire as quickly as possible.

4.5 P.M. The 15 pdr. Batteries and the one gun of No. 2 Mountain Battery, R.G.A., will cease fire and will "stand by" ready to continue the bombardment should the enemy reply.

4.10 P.M. The Howitzers and Trench Mortars will cease fire and stand by in their turn.

Each 15 pdr. Battery will be allowed . . . . 28 rounds.
5th. Durham (How.) B'ty. " " . . . . 20 "
4th. " " " " " . . . . 10 "
The 1 gun of No. 2 Mountain Battery, R.G.A.,
     will be allowed . . . . 10 "
The Trench Mortars " " " . . . . 18 "

The remaining 15 pdr. Batteries, the 2 guns of 4th Durham (Howitzer) Battery, R.F.A., the 31st. Trench Mortar Battery and the other gun of No. 2 Mountain Battery, R.G.A., will be ready to open fire at once on points that must be previously selected for them by their respective Brigade Commanders in the event of any retaliation being attempted by the enemy. 3 rounds per gun will be allowed them as a preliminary measure.

D.3. continued

The 9th. Heavy Battery will also be ready to crush any reply on the part of the enemy's batteries.

The SIGNAL TIME will be sent from this Office between 3.15 and 3.30 P.M. on Monday 20th. inst., to everybody concerned.

                                                A.G. Thomson.
                                                   Major, R.A.,
                                                B.M., 50th. D.A.

H'q. 50th. D.A.,
17-9-15.

Secret

3rd Northumbrian Bde RFA
War Diary

Copy No. 8

D.4

OPERATION ORDERS No. 19,

by

Brigadier General J.S.M. Shea, C.B., D.S.O.

2 sheets

Commanding 151st Infantry Brigade.

Reference
Trench
Map.

22nd September 15.

1.   The Brigade will be relieved by the 149th Brigade on the night of the 23rd/24th Sept. as under, -

5th Northumberland Fusiliers will take over trench 74 and right half of trench 75.

5th Border Regiment will take over left half of trench 75, trenches 76, 77, and S.P. Y.

4th Northumberland Fusiliers will take over trench 78, 79 less six bays, and S.P. Z.

6th Northumberland Fusiliers will take over six bays of trench 79, and trench 80.

2.   Guides are required as under, to be at the level crossing C.27.a.2.2.

For the 5th Northumberland Fusiliers at 7.15 p.m.

One guide for trench 74.
One guide for 74 S.
One guide for the right of trench 75.
One guide for new support trench at
    CHICKEN FARM.
One guide for 75 S.

The above will be furnished by the 6th Bn D.L.I.

For the 5th Border Regt. at 7.30 p.m.

One guide for S.P. Y from the 6th Bn. D.L.I.

One guide for the left of trench 75.
One guide for trench 76.
One guide for 76 S.
One guide for trench 77.
One guide for 77 S.

The above to be furnished by the 5th Loyal. N. Lancs. Regt.

3.   Battalions on relief will proceed to billets in ARMENTIERES.

/Order No. 4.

Sheet No. 2.

OPERATION ORDERS No. 19. (Cont:).

D.4.
continued

4. Brigade Headquarters on completion of reliefs will move to 3 RUE BAYARD.

5. Completion of reliefs to be reported to this office.

E.R.Clayton,
Major,
Brigade Major,
151st Inf. Brigade.

Copy No. 1 Filed.
" " 2 to 6th Bn. D.L.I.
" " 3 to 7th Bn. D.L.I.
" " 4 to 8th Bn. D.L.I.
" " 5 to 9th Bn. D.L.I.
" " 6 to 5th L.N.Lancs Regt.
" " 7 to 1st Northbn Field Coy. R.E.
" " 8 to 3rd Northbn Brigade R.F.A.
" " 9 to 149th Inf. Brigade.

3rd Northumbrian Bde R.F.A.
War diary

D.5
COPY No. 10
2 sheets

50th. DIVISION OPERATION ORDER No. 13.
****

24 - 9 - 15.

1. The 1st. and 3rd. Armies are about to assume the offensive.

2. The 2nd. Army is to hold the enemy to its front and to be prepared to take the offensive rapidly if the enemy retires.

3. Special instructions have been issued to the C. R. A. and Infantry Brigade Commanders as to the action to be taken by the Artillery and Infantry of the Division.

4. 1st. and 2nd. Northumbrian Field Coys. R.E. will remain affiliated to the 149th. and 150th. Infantry Brigades respectively, and will be prepared to carry out demolitions in any of the enemy's trenches that may be temporarily occupied by our Infantry.

5. 151st. Infantry Brigade will be in Corps Reserve, and will remain in billets ready to move.

6. Advanced Dressing Stations will be established from night 24th/25th. September at :-
   (1) The BRICQUERIE - I. 8. b. 3. 7.
   (2) 55 RUE VOLTAIRE - C. 26. b. 6. 6.

7. Barrel pier bridges will be thrown across the R. LYS on night 24th/25th. September as under :-
   One bridge at B. 29. b. 2.2. for train vehicles only.
   One bridge at B. 24. a. 6. 8.) For Artillery and
   One bridge at B. 18. c. 8. 3.) Ammunition only.
   These bridges will be used only in the event of the main ARMENTIERES - NIEPPE road being shelled.

8. "A" Sqdn. Yorks. Hussars will move on afternoon 24th. September to PONT DE NIEPPE.

9. All units of the Division will be prepared to move forward at short notice.

10. H. Q. of 149th. and 150th. Infantry Brigades will move to Advanced H. Q. night of 24th/25th. September.
    Div. H. Q. at ECOLE NATIONALE.

G.V. Hordern.
Lt.Col.,
General Staff,
50th Division.

Issued at 9.0 a.m.

SPECIAL INSTRUCTIONS TO C.R.A. AND INFANTRY BRIGADE COMMANDERS.

(Ref: Para. 5, Operation Order No. 13).

D.S. *[signature]*

1. At 4.56 a.m. on 25th September, if the wind is favourable, a wall of smoke will be started all along the front held by the Division, in accordance with the instructions already issued to 149th and 150th Infantry Brigades (G.X.482).

2. As soon as the smoke has been started rifle and machine gun fire will be opened on the enemy's parapets, and an artillery bombardment of the enemy's trenches will begin (Artillery programme attached).

3. The smoke will be continued till 5.30 a.m.

4. Between 4.15 a.m. and 4.56 a.m. quiet will be maintained in the trenches.

5. No pre-arranged Infantry assault will be made on any portion of the enemy's line opposed to us, but the utmost activity is to be shown in minor enterprises not only on 25th September but also during subsequent days and nights, and every endeavour made to lead the enemy to believe we are about to attack.   Advantage will, therefore, be taken of any panic on the part of the enemy, which may possibly arise from our use of smoke grenades or other causes, to occupy trenches which he may have abandoned and thus induce counter attack and fighting.

6. Should any portion of our Infantry occupy hostile trenches they will be afforded all possible Artillery Support without restriction to the ammunition allotted specially for these operations.

7. The correct time will be signalled from Div. H.Q. on evening of 24th September.

8. Should any alterations in these instructions be received from Corps Headquarters they will be communicated as early as possible.

9. It is thought that in the event of a successful offensive on the part of our troops, arrangements may be contemplated by the Germans for the automatic evolution of poisonous gases in their trenches after they have been evacuated.
‡ All Officers, telephonists, and orderlies who may have to go forward with the Infantry must wear their tube helmets when the time comes to advance.   These helmets will be worn rolled up so as not to interfere with vision and breathing.

(sgd) G. V. Hordern, Lt.Col.
General Staff,
50th Division.

24th September, 1915.

‡ refers to Artillery.

Reference 1/20,000, Sheets 36 N.W. & N.E.   COPY NO. 5

3rd Northumbrian R.F.A.

D.6

50th DIVISIONAL ARTILLERY OPERATION ORDER No. 4.

24-9-15.

1. The 1st and 3rd Armies are about to assume the offensive.

2. The 2nd Army is to hold the enemy to its front and to be prepared to take the offensive rapidly if the enemy retires.

3. The action of the Artillery between 5.0a.m. and 5.30a.m. on the 25th September, 1915, is given in the Programme of tasks sent you this afternoon.

4. Ammunition in addition to that in the limbers and wagons will be dumped as follows on the gun positions :-
    (i)   20 rounds per 15-pdr.
    (ii) 15 rounds per 5" B.L.Howitzer.
    (iii) 25 rounds per Mountain Gun.

5. The Artillery will be under the immediate orders of the C.R.A., but Infantry Brigadiers may call upon the Brigades affiliated to them in case of necessity.
    O.C.

6. The 1st Northumbrian Brigade will send a "liaison" officer to the Headquarters of the G.O.C., 150th Infantry Brigade.
    The O.C., 3rd Northumbrian Brigade will send a "liaison" Officer to the Headquarters of the 149th Infantry Brigade.

7. The 1st Northumbrian Brigade Ammunition Column will supply the 150th Infantry Brigade.
    The 3rd Northumbrian Brigade Ammunition Column will supply the 149th Infantry Brigade.
    The 2nd Northumbrian Brigade Ammunition Column will be ready to supply the 151st Infantry Brigade, which is at present in Divisional Reserve.

8. Barrel pier bridges will be thrown across the R. LYS on night 24th/25th September as under :-
    One Bridge at B.29.b.2.2. for train vehicles only.
    One bridge at B.24.a.6.8.) For Artillery and
    One Bridge at B.18.c.8.3.) Ammunition only.
    These Bridges will be used only in the event of the main ARMENTIERES - NIEPPE road being shelled.

9. All Units of the Division must be prepared to move forward at short notice.

10. The Advanced Dressing Stations will be established on the night 24th/25th September at :-
    1. The BRICQUERIE - I.8.b.3.7.
    2. 55 RUE VOLTAIRE - C.26.b.6.6.

11. From 4.30a.m. on September 25th, Divisional Artillery Head-Quarters will be at the ECOLE NATIONALE.

L.G. Thomson.
Major, R.A.,
Brigade Major, 50th D.A.

Issued at 5.0p.m.

Copies 1 and 2 - C.R.A.
Copy No. 3 - 1st Northbn. Bde. R.F.A. (Copy No.6 - 4th Northbn. Bde.RFA.
Copy No. 4 - 2nd Northbn. Bde. R.F.A. (Copy No. 7 - 16th Brigade R.G.A.
Copy No. 5 - 3rd Northbn. Bde. R.F.A. (Copy No. 8 - No. 2 Mountain Battery
                                                     R.G.A.

B.M./S.12/1.

D-7.
7 sheets

SECRET.

O.C., 3rd Northumbrian Brigade R.F.A.

The attached **programme of tasks** is now forwarded to you. At 5.0am, the Artillery will open with a rapid rate of fire on the targets first allotted to them - see programme attached.
5.5a.m. Fire will be lifted to the Artillery's second objectives, and will be maintained at a steady rate, until 5.30a.m.

The secondary objectives in the case of the 1st Durham Battery, 3rd Northumbrian Brigade are the communication trenches running from I.5 Central to I.6., and later on, CHIMNEY FARM.

In the case of the 1st Battery, 1st Northumbrian Brigade the secondary objectives will be either WEZ MACQUART or the Battery at I.23.b., if necessary.

In the case of the 2nd Battery, 1st Northumbrian Brigade, the secondary objectives will be the works at I.17. Central, or the guns in I. 23.b.

Should favourable targets present themselves, Battery Commanders can depart from the programme laid down, but Divisional Artillery Headquarters should, if possible, be notified when this has been done.

Allotment of Ammunition is attached.

Please acknowledge receipt.

R.G. Thomson.
Major, R.A.,
B.M., 50th D.A.

Hq. 50th D.A.
24. 9. 15.

※ The 2nd Durham Battery. R.F.A. will not fire on LE TEMPLE. Please amend original programme.

D7 cont.

50th DIVISIONAL ARTILLERY.

ARTILLERY PROGRAMME FOR SATURDAY, SEPTEMBER 25th, 1915.

LEFT SECTOR. Reference: Sheet 36. N.W. and N.E.

3rd Northumbrian Brigade.

    1st Battery :- Communication trench, I.5 Central to I.6.
        Support trenches opposite 76 and 75.
        Afterwards Cross-roads at LA FRESNELLE (I.12.b.9.9.)

    2nd Battery :- Communication trenches in C.29.d., and BRUNE RUE.
        Afterwards on the barrel breastwork, L'AVENTURE, and
        LE TEMPLE.

    3rd Battery :- Trenches and support trenches opposite 79 and 80.
        Afterwards L'AVENTURE and WHITE CHATEAU (J.1.a.9.0.)

5th Durham (Howitzer) Battery.:-

    One Section on support trench opposite 79.
    One section on BRUNE RUE, and FARM "A".
    Afterwards Farm and Redoubt, I.12.a.2½.7., and
    I.6.a.5½.1. (CHIMNEY FARM).

Mountain Gun near HAYSTACK FARM (I.10.d.2.7.) :-

    Enfilade trenches opposite 74, 75, and 77, and
    Support trenches in rear.

Mountain Gun near DURHAM CASTLE (C.22.c.1.7.):-

    Enfilade trenches opposite 79, 78 and 77, and
    support trenches in rear.

2nd Northumbrian Brigade:-

    A gun at I.2.c.2.3. to fire at barrel breastwork,
    and communication trench running N.E. from BRUNE RUE.

    One gun at C.22.a.2.4. to enfilade trenches opposite
    79, 78, and 77.

The two Mountain Guns will be at the disposal of the Infantry Brigadier commanding the Left Sector.

D.7.
cont.

Reference 1/20,000 Sheets 36 N.W. & N.E.   50th DIVISIONAL ARTILLERY OPERATIONS. 25.9.15.

FIRST PHASE.

UNIT.	TIME.	TASK.	ROUNDS PER GUN.
Gun at C.22.a.2.4.	5.0a.m. to 5.5a.m.	Enfilading trenches opposite 79, 78, & 77.	6
Gun at I.2.c.2.3.	-do-	Fire at Barrel Breastwork and communication trench running N.E. from BRUNE RUE.	6
Gun at C.22.c.1.7.	-do-	Enfilade trenches opposite 79 and 77, and support trenches in rear.	6
Gun at I.10.d.3.7.	-do-	Enfilade trenches opposite 74 and 75, and support trenches in rear.	6
Battery at I.2.c.7.0.	-do-	Fire on the trenches opposite 79 and 80.	7
Battery at C.27.b.2.0.	-do-	Fire on the communication trenches in C.29.d., and BRUNE RUE.	7
Battery at C.27.d.2.8.	-do-	Fire on the support trenches opposite 75 and 76.	
Battery at C.27.d.7.6.	-do-	1 Section to fire on support trenches opposite 79. 1 Section to fire on BRUNE RUE.	5
Battery at C.26.d.5.5.	-do-	Fire on communication trench from SPARROWS WEST to I. 12 Central.	7
Battery at I.9.a.7.8.	-do-	Fire on support trenches opposite 71 & 72.	7
Battery at I.8.b.3.2.	-do-	" " " " 67 & 68	7

SHEET 2.

FIRST PHASE (cont/d)

UNIT.	TIME	TASK.	NUMBER OF ROUNDS.
Battery near ASHLUM.	5.0am to 5.5a.m.	Fire on support and communication trenches opposite 69 and 70.	7
Battery at I.9.c.5.8.	–do–	1 Section to fire on support trenches opposite 70.	5
		1 Section to fire on support trenches opposite 67.	6
9th Heavy Battery.	–do–	To fire on FORT SEHARMONT.	As rapidly as possible.

SECRET.

B.M./S.12/2.

O.C.,
    3rd Northumbrian Brigade R.F.A.

Ammunition is allotted to your Batteries as follows:-

To the 1st Durham Battery,   60 rounds.
To the 2nd Durham Battery,   70 rounds   (70)
To the 3rd Durham Battery,   62 rounds.

    28 rounds will be fired by Each Battery in the First Phase of the bombardment, i.e., from 5.0am to 5.5a.m.

    The remainder will be fired between 5.5a.m. and 5.30a.m.

L.G. Thomson.
Major, R.A.,
B.M., 50th D.A.

Hq. 50th D.A.
24. 9. 15.

Ref: 1/20,000 Sheets 36 N.W. & N.E.   50th DIVISIONAL ARTILLERY OPERATIONS. 25.9.15.

SECOND PHASE.

UNIT.	TIME.	TASK.	ROUNDS PER GUN.	REMARKS.
Battery at I.9.c.5.8.	5.5am to 5.30am.	One Section to fire on LA HOUGNIE, and trenches in vicinity. One Section to fire on VEZ MACQUART and I.17 Central.		In the two phases, each 18-pdr gun will fire on the average 17 rounds, each 5" B.L. Howitzer will fire 12 rounds, and each Mountain Gun will fire 25 rounds.
Battery at I.8.b.3.2.	-do-	To fire on VEZ MACQUART and on the Battery in I.23.b. if necessary.		
Battery at I.9.a.7.8.	-do-	To fire on works in I.17 Central, or if necessary, the Battery in I.23.b.		
Battery at C.26.d.5.5.	-do-	Fire on the communication trench running from SPARROWS NEST to I.12 Central, and KXXXXXXXXXETALIATION FARM.		
Battery near ASYLUM.	-do-	Fire on communication trench opposite Trenches 69 and 70, works in I.17 Central, and LA HOUGRIE.	Remainder of ammunition allotted.	
Battery at C.27.d.2.8.	-do-	Fire on communication trench running from I.5 Central to I.6, and CHIMNEY FARM.		
Battery at C.27.b.2.0.	-do-	Fire on Barrel breastwork and on L'AVENTURE.		
Battery at I.2.c.7.0.	-do-	Fire on L'AVENTURE and WHITE CHATEAU (J.1.a.9.0.)		
Howitzer Battery at C.27.a.7.6.	-do-	Fire on farm and redoubt at I.12.a.2½.7. and on CHIMNEY FARM.		
Gun at I.10.d.3.7.	-do-	Enfilade trenches opposite 74, 75 and 77, and support trenches in rear.		
Gun at C.22.c.1.7.	-do-	Enfilade trenches opposite 79, 78 and 77, and support trenches in rear.		
Gun at I.2.c.2.3.	-do-	Fire at Barrel breastwork and communication trench running N.E. from BRULE RUE.		
Gun at C.22.a.2.4.	-do-	Enfilade trenches opposite 79, 78, and 77. Will continue firing on FORT SEHARMONT. One section will be ready to reply if the enemy's artillery opens fire.	For the guns firing on FORT SEHARMONT, 25 rds per gun, H.E.
9th Heavy Battery.	-do-			

B.M./S.12.

Headquarters,
　　50th Division.
　　―――

　　With reference to your letter (un-numbered) dated 24th September, 1915, herewith another Programme shewing the two phases for artillery fire.

　　From 5.0a.m. to 5.5a.m. the artillery will fire on certain points of the front which are shewn in the programme headed "First Phase".

　　From 5.5a.m. to 5.30a.m. the artillery will lift on to other objectives according to the programme headed "Second "Phase".

　　If fire is required after 5.30a.m. the G.Os. C. Infantry Brigades can call upon their affiliated artillery Brigades to fire on any objective they may consider necessary. Similar action may be taken as regards the two howitzer batteries.

　　The O.C., Artillery Brigade concerned will inform the C.R.A. of the action taken by him.

　　If an attack by our Infantry is contemplated, the Officers Commanding Field Artillery Brigades will, on this being made known to them by the Infantry Brigadiers, make the necessary arrangements to support it, either by creating a "barrage" of fire, or by concentrating on the enemy's parapets.

R.G. Thomson.
Major
for Brig. Genl.,
C.R.A., 50th Division.

Hq. 50th D.A.
24. 9. 15.

D.8.

Copy No. 10

50th. DIVISION OPERATION ORDER No. 14.

26 - 9 - 15.

1. On night 26th/27th. September the 151st. Infantry Brigade will take over the line from left of 149th. Infantry Brigade to the R. LYS (trenches 81 to 89 inclusive) from 36th. Infantry Brigade of 12th. Division.

   Details of relief to be arranged between Infantry Brigades concerned.

2. The G. O. C. 50th. Division will assume command of this portion of the line on completion of relief.

3. The 62nd. Brigade R. F. A. (less "A" Battery) and "A" Battery 65th. (How.) Brigade R. F. A. 12th. Division will continue to cover this front.

4. The 70th. Field Coy. R. E. 12th. Division will be attached to the Division until relieved by the 7th. Field Coy R. E. and will continue to work in the sector held by 151st. Infantry Brigade.

5. The Battalion 151st. Infantry Brigade billetted in ARMENTIERES will be in Divisional Reserve. The name of this Battalion and position of its H. Q. will be reported to Div. H. Q..

6. The bridges referred to in para. 7, Operation Order No. 13, will be dismantled tonight.

7. The terms "Right", "Centre", and "Left" will be used to denote Brigade Areas in future.

[signature]

Lt.-Col.
General Staff,
50th. Division.

Issued at 4.30 p.m.

D.9

Copy No. 10.

50th DIVISION OPERATION ORDER No. 15.
----

27 - 9 - 15.

1. The 151st Infantry Brigade will tonight take over the line from R. LYS to C.4.a.4.7 (trenches 90 to 101 inclusive) from 37th Infantry Brigade of 12th Division.

2. G.O.C. 50th Division will assume command of this portion of the line on completion of relief.

3. The 13th Battalion, Canadian Division, is attached to the 151st Infantry Brigade and will relieve the left Battalion of 37th Infantry Brigade in the trenches.

4. The Artillery of 12th Division will continue to cover the same zones as at present. This Artillery will be attached to 50th Division forthwith.

5. The Pioneer Battalion, 12th Division, is attached to 50th Division and will billet tonight at LE BIZET.

6. The 7th Field Co. R.E. (less 1 Section) will rejoin the Division tomorrow.

G. V. Horden.

Lt.-Col.
General Staff,
50th. Division.

Issued at 5 p.m.

21/7333

50th Divn

3rd Northn'mbn Bde RFA.

Vol VI

Oct 15

WAR DIARY
of
III NORTHUMBRIAN BRIGADE R.F.A. 50th DIVISION
INTELLIGENCE SUMMARY

Army Form C. 2118.

Ser No. 17

Hour, Date, Place	Summary of Events and Information	Remarks and references to Appendices

ARMENTIERES

October 1st 1915

1. Batteries fired 32 rounds in retaliation to 1st report of an infantry.
2. Batteries fired 7 rounds.
3. Left 0 W/F H.A. Usherwood Slayford ordered to join 24th Division at once.
4. Batteries fired 11 rounds.
   Ammunition allowance at present being Nil, no firing can take place until further orders except in case of attack. Division of Trenches amongst Gulf Brigades taken into consideration. — Marked E.1.
   149th Inf Bde Brigade take over Trench 50 from 149th Inf Bde Brigade.
8. One section of No. 1, 3rd Durham Battery is relieved by D Battery 96th Bde RFA.
9. Remaining sections of 3rd Durham Battery is relieved by D Battery 96th Bde RFA.
10. An Artillery demonstration by the Artillery on our sector — Marked E2. duration ¾ hour herewith.
11. 2nd Lieut Wilson joined the Brigade as a reinforcement from 2nd Heavy & Cumbrian firing raid to the South during last 24 hours.
12. (2 p.m.) Ammunition allowance for 50th D.A. Nil.
13. Artillery demonstration by 18 pr batteries attached to Div. Operation orders marked E.3.

[signature] Lt Col
Comdg III N Bde RFA

RFA
WAR DIARY IIIrd NORTHUMBRIAN BRIGADE RFA Army Form C. 2118.
50th DIV

Sheet No 18

INTELLIGENCE SUMMARY

Hour, Date, Place	Summary of Events and Information	Remarks and references to Appendices
ARMENTIERES October 13th 1915	Disposition of Infantry Brigade over front as per Operation Order herewith.	marked E4
14	Artillery demonstration in wire cutting by 18 pr batteries resumed. Operation order herewith.	marked E5
	Any F.O.O. reported on the result of the demonstration that artillery fire against machine guns below the German lines might be used to good advantage.	
18	Ammunition allotment NIL	
20	D Battery 96th Bde R.F.A. is grouped under my command for tactical purposes.	
21	Relief in section by 94th Bde RFA begins as per Operation orders herewith.	Marked E6.
23	Relief by 94th Bde R.F.A. completed 6 p.m. Col Bannister took over Lt W.T. Young from C/110th Bde RFA appointed Adjutant vice Major for Brady. The Brigade marched to area 1 mile N.E. HAZEBROUCK bivouacing in route to new METEREN.	
24	Brigade billetted in new area by 1 p.m.	
26	Brigade ordered to move to an advanced reserve position near BAILLEUL.	
27 8.20 A.M.	Brigade marched about 3 miles S.W. of BAILLEUL. to an billetting area where it arrived about mid-day.	
28-31	3rd Northumbrian Bde RFA in forward reserve area.	

[signature] M^c? Renard?
Lieut. Col.
Commdg 3rd N^rn Bde RFA

SECRET. B.M./588.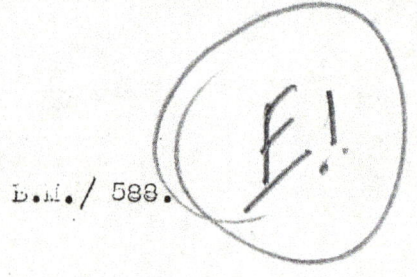

O.C.,
    3rd Northbn Bde R.F.A.

    The front of the Division having been extended as far as the R. LYS as a permanent arrangement, a definite portion of the line has now been allotted by the G.O.C., Division, to each Infantry Brigade, viz :-

Trenches 67 to 73 to 150th Infantry Brigade.
    "   74 to 80 " 149th   "   "
    "   81 to 89 " 151st   "   "

    For the future the above Brigades will be responsible for their own reliefs.

                          R.G. Thomson.
                          Major, R.A.,
                          B.M., 50th D.A.

Hq. 50th D.A.
4. 10. 15.

SECRET.  B.M./6...

O.C.,
3rd Northbn Bde R F A

Herewith the following :-

(a) Arrangements for demonstration on our front.
(b) Objectives.
(c) 2nd Corps G. 960 in regard to above.

No date has yet been fixed for this demonstration to take place..

L.G. Thomson.
Major, R.A.,
B.M., 50th D.A.

Hq.50th D.A.
11. 10. 15.

SECRET

(E3)

OPERATION ORDERS

An Artillery demonstration will take place today by the 95th, 26th Brigade R.F.A., 2nd Battery 3rd Northumbrian Brigade R.F.A. and 4th and 5th Durham Howitzer Batteries.

2.0pm to 3.30pm. Batteries will fire on allotted targets - 2nd Durham Battery will <u>stand by</u> ready to open fire on L'AVENTURE or other target as may be later ordered. The ammunition allowance for this purpose will be 102 rounds. These will be handed over by the O.C., 1st Battery

---

3.30pm Infantry Brigadier may decide to launch a fumite bomb smoke for 30 minutes, with heavy machine gun and rifle fire to simulate an attack. If the smoke is not started the enemy's front line parapets will not be bombarded by Artillery.

3.45pm to 4.0pm "A" Battery and two guns of 95 th Brigade will open fire on the salient C.29.a.5.0. with H.E.

4.0pm to 4.15pm "D" Battery 96th Brigade will open on same point.

The correct time will be signalled at 12 noon today
Battery Commanders will report to Headquarters every 20 minutes between 2.0pm and 4.0pm what is happening on their front. After 4.0pm as my may be necessary.
A Liaison Officer from 3rd Northumbrian Brigade R.F.A. will be attached to Battle Headquarters 149th Infantry Brigade at 1.30pm.

                                    Lieut Col,
Commanding 3rd Northumbrian Brigade., R.F.A.

13 Oct 1915

SECRET.

B.M./612/3.

O.C.,
3rd North'b Bde R.F.A.

The demonstration referred to in my B.M.612, dated 11/10/15 will take place to-morrow, 13th October.

1. The attached Programme, Marked "X", shews the procedure for the batteries detailed to cut the wire.

   These batteries will open fire at 2.0p.m. and continue firing until 3.30p.m.

2. (a) At 2.0p.m. "D" Battery, and the rear section of "C" Battery, 95th Brigade R.F.A. will fire on LES OURSINS FERME and on C.17.d.0.7. respectively. 10 rounds per gun of H. E. will be allotted for these tasks.

   (b) The 4th and 5th Durham (Howitzer) Batteries R.F.A. will be ready to open fire immediately on WEZ MACQUART and on C.30.a.9.2. respectively.

   (c) "A" Battery, 96th Brigade R.F.A. will guard against activity on the part of the Battery at I.23.b.9.3.
   Twenty rounds per gun of 18-pdr shrapnel will be allotted for this task.
   "B" and "C" Batteries, 96th Brigade R.F.A. will, in the event of any retaliation on the enemy's part, fire on LA HONGRIE FERME and the work at I.12 Central, respectively.
   10 rounds of H.E. per gun will be allotted for this purpose.

   (d) The remainder of the ammunition, (H. E. and shrapnel), allotted to the 18-pdr Brigades will be distributed at the discretion of the Officers Commanding those Brigades.
   Particular attention will be paid to the Salient at C.23.c.8.7., the communication trench between I.5.d.1.1. and I.12 Central, the work at I.12 Central, L'AVENTURE, and the enemy guns near I.17 central, and in I.23.b.

   As the demonstration proceeds, fresh targets will be assigned to batteries by the C.R.A.

   (e) The allotment of ammunition, previously notified, will hold good, i.e.,
   4,000 rounds shrapnel.
   800   "   H. E.

   of this,   480 rounds shrapnel, and
              200   "   H. E. will be kept in reserve.

   (f) The salient at C.29.a.5.0. will be attacked with H. E. as follows :-

   From 3.45p.m. to 4.0p.m., by { "A" Battery, and 2 guns of
                                          { "C" Battery, 95th Brigade RFA.

   From 4.0p.m. to 4.15p.m. by "D" Battery, 96th Brigade RFA.

Sheet 2.

3. At 3.30p.m., if the wind is favourable, "fumite" bombs will be discharged along the front between trenches 74 and 89, both inclusive.

   The smoke will be continued for 30 minutes.

   The G.Os.C. 149th and 151st Infantry Brigades will decide whether to start the smoke or not, and will notify the C.R.A. and Div. H.Q. of their intentions by 2.0p.m.

4. When the smoke is seen to be nearing the enemy's line shrapnel, machine gun and rifle fire will be turned on to his parapets and communication trenches, and every means taken to make the enemy believe an assault is intended.

5. If the smoke is not started, shrapnel will not be fired at the enemy's front parapets but his communication trenches and the works behind his line must be kept under fire.

6. The correct time will be signalled at 12 noon, October 13th.

7. Certain portions of our front trenches must be kept clear of troops during the wire-cutting.
   Os. C. 95th and 93th Brigades must arrange this with the G.O.C. 151st and 150th Infantry Brigades respectively.

8. The Os. C. 3rd and 4th Northumbrian Brigades R.F.A. will arrange to let the C.R.A. have a detailed report of what is happening on their respective fronts every twenty minutes from 2.0pm until 4.0pm.
   After 4.0p.m. they will only report as may be necessary.

9. Liaison Officers will be detailed as follows :-

   By the O.C., 93th Brigade R.F.A. to the H.Q. 150th Inf. Bde.

   "   "   "   95th   "   "   "   H.Q., 151st "   "

   "   "   "   3rd Northbn. Bde   "   H.Q., 149th "   "

   They should be at those Headquarters by 1.45p.m. on 13th October.

10. Reliefs will be arranged for the detachments serving the guns of the wire-cutting batteries. Particular attention must be paid to keeping the gun-layers as fresh as possible.

11. The communications between the Headquarters of Artillery Brigades and the Battle Headquarters of the Infantry Brigades with which they work are to be carefully looked to to-morrow morning.

12. Please acknowledge receipt.

A copy of 2nd Corps / G.8 dated 11/10/15 is attached.

R.G. Thomson.
Major, R.A.,
B.M., 50th D.A.

Hq. 50th D.A.
12. 10. 15.

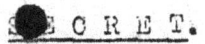SECRET.

2nd Corps
G. S.

50th Division.

1. Reference my G. 960 of the 10th instant.

The wire cutting and breaching of the enemy's trenches at the selected spots opposite the 2nd Corps front will commence at 2.0p.m. on the 13th. In order to be independent of weather the artillery told off for these tasks should have been previously registered, and this registration should be verified on the morning of the 13th if conditions are favourable: otherwise no indication of the covering artillery action should be given before 2.0p.m.

2. Smoke on the fronts arranged for should, unless the weather is unfavourable, be commenced at 3.30p.m. at which hour the German trenches will be subjected to shrapnel fire and every means taken to make the enemy believe that an assault is intended.

(sgd) P. de B. Radcliffe,
B.G.G.S.

11. 10. 15.

Reference Sheet 36, N.W.　　　　　　　Sheet 3.

1st P H A S E.
2.0p.m. to 2.15p.m.

Battery.	Objective.	Rate of fire.	No. of Rounds.
B/95.	C.29.a.4½.3½. to C.29.a.6½.5½.	Start with 3 rounds of Battery Fire, 10 Seconds. Then go to Section Fire, 20 seconds.	About 93.
Section C/95.	C.29.a.6½.5½. to C.29.a.7.7½.	Section Fire, 20 seconds.	45.
A/95.	C.29.a.7.7½. to C.29.a.7½.9.	Start with four rounds of Battery Fire, 10 Seconds. Then Right Section goes to Section Fire, 20 seconds. No. 3 Gun to Gun Fire, 20 seconds.	About 93.
D/96.	C.29.c.5.8½ to C.29.c.6½.7.	Start with 3 rounds of Battery Fire, 10 seconds. Then go to Section Fire, 20 seconds.	About 93.

A pause of 10 minutes.

2nd PHASE, 2.25p.m. - 2.40p.m.
(As for 1st Phase).

A pause of 10 minutes.

3rd PHASE, 2.50p.m. - 3.5p.m.
(As for 1st Phase).

A pause of 10 minutes.

4th PHASE, 3.15p.m. to 3.30p.m.
(As for 1st Phase).

From 2.17p.m. to 2.23p.m., One gun of advanced section C/95 will enfilade the wire in front of 80 Trench, at Gun Fire, 30 seconds.

At 2.23p.m. it will switch back to its former line of fire.

From 3.7p.m. to 3.13p.m. the same gun will carry out the same procedure.

From 2.42p.m. to 2.48p.m. One gun of "D" Battery, 96th Brigade will enfilade the wire in front of 81 trench, at Gun Fire, 30 seconds.

Sheet 4.

After 3.30p.m. Batteries, except those referred to in Para: 2 (f) of the accompanying letter, will fire on orders given them through their Brigade Commanders by the C. R. A.

If ordered to fire, they will open out their lines of fire, and sweep in between.

B.C.'s must select their objectives before-hand.

The O.C., Advanced Section C/95 will arrange with O.C. B/95 that their lines of fire do not clash.

Detachments will be changed after each phase.

As many men as possible will be collected for the supply of ammunition, and to relieve those serving the guns.

Ammunition.

Ammunition will be carefully sorted into lots.

Fuze 85 will be used for cutting wire.   Dates of fuzes should be ascertained.

Loading.

When loading 85 fuzes the stud on the fuze will be kept uppermost.   Should the fuze strike the breech the round will be at once unloaded and examined.

S E C R E T.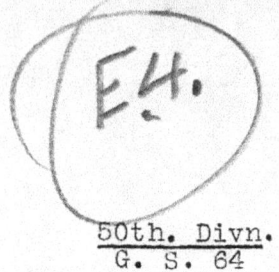

50th. Divn.
G. S. 64

The following will be substituted for para. 1 of
50th. Divn. of 2nd. July.
G. X. 85

1. The front held by the Infantry is divided into 3 sections, viz:-

Right Section - Trenches held by 150th. Infantry Brigade.
Centre Section-   "   "   " 149th.   "   "
Left Section -   "   "   " 151st.   "   "

Each of these sections is covered by the fire of one Brigade R. F. A..

13th. October 1915.

Lt.-Col.
General Staff,
50th. Division.

S E C R E T.   50th. Divn.
                                                            G. S. 64

The following will be substituted for para. 1 of
50th. Divn. of 2nd. July.
 G. X. 85

1.   The front held by the Infantry is divided into 3
sections, viz:-

Right Section - Trenches held by 150th. Infantry Brigade.
Centre Section-   "   "   " 149th.   "   "
Left Section -   "   "   " 151st.   "   "

Each of these sections is covered by the fire of one
Brigade R. F. A..

                                    [signed] J. V. Hordern
                                                Lt.-Col.
                                             General Staff,
13th. October 1915.   50th. Division.

B.H./612/5.

O.C.,

B.E.5.

The demonstration referred to in my B.H.312 dated 11/10/15 will be resumed by the Batteries of the 95th and 96th Brigades R.F.A..

1. The attached programme marked "Y" shews the procedure for the batteries detailed to cut the wire.
    These Batteries will start firing at 2.30p.m.

2. (a). While wire cutting is proceeding, "D" Battery, and the rear section of "C" Battery, 95th Brigade R.F.A. will fire at targets which may be allotted to them by the Brigade Commander.
    (Howitzer)
    (b). The 4th and 5th Durham Batteries R.F.A. must stand by ready in case they are called upon to open fire in retaliation.

    (c). "A" Battery, 96th Brigade R.F.A. will guard against activity on the part of the battery at I.23.b.9.3.
    "B" and "C" Batteries, 96th Brigade R.F.A. will fire on targets as allotted to them by the O.C. Brigade.

    (d). The ammunition for the 95th and 96th Brigades R.F.A. is allotted as follows :-

    For the wire cutting,   95th Brigade - 312 rounds. ⎫ shrapnel.
                            96th Brigade - 132   "   ⎭

    For general purposes,   150 H.E. to each Brigade, and Shrapnel at the discretion of Brigade Commanders

3. The correct time will be signalled to you at 2.0pm, October 14th.

5. Please acknowledge receipt.

L.G. Thomson.

Major, R.A.,
B.H., 50th D.A.

Hq. 50th D.A.
14. 10. 15.

Shoot 2.

Reference Sheet 33, N.W.

1st PHASE.
2.30p.m. to 2.45 p.m.

Battery.	Objective.	Rate of fire.	No. of Rounds.
B/95.	C.29.a.4½.3½ to C.29.a.6½.5½.	Start with 3 rounds of Battery Fire, 10 seconds. Then go to Section Fire, 30 seconds.	60
Section C.95.	C.29.a.6½.5½. to C.29.a.7.7½.	Section fire, 30 seconds.	30
A/95.	C.29.a.7.7½ to C.29.a.7½.9.	Start with four rounds of Battery Fire, 10 Seconds. Then right section goes to Section Fire, 30 seconds. No. 3 gun to Gun Fire, 30 seconds.	30
D/96.	C.29.c.5.8½ to C.29.c.6½.7.	Start with 3 rounds of Battery Fire, 10 seconds. Then go to Section Fire, 30 seconds.	60

A pause of 10 minutes.

2nd PHASE,. 2.55p.m. to 3.10p.m.
(As for 1st Phase).

From 2.47pm to 2.53pm one gun of "D" Battery, 96th Brigade will enfilade the wire in front of 81 trench at Gun Fire, 30 seconds.

From 3.12p.m. to 3.18p.m. one gun of Advanced Section C/95 will enfilade the wire in front of 80 trench at Gun Fire, 30 seconds.

S E C R E T

F.6

OPERATION ORDERS BY LIEUT COL G.T. PEARSON R.F.A.
FOR 21st October 1915

ORDERS FOR THE RELIEF OF 3rd NORTHUMBRIAN BRIGADE
R.F.A. by the 94th BRIGADE, R.F.A.

1. The move will be effected by sections the first section being relieved at 6pm on the night of Oct 21st and the rear section at 6pm on the night of Oct 23rd.

2. 1st Durham Battery will be relieved by "A" Battery 94th Bde R.F.A.
   2nd Durham Battery will be relieved by "B" Battery 94th Bde R.F.A.
   THE same applying to wagon lines.

3. 1st and 2nd Durham Batteries will have two guides at the cross roads at PONT DE NIEPPE, B.23.a.8½.3½. Sheet 36.N.W. at 2pm to lead incoming Batteries to their wagon lines and the Battery Staffs to the gun positions.

4. The incoming sections will have their leading sections guns and F.B. wagons brought up by the teams and drivers of the outgoing sections and these teams will the guns and wagons of the outgoing sections away.

5. Battery Commanders will hand over all 1/10,000 maps, telephone charts and any documents likely to be of assistance to the incoming Batteries also their 1/20,000, Sheet 36 N.W. & N.E., if the incoming Batteries do not already possess each.

6. The 2nd Brigade Ammunition Column will be responsible for ammunition supply to rear sections after 8am 22/10/15.

7. The 3rd Durham Battery will move with the 1st and 2nd Batteries, 2nd Northumbrian Brigade on 22nd Oct 15. Marching orders later.

8. The leading sections of the 1st and 2nd Batteries will be under O.C., 1st x Battery. They will stay the night 21/22 Oct at X.5.c.3.2. Sheet 27. Marching orders will be issued later.

9. Ammunition Column will stand by, ready to move at two hours notice from to-morrow morning.

Further operation orders will be issued for the relief of the rear sections.

Lieut Col.
Commanding 3rd Northumbrian Brigade., R.F.A.

X 10.30am
21st October 1915.

Copy No.1   C.O. 3rd Nbn Bde R.F.A.
"   No.2   O.C. 1st Durham Battery
"   No.3   O.C. 2nd Durham Battery
"   No.4   O.C. 3rd Durham Battery
"   No.5   O.C. 3rd Nbn Bde Ammunition Col R.F.A.

21.10.15   B.M./647.

O.C.,
3" North" Bde R. F. A.

The batteries of the 50th Divisional Artillery and "D" Battery, 96th Brigade R.F.A. will shortly be relieved by Batteries of the 31st Divisional Artillery.

The relief will commence with one section per Battery on the night 21st/22nd October. The remaining section in each Battery will be relieved on the night 23rd/24th October.

The relieving batteries are "A", "B" and "C" of the 94th Brigade R.F.A., and "B" and "C" of the 97th (Howitzer) Brigade R.F.A.

A/94 will relieve the 1st Durham Battery, 3rd Nbn. Bde. R.F.A.
B/94   "   "   " 2nd Durham Battery,   "   "   "
C/94   "   "   "D" Battery, 96th Brigade R.F.A.
D/96   "   "   (H.R.) Battery, 2nd Northbn. Bde. R.F.A.
B/97   "   "   4th Durham Battery, 4th Northbn. Bde. R.F.A.
C/97   "   "   5th Durham Battery,   "   "   "   "

The relief on each night will be commenced at 6.0p.m.

In accordance with the above, A & B Batteries, 94th Brigade R.F.A. will take over the wagon lines of the batteries they are relieving.

C/94 will take over the wagon lines of the 3rd Durham Battery, 3rd Northumbrian Brigade R.F.A.

By arrangements made between the O.C., 2nd Northbn. Bde: and O.C. 96th Brigade, D/96 will move its wagon lines to one of the 2nd Northbn. Bde's battery wagon lines.

B. & C. Batteries, 97th Brigade will take over the wagon lines of the 4th and 5th Durham Batteries, 4th Northumbrian Bde.

The advanced sections of the incoming batteries will be met by a guide from each of the batteries mentioned above, at 2.0p.m. on October 21st, at the Cross-roads at B.23.a.8½.3½, Sheet 36 N.W.

The two Brigade Commanders, and Battery Commanders of the 94th & 97th Brigades R.F.A. will be at these Headquarters at 11.0a.m. to-day, 21st instant. I will bring them on to the different Headquarters, immediately afterwards.

They will

Sheet 2.

They will bring the whole of their Battery staffs with them.

Will you, therefore, please have the Officers Commanding the Batteries under your command at your Headquarters at about 11.30a.m. to take these officers round your batteries.

The O.C. D/96 and O.C. (H.R.) Battery, 2nd Northbn. Bde., will both be at the Headquarters, 3rd Northbn. Bde. at 11.0a.m. to-day, 21st instant.

You will arrange to hand over the following maps :-

Sheet 36 (with the exception of two).

All Sheets 36 N.W., 36 N.E., 36 S.W. and 36A., S.E.

Sheets Nos. 2x and 4 of Sheet 36 N.W., (Scale 1/10,000) CHAPELLE - HOUPLINES map. The plan of WEZ MACQUART, and any other information in your possession in the shape of panoramas, registration cards, trench maps, tracings, that will be useful to the incoming batteries, also all secret documents relating to the Bridges over the R. LYS., battery positions to cover the Subsidiary Line and G.H.Q. 2., Reserve positions, and O.P.'s for these positions

On the completion of the relief on the night 23rd/24th October, one selected officer per battery will remain behind until such time as the new Battery Commander is thoroughly familiar with the front he is covering.

22/10/15.   The Brigade Ammunition Columns will arrive on the 22nd inst: They will be met as follows :-

The Brigade Ammunition Columns of the 94th Brigade R.F.A. will be met at the Cross-roads in NIEPPE (B.16.a.3.0) at 2.0p.m. on 22nd instant, by a guide from the 50th Divisional Ammunition Column.

The Brigade Ammunition Column of the 97th Brigade R.F.A. will be met at the Cross-roads (B.23.a.8½.3½) at 2.30p.m. on the 22nd inst., by a guide from the 4th Northumbrian Brigade.

The 2nd Northumbrian Brigade Ammunition Column will supply all the 15-pdr guns still in action, from 8.0am on 22/10/15.

If the 94th Brigade R.F.A. cannot supply the 149th Infantry Brigade with S.A.A. immediately after its arrival in this area, the O.C., 2nd Northumbrian Brigade will arrange to do this on being so informed by the O.C., 3rd Northumbrian Brigade R.F.A.

24/10/15.   One section of the 21st Divisional Ammunition Column will arrive at the Cross-roads, B.16.a.3.0. at 2.0p.m. on 24th instant, and will go into the field and billets now occupied by the advanced section of the 50th Divisional Ammunition Column.

The advanced section of the 50th Divisional Ammunition Column will arrange to be clear at 9.0a.m. on 24th instant, and will leave one officer behind to give what help he can to the incoming section.

The Batteries -

Sheet 3.

The batteries and Brigade ammunition columns will probably march on the days mentioned below, but detailed instructions will be issued to everybody concerned as soon as possible.

The 3rd Northumbrian Brigade Ammunition Column and 4th Northumbrian Brigade Ammunition Column will each leave two G.S. wagons for gun ammunition behind. Those of the 3rd Northbn. Bde. Ammn. Col. will go to the lines of the 2nd Northbn. Bde. Ammn. Col. during the morning of the 22nd. Those of the 4th Northbn. Bde. Ammn. Col. will stay on their own lines.

Night 21st/22nd.
The two sections of the 4th Northumbrian (H) Brigade R.F.A. after being relieved on the night 21st/22nd will go to their Wagon-lines.

They will march at 9.0a.m. on 22nd instant, in company with the 4th Northumbrian Brigade Ammunition Column (less two G.S. wagons for gun ammunition).

The 2 sections of the 3rd Northbn. Bde. R.F.A. and the section of the (N.R.) Battery, 2nd Northumbrian Brigade will, on relief on night 21st/22nd, march to the billets of the 50th Divisional Ammunition Column, near X.5.c.3.2. (Sheet 27). On arrival in the square at BAILLEUL they will be met by a guide.

They will resume the march into the new area on the 22nd inst.

23rd.
The Headquarters, 2nd Northumbrian Brigade, The 1st and 2nd East Riding Batteries (less one gun each) and the 3rd Battery, 3rd Northumbrian Brigade R.F.A. will march into the new area on the 23rd instant. Hour of start will be at 9.0a.m.

Night 23rd/24th.
The two single guns will be pulled out on night 23rd/24th and will proceed to the lines of the 2nd Northumbrian Brigade Ammunition Column.

The remaining section of the (N.R.) Battery will also go to the lines of the 2nd Northumbrian Brigade Ammunition Column after being relieved.

The remaining sections of the 1st and 2nd Durham Batteries will, on relief, go to the billets of the 50th Divisional Ammunition Column at X.5.c.3.2. (Sheet 27) under the same arrangements as laid down for the sections first relieved.

The remaining sections of the 4th and 5th Durham Batteries will go to their wagon-lines after being relieved.

24th.
The two single guns, the section of the (N.R.)Battery, the 2nd Northumbrian Brigade Ammunition Column, the wagons for gun ammunition of the 3rd Northumbrian Brigade Ammunition Column will march as one body on 24th instant, under arrangements that will be made later.

The remaining two sections of the 4th Northumbrian (How) Brigade and the two wagons of the 4th Northumbrian Brigade Ammunition Column will also march on 24th instant.

H.Q. 50th D.A. -

Sheet 4.

Headquarters, 50th Divisional Artillery will probably move to the new area on 24th instant.

I am trying to get you some Maps, Sheet 27.

R.G. Thomson

Hq. 50th D.A.
21. 10. 15.

Major, R.A.,
B.M., 50th D.A.

Copy No. _1_

SECRET.

OPERATION ORDERS BY LIEUT COL G.T.PEARSON R.F.A.(T) COMMANDING
3rd NORTHUMBRIAN BRIGADE R.F.A. FOR SATURDAY OCT 23rd AND
SUNDAY 24th OCT 1915

----

1. Brigade Headquarters and the rear sections of the 1st and 2nd Durham Batteries will march into the new area on the night of 23/24th October 15.

2. Time of start 7.15pm October 23rd '15
Head of Column at B.16.d.0.6., facing NIEPPE, on the NIEPPE - ARMENTIERES Road.

3. Order of march :-
    (i)   Brigade Headquarters
    (ii) Section 1st Durham Battery
    (iii) Section 2nd Durham Battery

4. The column will be met by a guide in BAILLEUL SQUARE at 9.15pm and led to billets at X.5.c.3.2, Sheet 27.

5. The march will be resumed at 9am, on October 24th.

6. The relief will be at 5.30 pm Oct 23rd, & the 3rd Nbn Bde RFA sections will provide teams & drivers to bring up the sections of A/94 and C/94 & take their own away.

            E.H.Johnson
            2/Lieut R.F.A.
      a/Adjutant 3rd Northumbrian Brigade., R.F.A.

10.30am
22nd October 1915.

Copy No.1   C.O., 3rd Nbn Bde R.F.A.

Copy No.2   O.C., 1st Durham Battery

Copy No.3   O.C., 2nd Durham Battery

SECRET.   B.M./b12/5.

O.C. 3rd Hv: Bde: R.F.A.

I beg to inform you that the demonstration, referred to in my B.M./b12. Dated 12/10/15. will be resumed this afternoon.

Exactly the same portions of the enemy wire will be cut.

1st Phase.   2.30. P.M. to 2.45. P.M.
           Pause of 10 minutes.
2nd Phase.   2.55. P.M. to 3.10. P.M.

From 3.12. P.M. to 3.18. P.M. a single gun will enfilade the ~~enemy trench~~ wire in front of the enemy trench 80.

The 1st & 2nd Durham Batteries will stand by ready to open fire in retaliation. They will only do so, however, in cases of the most extreme necessity.

$14\tfrac{10}{15}$

A

Arrangements for demonstration on our front :-

Ammunition allotted :-

    4,000 rounds 18-pdr Shrapnel.
     800 " " H.E.

How divided :-
 (a) For cutting wire, 2,520 18-pdr Shrapnel.
 (b) For retaliation 1,000 " Shrapnel.
        600 " H.E.
 (c) In reserve, 480 " Shrapnel.
        200 " H.E.

Batteries engaged in cutting wire :-

 "A", "B", and 2 guns of "C" Batteries, 95th Brigade, R.F.A.

 "D" Battery, 96th Brigade R.F.A.

A total of 14 guns. This gives roughly (vide (a)), 180 rounds per gun.

Batteries engaged in retaliation :-

 "A", "B", "C", & "D" Batteries, 95th Brigade R.F.A.

 "A", "B", "C", & "D" Batteries, 96th Brigade R.F.A.

for this, ammunition allotment is as follows :-

 720 rounds for "A", "B", & "C" Batteries, 96th Brigade, and "D" and 2 guns of "C" Battery, 95th Brigade, i.e., 18 guns, or 40 rounds per gun.

The remaining 280 rounds will be allotted to 2 guns of "C" Battery, "A" and "B" Batteries, 95th Brigade, and "D" Battery, 96th Brigade.

To "D" Battery, 96th Brigade will be allotted 120 rounds, or 30 rounds per gun.

To the remainder, 160 rounds, or 16 rounds per gun.

(Objectives on attached list) -

NOTE :-

Allotment of H.E is as follows :-
 300 Rounds to 95th Brigade R.F.A.
 300 Rounds to 96th Brigade R.F.A.
The re-allotment of this ammunition to Batteries will be left in the hands of the Officers Commanding these two F.A. Brigades.

B

OBJECTIVES.

The 95th Brigade will cut wire from C.29.a.5½.2½ to C.29.a.8½.8½.

The 96th Brigade will cut wire from C.29.c.5.8½ to C.29.c.8½.7.

Targets for the 5" B.L. Howitzer Batteries will be allotted separately.

Targets for the 95th Brigade R.F.A. :-

    LES OURSINS FME.
    C.23.c.8.7.
    C.17.d.0.7.
    C.30.a.6.4.
    FME DU CHASTEL
    BRUNE RUE

96th Brigade R.F.A. :-

    LA HONGRIE.
    I.17. Central, and guns in vicinity.- (One gun suspected to be in I.17.d.0.8. and guns at I.17.b.7.2.)
    Supports near enemy trench 67.
    I. 23.b.9.3 (a battery)
    Communication trench running from I.5.d.1.1. to I.12. Central, and works at I.12 Central.
    LA FRESNELLE CROSS-ROADS.
    I.11.a.4½.2¼.

A Target common to both 95th and 96th Brigades, R.F.A. :-

    C.29.a.5.0.

Batteries will proceed to register to-day under Brigade arrangements.

If possible, the guns reported to be at D.25.a.7.3. will be engaged by the Heavy Artillery.

Hq. 50th D.A.
11. 10. 15.

SECRET

2nd Corps
G 960

50th Division

1. The 50th Division will arrange to carry out a demonstration on as large a portion of its front as possible at a date which will be notified later, but preparations should be made to begin wire cutting on October 11th.

2. The demonstration will take the form of cutting the enemy's wire, and breaking his parapets, in combination with the use of smoke if the wind serves.

   Infantry and machine gun fire will be brought to bear on the damaged sections to prevent the enemy repairing them.

3. The following ammunition will be available:—
   4,000 Rounds 18 pdr Shrapnel
   800   "   "   " H.E.

4. For the production of smoke 3000 Thermite Bombs will be issued from 1st Army Railhead at ST. VENANT.

   It is hoped that about 3000 local pattern smoke ~~pattern smoke~~ bombs will also be available.

   The object of the smoke is to simulate a gas attack, so as to make the enemy line his parapets and offer a target to our guns. The smoke should therefore be prepared opposite that portion of the lines where the wire has been cut and guns held in readiness to turn on to it with shrapnel when the smoke cloud starts.

- 2 -

It is expected that the enemy's guns will turn on to our trenches if he is induced to expect an attack.

Steps should be taken, therefore, to hold the front trenches very lightly opposite the portion of the line selected, and to get the garrison under as good cover as possible.

A proportion of the ammunition, especially H.E. should be kept handy to reply to this bombardment

———

Dr Nominierung des RfA.

Dez
Vol. VIII

D/
7957

50/h/54

Army Form C. 2118.

50th Division

WAR DIARY
or
INTELLIGENCE SUMMARY.

(Erase heading not required.)

3RD NORTHUMBRIAN BRIGADE R.F.A. [T] 121/7637

50TH DIVISION

Vol VII

NOVEMBER 1915

Army Form C. 2118.

WAR DIARY
or
INTELLIGENCE SUMMARY.   3RD NORTHUMBRIAN BRIGADE RFA
(Erase heading not required.)   Sheet No 19.

Place	Date	Hour	Summary of Events and Information	Remarks and references to Appendices
NOOTE BOOM	Nov 1st 1915		Brigade H.Q. in NOOTE BOOM [F.17 a 7,8 sheet 36 A 1/40000] Batteries & Amm Col in Neighbourhood. The Brigade is attached to 157th Inf Bde as forward reserve.	
	Nov 17th		Lt C.F HORNSBY joined from 3rd line & was posted to ~~Amm Col~~ supernumary to establishment	
			2 Lt W R HORNSBY " " " " " " 3rd Bty " "	
	Nov 25		The Brigade was rearmed with 18 pounder Q.F Ordnance which was drawn at HAZEBROUCK.	
	Nov 27		Brigade Amm Col. S.A.A. section took part in scheme of S.A.A. supply with 157th Inf Bde.	
	Nov 30	10.30 AM	The Divisional Artillery was inspected by the Army Commander General Sir HERBERT PLUMER near STRAZEELE	

J.T Pearson
Lieut. Col.
Commdg. 3rd Nbn. Bde. R.F.A.

Army Form C. 2118.

WAR DIARY
or
INTELLIGENCE SUMMARY.

(Erase heading not required.)

3RD NORTHUMBRIAN BDE R.F.A.

Sheet No. 20.

Instructions regarding War Diaries and Intelligence Summaries are contained in F. S. Regs., Part II. and the Staff Manual respectively. Title pages will be prepared in manuscript.

Place	Date 1915	Hour	Summary of Events and Information	Remarks and references to Appendices
NOOTE BOOM	Dec 1st to 5th		Brigade H.Q. in NOOTE BOOM [F 17 a 7, 8 sheet 36A 1/40000] Batteries and Amm. Col. in neighbourhood.	
	5th		Headquarters and the three batteries moved to the 2nd Army Artillery Training Camp near WATTEN. The night of the 5th was spent in billets in the neighbourhood of LA KREULE	Operation Orders herewith marked "G"
	6th		Headquarters & the batteries proceeded to BOLLEZEELE [A 24 c Sheet 27 1/40000]	
	7		Training — hampered by bad weather conditions — proceeded with	
	8		ditto	
	9		The G.O.C. 50th Div Major gen WILKINSON inspected the batteries	
	10		" Training	
	11		"	
	13		G.O.C. 2nd Army gen Sir HERBERT PLUMER inspected the batteries during training.	
HONDEGHEM 17			The Brigade moved to HONDEGHEM [Sheet 27 V 2 b] [M17/xxxx]	Operation Order marked 92

Army Form C. 2118.

Sheet No 21

WAR DIARY
or
INTELLIGENCE SUMMARY.

3RD NORTHUMBRIAN BRIGADE R.F.A. [T]

(Erase heading not required.)

Place	Date	Hour	Summary of Events and Information	Remarks and references to Appendices
HONDEGHEM	Dec 1915 18		Brigade Commander & Adjutant visited KRUISSTRAAT to see the C.O 52nd Bde Brigade whom the Brigade is taking over.	
	19	7AM	Brigade Ammunition Column moved to new area	
	20	7AM	Brigade H.Q. & Batteries moved to wagon lines in 5th Corps area.	Operation Orders attached G3
KRUISSTRAAT	21	12 noon	Batteries took over. Ammunition expended 27 HE. 13 Shrapnel.	
	22	10AM	H.Q. took over & 52nd Bde R.F.A. rear parties left. Ammunition expended NIL	
	23rd		" " " NIL. Brigadier Genl Robinson assumed command of 50th D.A.	
	24th		Ammunition expended 34 HE and 80 Shrapnel	
	25th		" " 67 HE " 79 "	
	26th		" " 26 " " 68 "	
	27th		" " 45 " " 103 "	
	28th		" " 53 " " 111 "	
	29th		" " 21 " " 44 "	
	30		" " NIL " " 53 "	

J. Fleward

SHEET No 22

Army Form C. 2118.

WAR DIARY
or
INTELLIGENCE SUMMARY.
(Erase heading not required.)

Place	Date	Hour	Summary of Events and Information	Remarks and references to Appendices
KRUISSTRAAT	Dec 31	11 P.M. 12 m.night	Ammunition expended. 4 H.E. 398 Shrapnel. Each battery fired 60 rounds between 11 P.M. and 11.5 P.M. and the same between midnight and 12.5 A.M., without provoking retaliation.	

OPERATION ORDERS BY LIEUT.-COLONEL G.T.PEARSON, R.F.A. (T)
COMMANDING 3rd NORTHUMBRIAN BRIGADE, R.F.A.
----

1. The Brigade will leave this area on the 5th inst., to undergo a course of ten days' training at the Artillery Camp in the neighbourhood of WATTEN, N.W. of ST. OMER.

2. The Brigade will move off in the following order:-
    Headquarters
    1st Battery
    2nd   "
    3rd   "

3. Head of the column to be at the Railway Crossing north of 1st Battery billets (F.10.a.4.2.Sheet 36a 1/40,000) at 10.0 a.m. on the 5th instant.

4. Dress:- Full marching order.

5. Haversack ration and nose-bag feeds for one meal to be carried.

6. The march will occupy two days. Billets for the 1st night will be somewhere in the vicinity of La Kraule.

7. O.C., Ammunition Column will arrange to supply one G.S. wagon four-horse team to convey horse rugs of the Brigade.

8. Brigade Ammunition Column will remain in their present billet with the exception of the following, who will proceed with the Brigade for training:-
    Captain Common (attached to 2nd Battery)
    Lieut. Hornsby ("   " 3rd   "   )
    1 Sgt, 1 Cpl and 5 gunners (attached to 1st Battery)
    1 "   1 Bdr "   "   "   ("   " 2nd   "   )

9. Under no circumstances will private vehicles be allowed on the line of march or on the new area. They must remain behind.

10. O.Cs Batteries will arrange to leave one competent man in charge of kit &c left behind in the present billets. This man together with the sick will be rationed by the Amm.Column.

Lieut.-Colonel,
Commanding 3rd Northumbrian Brigade, R.F.A.

3rd December 1915.

OPERATION ORDERS BY LIEUT.-COLONEL G.T. PEARSON, R.F.A. (T)
COMMANDING 3rd NORTHUMBRIAN BRIGADE, R.F.A. FOR FRIDAY 17th DECR
————————————————————

1. The Brigade will return to their former billets in 2nd Corps Rest Area on December 17th.

2. Batteries in all probability will take over the same billets near MONDEGHEM which they occupied on the march up to this training camp.

3. Gun limbers, firing battery wagons, and first line wagons only to be taken.
All guns to be parked in the market square, BOLLEZEELE, by 1.45 p.m. to-morrow the 16th inst.

4. All gun stores, dial sights, adapters and carriers, and sight clinometers to be taken.

5. The Brigade will move off in the following order:-

    Headquarters.
    1st Durham Battery.
    2nd Durham Battery.
    3rd Durham Battery.

Head of the column to be at the red roofed house, situated in G.6.a.0.9. at 9.15 a.m.

7. Haversack rations and one feed in nosebags to be taken.

              Lieut.-Colonel,
         Commanding 3rd Northumbrian Brigade, R.F.A.

16th December 1915.

ROUTE TABLE FOR 3RD MTN. LT. INF. R.O.K.

DATE	UNIT	STARTING POINT	TIME OF DEPARTURE	ROUTE TO BE FOLLOWED & APPROX HOURS
20th Oct	3rd Mtn. Regt. R.O.K.	Camp near rd. CHESTER N3 - 4-5 Sheet 21	8:30 AM	Route to Godmakersville Station, Godmakersville - Bosshispa Sheet 21, Westout - Waken - Rainachelt Sheet 28

TABLE OF ROUTES

DATE	UNIT	TO FOLLOW	PLACE	REMARKS
20th Oct	3-1 Mtn. R.u.R. 3rd Co.	Cross green march to ridge line north of Boughton	Co's control Sheet 28	Will stop for the night
21st		The amount of horses of R.18/ of Buttons refused when J Battery Sup. and men arrive on returning Storm compass deflate of R. 53 ½ ...		
22nd		The remaining sections of R. 18th Buttons attempting to sweep F & H the J.F. 18th Battery ...		

Reference :- Sheet 27 and 28. 1/40,000

G3

Copy No. 9

50th DIVISIONAL ARTILLERY OPERATION ORDER NO. 8.

Headquarters,
50th Divisional Artillery.

16. 12. 15.

1. The Division is to be transferred to the 5th Corps. This Divisional Artillery will relieve that of the 9th Division.

2. Reliefs will be carried out as shewn in Table of Reliefs attached.

3. The move to the 5th Corps area will be carried out as laid down in the March Table attached.

4. The personnel of the 23rd and 31st Trench Mortar Batteries will march with the 2nd Northumbrian Brigade Ammunition Column on December 19th.

5. All movements East of ST.HUBERTUSHOEK and VLAMERTINGHE are to be concealed from the enemy.

6. All completion of reliefs to be reported to this Office by wire.

7. Headquarters 50th Divisional Artillery will be established at G. 26.c.2.7. at 1.0pm on December 22nd.

Issued at 12 noon.

R.G. Thomson.

Major R.A.
B. M. 50th D.A.

OPERATION ORDERS BY LIEUT.-COLONEL G.T.PEARSON, R.F.A. (T)
COMMANDING 3rd NORTHUMBRIAN BRIGADE, R.F.A. FOR MONDAY 20th DECR.
----

1. This Brigade is transferred to the 5th Corps.
The 3rd Northumbrian Brigade will relieve the 52nd Brigade R.F.A. at YPRES.

2. Reliefs will be carried out as shewn in attached relief table.

3. The move to the new area will be carried out as per attached March Table.

4. Batteries will march <u>independently</u> to the starting point in CAESTRE. They will march from CAESTRE in order of arrival at the Starting Point.
It is absolutely necessary for the whole column to move off from CAESTRE at the time laid down in attached table i.e. 8.30 a.m.

5. Soyers stoves and braziers will be taken unless notified to the contrary.

6. Strict march discipline must be maintained.

[signature]
Lieut. R.F.A.
Adjutant 3rd Northumbrian Brigade R.F.A.

19th December 1915.

Copy
1 Brigade H.Q.
1 1st Battery
1 2nd Battery
1 3rd Battery

1/3rd Nineteenth Bde. R.G.A.

Jan / Vol IX

50

Army Form C. 2118.

WAR DIARY
or
INTELLIGENCE SUMMARY.

SHEET No 23

3rd NORTHUMBRIAN BDE R.F.A. T.F.

(Erase heading not required.)

Instructions regarding War Diaries and Intelligence Summaries are contained in F. S. Regs., Part II. and the Staff Manual respectively. Title pages will be prepared in manuscript.

Place	Date	Hour	Summary of Events and Information	Remarks and references to Appendices
KRUISSTRAAT Sheet 28. H24a.6.8.	1916 JAN 1		Ammunition Expended NIL.	
	2		No 1286 Sgt KIRTON J. wounded in chest by rifle bullet. Ammn Expended Shrapnel 69	
	3		No 1249 Bdr BAINBRIDGE J. wounded by shrapnel (died after 10 hrs) 1177 Gr FIFE wounded slightly in head 32 H.E. 105 Shrapnel Burned Sh.27 L.22.d.63 grave N71	
	4		Ammn Exp 6 H.E. 25 Shrapnel	
	5		" " 4 " 118 "	
	6		" " 38 " 205 "	
	7		" " 1 " 54 "	
	8		Barrage practise Ammn Exp 54 H.E. 169 Shrapnel	
	9		Major GUTHE T.P. & 2 Lt BUSHELL E.R. wounded by same shell 557 Armament Staff Sgt KEMP J. wounded by bullet in thigh Ammunition Expended 32 H.E. 36 Shrapnel	
	10		1357 Gr Staincliffe C. wounded. Ammn Expended. 142 H.E. 157 Shrapnel . Died same day. Burned Sh.28 I40000 L.21.c.68	
	11		Ammn Exp 34 H.E. 52 S.	
	12		" " 71 " 77 "	
	13		" " 14 " 30 " Major T.P. GUTHE died of wounds at hospital at LE TOUQUET	

SHEET No 24
Army Form C. 2118.

WAR DIARY
or
INTELLIGENCE SUMMARY.

3RD NORTHUMBRIAN BDE R.F.A.

Place	Date	Hour	Summary of Events and Information	Remarks and references to Appendices
KRUISSTRAAT SHEET 28 H24a68	14		Amm Expended 65 HE 70 S	
	15		" " 74 HE 63 Shrapnel	
	16		" " 118 " 158 "	
	17		" " 233 " 227 "	
	18		" " 178 168 " 179 169 "	
	19		" " 73 " 55 "	
	20		" " 107 " 48 51 "	
	21		" " 93 " 21 "	
	22		" " 55 " 41 "	
	23		" " 27 " 39 "	
	24		" " 16 " 30 "	
	25		" " 3 " 9 "	
	26		" " 32 " 42 " . Lieut-Col G.T. Pearson proceeded to England on sick leave, command of Brigade taken over by Major F.L. Pickersgill. During evening Lieut. S.W. Milburn slight G.S. wound on chest, did not leave duty. + Gnr 1093 Gr Bear) G.S. wound in side on Battery position. Lieut Col Francis Pickersgill Major Commanding 3rd Nbn. Bde. R.F.A.	

Army Form C. 2118.

WAR DIARY
or
INTELLIGENCE SUMMARY.

SHEET No 25

3rd NORTHUMBRIAN Bde RFA

Place	Date	Hour	Summary of Events and Information	Remarks and references to Appendices
	JAN/16			
KRUISSTRAAT	27		Ammunition expended 36 HE 18 Shrapnel	
SHEET 28	28		" " 39 " 34 "	
H24a 6.8.	29		" " 28 " 23 "	
	30		" " 76 " 14 "	
	31		" " 17 " 1 "	

Bramwell Pickersgill
Lieut. Col.
Commdg 3rd N'bn Bde. R.F.A.

WAR DIARY
INTELLIGENCE SUMMARY

Sheet No 27. 3rd NORTHUMBRIAN BDE RFA

Army Form C. 2118.

Place	Date	Hour	Summary of Events and Information	Remarks and references to Appendices
Sheet 28 H24a68	Feb 13		Ammunition expended 63 HE 27 Shrapnel. Capt Boyd Cunningham slight G.S wound in hand, not off duty.	
	14		Am. Expended 344 < HE 90 Shrapnel. 117 Sergt Saddler Thirlwell G.S wound in foot	
	15		Amm Expended 98 HE 203 Shrapnel	
	16		" " 33 " 30 "	
	17		" " 66 " 66 "	
	18		" " 51 " 77 "	
	19		" " 25 " 10 " 1941 Gr Thompson Rifle bullet in the groin	
	20		" " 26 " 60 "	
	21		" " 92 " 36 "	
	22		" " 80 " 53 "	
	23		" " 45 " 21 "	
	24		" " 24 " 26 " Gr Lawn H slight wound on Thumb	
	25		" " 22 " 24 "	
	26		" " 57 " 70 " 1209 Gr Davidson G.S wound in back	
	27		" " 73 " 4 "	
	28		" " 52 " 19 " Branch Pickersgill	
	29		" " 34 " 30 " Major Comdg 3 Nm Bde RFA	

Army Form C. 2118.

SHEET No 26
3rd NORTHUMBRIAN BDE
R.F.A.

WAR DIARY
or
INTELLIGENCE SUMMARY.
(Erase heading not required.)

Place	Date	Hour	Summary of Events and Information	Remarks and references to Appendices
KRUISSTRAAT Sheet 28 H24a68	FEB 1916 1		On night 31st Jan - 1st Feb 15 in Act divided into Right and Left Groups. O/C 3rd N'um Brig R.F.A. taking command of Left group i/c 1/2; 3rd Durham Bty, 4th Dur How Bty, 2nd N'um'land Bty.	
	2		Ammunition Expended 71 HE 5 Shrapnel. Left group supporting 151 Inf. Brig.	
	3		" " 46 " 10 "	
	4		" " 49 " 7 "	
	5		" " 52 " 16 "	
			" " 66 " 11 " 1282 Gr McKeuren J.G.S. wound in	
	6		foot during shelling of BLAUWEPOORT Farm.	
	7		Ammunition expended 24 HE 6 Shrapnel	
	8		" " 105 " 46 "	
	9		" " 291 " 32 "	
	10		" " 86 " 25 "	
	11		" " 73 " 23 "	
			" " 133 " 17 " 356 Bn Hutchinson J. 309 Br	
			Bators J. + 563 Driver Full W wounded, in order named G.S. wound in face, G.S. wound in head + legs, G.S. wound head, at LILLE GATE, first + last named reporting with return cart back to H.Q.	
	12		Ammunition Expended 155 HE 176 Shrapnel	

Branch Pickersgill.
Major Comdg
3 N'um Bde RFA

WAR DIARY or INTELLIGENCE SUMMARY

Army Form C. 2118.

SHEET No. 28
3rd NORTHUMBRIAN BDE. R.F.A.

Place	Date	Hour	Summary of Events and Information	Remarks and references to Appendices
Shot 28.5.9.	March			Operation Orders Attached
H.23.B.5.9.	1		Ammunition expended 30 A. H3 A x.	2 n P
	2		" 845 A. 1048 A x Bombardment of "Bluff" in conjunction with inf.	
	3		14th & 9th Division	
			Amm. expended 157 A. 181 A x	
	4		" 3 A. 23 A x 5.9" How obtained direct hit on Sunk. hill.	2 n P
			Relieved officers mess, 1 field rifle in front of redoubt being put 4.15 p.m. H.2 n heavily	
			shelled with 5.9"	
	5		Amm. expended 18 A. 43 A x Ready to turnover to H.23.B.5.9.	2 n P
	6		" 21 A. 123 A x	2 n P
	7		" - 44 A x	2 n P
	8		" - 25 A x	2 n P
	9		" 2 A. 9 A x	2 n P
	10		By the night of the 9th S. Batteries of the 3rd Nth. relieved Batteries of enemy's group.	2 n P
			left their command taken over by 104 Bde. R.F.A. 12 noon.	
			Change turnover to wagon lines H.30A.9.5.	
			Relief complete.	
	10		Guns and Amm. taken over from the 3rd Bde. at wagon lines	2 n P
	11		Two guns of "106 Bdy. relieved D.Bdy. 105 Bde. R.F.A.	2 n P
	17		Kerl Section and D.6's into Bdy. positions of night g. group.	2 n P
	21		Removing section into like Bdy. positions of night g. group, relief completed 11.45 p.m.	2 n P
	22			2 n P

WAR DIARY or INTELLIGENCE SUMMARY

Army Form C. 2118.

SHEET N° 29
3rd Northumbrian RFA
(TF)

Place	Date	Hour	Summary of Events and Information	Remarks and references to Appendices
Sheet 28 H23 B59	1916 March 23		Nil	
	24		Ammn expended 26A 6AX	JHP
			do 54A 159AX	JHP
	25		Gnr Law H.W. N° 1140 a casualty – shell shock.	JHP
	26		Ammn expended 23A 6AX	JHP
			do 66A 69AX	JHP
	27		Lt J R Platt, 2nd Battery, wounded by shell pce while on duty same day.	
			Corporal JA Shaw N°942, 1st Bty do dies following day.	
			Gr Turnbull J N°1617 2nd Bty do and sent to Hospital	
	28		Ammn expended 63A 89 AX	JHP
			Cpl JA Shaw N°942, 1st Bty died of wounds.	JHP
	29		Ammn expd 22A 24 AX	
			Gr Ferguson I N° 2nd Bty killed by rifle bullet near Klaverpoort Farm.	JHP
	30		Ammn expd 19A 13 AX	JHP
	31		do 38A 4AX – Bomr J W Magee N°1645 killed by shell pce near Swan Chateau.	Ref. JHP
				Bnr Lt Pickersgill

B.M. 900/3.

Officer Commanding, Left Group, 50th D.A.

The following are the positions of the wagon lines of the 54th Divisional Artillery :-

  G.22.b.5.7. - Wagon Line of C/126 Battery.
  G.24.b.4.9. - " " " A/157 "
  G.24.b.5.8. - " " " B/157 "
  G.24.d.1.0. - " " " D/157 "
  G.12.a.7.0. - " " " D/157 "

  C/126 relieves 1st Durham Battery.
  A/157   "   3rd   "   "
  B/157   "   2nd   "   "
  D/157   "   2nd Northumberland Battery.
  D/159   "   4th Durham Battery.

The four guns belonging to each of the above mentioned batteries together with 120 rounds per 18-pdr gun and 60 rounds per 4.5" Howitzer will be brought away at 10.0 a.m. on March 11th by the corresponding Battery which has just been relieved in our Left Group.

An Officer is to go with each Battery's party, and will be responsible for the taking over of the guns and the ammunition. This party will consist of four gun limbers and four ammunition wagons with limbers for each battery. A small detachment of gunners should also be taken to help in the unloading.

The remaining rounds per gun and howitzer handed over at 12 noon on March 10th will be collected at 11.0 a.m. on March 11th by the 54th D.A.C. The O.C. 54th D.A.C. has been so instructed.

      (Sgd) R.C. THOMSON, Major.
      B.M. 50th D.A.

7/3/16.

O.C.

  For information, and report in writing to 3rd Adjutant Wagon Lines at B.09.a.9.5. as soon as the above has been completed.

           Lieut., R.F.A.
     Adjutant 3rd Northumbrian Brigade., R.F.A.

8/3/16.

COPY No. 2

OPERATION ORDER No 2.

- BY -

MAJOR F.L.PICKERSGILL, R.F.A. (T) COMMANDING LEFT GROUP 50th D.A.

Reference:- 1/10,000 Trench Map - HOOGE & ZILLEBEKE.　　　　　7-3-16.

1.　　　　The 24th Division will take over the LEFT SECTOR of the 50th Division front from trench B.7. (J.13.c.2.2.) to Trench A.4. (I.30.b.0.4.) both inclusive, on the night of the 8th/9th March, together with the supporting points now held by the 150th Infantry Brigade.

2.　　　　Five batteries of the 24th Division will relieve the Batteries of the Left Group, 50th Divisional Artillery, commencing on the night of the 9th/10th March and completing the relief on the night 10th/11th March.

3.　　　　The C.R.A. 24th Division will assume command of the Artillery covering the Left Sector at 12.0 noon on 10th March. All details of the handing over will be arranged direct between the Group Commanders concerned.

4.　　　　The Headquarters of the 50th Division and 50th Divisional R.A. will remain in their present quarters.

5.　　　　The relief will commence with one section per Battery on the night 9th/10th March. The remaining section per Battery will be relieved on the night of the 10th/11th March. The reliefs on these two nights will not start before 7.0 p.m. Of course Battery Commanders will use their own discretion as to the exact times and as to getting cumbersome stores and kits away as soon as possible irrespective of above time and dates.

6.　　　　Battery Commanders of incoming Batteries will take over command at 12.0 noon on March 10th.

7.　　　　Only the guns will be handed over and they will be handed over stripped of everything. Every single small store, sight, strap, aiming post is to be taken away before the guns pass to the 24th Divisional Artillery.

8. The ammunition that is with the guns at 12.0 noon on March 10th will be handed over, and the amount so handed over will be notified to this Office as soon as possible. A and Ax to be stated separately.

9. All trench maps, zone charts, panoramas, list of squares allotted to selected batteries for firing on with an aeroplane, overlap of fire, position of O.Ps and F.O.O's dugout, extent of barrages, and any other information that may be useful to incoming B.Cs. Copies of Defence Scheme for Left Sector. All trench stores, gum boots thigh &c are to be handed over. Receipt of complete list handed over must be taken in triplicate, one copy for retention by Battery Commanders and two copies to be sent to this office at earliest possible opportunity, but at latest by 4.0 p.m. on the 10th March.

10. A selected officer will stay behind in each battery to help the Battery Commander taking over in every possible way, and, until the said Battery Commander is satisfied that he is fully conversant with all appertaining to the Battery position and its zone.

11. No wire is to be reeled in.

12. .Battery Commanders are to return to their own respective wagon lines, and all details concerning the above arrangements and any points that may arise afterwards re this handing over are to be settled direct between Battery Commanders concerned.

13. Arrangements are being made for requisite extra accommodation in wagon lines.

14. Forward gun of 2nd Northumberland Battery will remain in its forward position.

15. Battery Commanders will take over from the 24th Division on March 11 at a time and place to be notified later the same number of rounds, both 18-pdr and 4.5" how. as they hand over to them with the guns (verb. sap. we don't want to carry an ammunition park, but don't run them short at the guns). The guns to be taken over will also be collected at the same time.

16. All Battery Commanders will report as soon as the handing over is completed.

17. Reports to be sent to H.20.a.9.5. (Ref. 1/20,000 Sheet 28

N.W. BELGIUM). *after 12.0 on the 10/3/16*

                                                                            Major,
3rd Northumbrian Brigade, R.F.A.

Issued at *3rd Nthn Bde Hqrs 1.0 pm 7/3/16.*

                      Copy No. *1 — N.D.A.*
                              2 — Hqrs.
                              3 — 1st Nthn Bty
                              4 — 2nd Nth Bty
                              5 — 2nd Bty
                              6 — 4th How
                              7 — 3rd Battery

WAR DIARY or INTELLIGENCE SUMMARY

Shul M30 3rd Northumbrian RFA Army Form C. 2118.

Place	Date 1916	Hour	Summary of Events and Information	Remarks and references to Appendices
Shul 28 H23 B59	April 1		Amn. expd. 4 A	JNP
	1		105 A 136 A	JNP
	2		26 A 23 AX Dr Mason No 1337 3rd Bty wounded in the back by shrapnel at Kruisstraat.	JNP
	3		26 A 35 TA	JNP
	4		35 TA Half of Brigade relieved by 1st C.T.A.	JNP
	5		Half of Brigade relieved by 1st CTA	JNP
Steenvoorde	6		Brigade in rest at Steenvoorde. Colonel Pickersgill marches 4th C.T.A.	JNP
Nrd Oliffe	7		Half Brigade relieves Half of 3 Batterie 4th C+A. Whole of H.Q. moves	JNP
	8		do	JNP
	9		Amn. expended 805 A do AX Major Yeoman sent to hospital - sick -	JNP
	10		do 476 A 244 AX Gr Bostin No 1261 2nd Bty wounded by shrapnel in trenches	JNP
	11		do 450 A 420 AX 2nd Bty shelled out of their position.	JNP
	12		do 577 A 531 AX do moves to new position Ingul 11/12 - 4 - 16	JNP
	13		do 284 A 252 AX	JNP
	14		do 300 A 249 AX	JNP
	15		do 106 A 88 AX	JNP
	16		do 326 A 461 AX	JNP
	17		do 210 A 317 AX Dr E Mason No 1337 3rd Bty died of wounds	JNP
	18		do 35 A 54 AX	JNP
	19		do 360 A 634 AX Major K.S. Yeoman evacuated to England	JNP

J.W. Pickersgill

WAR DIARY or INTELLIGENCE SUMMARY

Army Form C. 2118.

Sheet No 31
3rd North'n R.F.A.

Place	Date	Hour	Summary of Events and Information	Remarks and references to Appendices
	1916			
Mdr Cayllo	April 21		Bomr expended 181 A 120 AX Major Vraman rejoins his Bty which was subjected to heavy fire & gas shells.	21P
"	April 22		Amn expended 86 A 70 AX	21P
"	April 23		Amn expended 287 A 315 AX	21P
"	April 24		" " 54 A 27 AX	21P
"	April 25		Amn. expended 109 A 112 AX	21P
	April 26		232 A 234 AX Co. 3 Bde R.F.A. + officers went round gun positions.	21P
	April 27		448 A 451 AX 1st Bty shells out. 1 man killed 3 wounded.	21P
			Cp. Bell 1841 killed. Cp. Brown RS 2855. Cp. Rend.?	21P
			Cp. Stain Frank wounded	21P
	April 28		Amm expended 174 A 182 AX	21P
	April 29		Amm expended 207 A 165 AX Enemy attacked French E1 at 2-15 AM	21P
	April 30		I got into the Bullring. Royal Welch Fusiliers at once counter attacked & enemy were driven out.	
			Amm expended 59 A, 312 AX 1st Section of Battery galloped by 42nd brigade quarters Frank Pickering	21P

50

Army Form C. 2118.

WAR DIARY
or
INTELLIGENCE SUMMARY.

Sheet 32
252 (Mor.) RFA
Lat 1/5 Nim B/m

Place	Date	Hour	Summary of Events and Information	Remarks and references to Appendices
La Clytte	1 May			2/Lt Mathews
Ecke	2		Remainder of Brigade moved into Rest Area	
	3			
	4			
	5		Brigade in Rest.	BaP
	6			
	7			
	8			
	28			
La Clytte	29		1 section for BCs moved into 42 RFA 3 DA at La Clytte	2/Lt Cope Operator
	30		Remainder of Brigade " do	2/Lt P " when attached
	31		Amm. expend: 170 A 42 AX 11 BX	2/Lt P

Stanwich Pickersgill
Lieut Col:
1/6/16.

COPY NO. 7.

OPERATION ORDERS BY MAJOR K.G.YEOMAN, R.F.A. (T) COMMANDING 3rd
NORTHUMBRIAN BRIGADE, R.F.A., T.F. 50th DIVISIONAL ARTILLERY.

1. The 50th Divisional Artillery will be relieved in action by the 1st Canadian D.A. on the nights of April 4th/5th and 5th/6th.
   No relief is to take place before 8.0 p.m.

2. That part of the D.A. not in action will move to Canadian Rest Area as laid down in the attached March Table "A" which must be strictly adhered to.
   Billets to be occupied in the Rest Area are shewn in Table "B"

3. Officers Commanding Batteries in action must arrange their reliefs so that the horses which bring the relieving sections up to the positions can take their men back to GODEWAERSVELDE. Motor buses will be in readiness in ODERSOM from H.Q.R.A. each night to convey personnel from gun positions to Rest Area.

4. The guns of relieved sections will march to Rest Area each night by the same route as laid down for the remainder of the Divisional Artillery.
   They will march by Sub-Sections under Officers to be specially detailed.
   Route to be followed POPERINGHE-ABEELE K.58.d.5.9.- G.D.d.5.1. - Rest Billets.

5. All ammunition at the gun positions will be handed over to relieving unit. Details of quantities of all natures accompanied by receipts will be sent to this Office as soon as possible after the relief is completed. All ammunition now in excess of units, including Brigade Ammunition Columns, will be taken to the new area. During the time that Units remain in the Rest Area arrangements will be made for all wagons to be filled to establishment as far as possible one of each nature from the Divisional Ammunition Column Headquarters from 4 p.m. 4th April. O.C.s.a.a.C. less if who are taking over in the Rest Area sufficient ammunition to complete units.

6. All maps registration records, panoramas, and aeroplane photographs will be handed over to incoming batteries.

7. All existing telephone lines will be handed over and no lines will be reeled up.

Major, R.F.A. (T),
Commanding, 3rd Northumbrian Brigade, R.F.A. (T.F.)

31st March 1916.

N.B. Trench stores, (Goyer's stoves, gum boots thigh &c &c) will not be handed over to incoming Units until further orders are issued to the contrary. Steel helmets are not trench stores. Great care must be taken in giving and obtaining receipts in triplicate signed by the O.C. of the incoming and outgoing batteries for all articles enumerated in No 6.

Copy No 1   HDA.
   " 2   Right Group
   " 3   1st
   4   2nd
   5   3rd
   6   O.C.

Copy No ..7..   SECRET.

OPERATION ORDERS NO 1a BY LIEUT COL F.L.PICKERSGILL.,R.F.A.(T)
COMMANDING 3RD NORTHUMBRIAN BRIGADE.,R.F.A.

Reference Map Sheets 27 and 28, 1/40,000 .

(1)   The Brigade will be relieved by 3rd D.A. on the
        nights of 30th April/1st May and 1/2 May and will
        proceed to V Corps Rest Area No 4, via WESTROUTRE -
        MT KOKEREELE - BOESCHEPE - Road Junction R.1.d.2.4.
        GODERSWAERSVELDE, as shown in tracing herewith .

(2)   Guns will not be exchanged unless under exceptional
        cases and by mutual arrangement .

(3)   Sections will move out of action as soon as possible
        after dark and proceed at once to Rest Area .

(4)   One section per battery will move on the night of
        30/1st. Brigade Headquarters and remaining Sections
        will move on the second night .

(5)   Sections will move independently under Command of
        an officer and the C.O. is confident that the strictest
        march discipline will be observed throughout .

(6)   Arrivals of sections moving on 30/1st to be reported
        to Capt W. Hilburn, who will be with section of 1st
        Battery moving that night . Arrivals of remainder to
        be reported to H.Q. in Rest Area .

(7)   "D" Battery will march on May 1st; details will be
        given O.C. in due course .

(8)   Ammunition Column will move on May 1st by half
        column. (See March Table "A" attached hereto for
        Ammunition Column only.) O.C. B.A.C. will move with
        last section .

(9)   All ammunition at gun positions will be handed over
        and receipts for it sent to H.Q. as soon as possible on
        arrival in rest billets .

        This Brigade will be responsible for ammunition
supply up to 10.30 a.m. 1st May.

(10) All ammunition with Battery Wagon Lines, Brigade Ammunition Column will be taken to Rest Area.

(11) Units will arrange to draw up to complete echelon as soon as possible after arrival in Rest Area.

(12) Advance parties of 3rd D.A. (B.Cs. and telephonists) will arrive on morning of 30th April.

(13) Log Books, Defence Schemes, Orders, Maps, Photographs and all useful available information will be handed over.

(14) An officer from each Battery will be left behind to assist the relieving Battery.

(15) Rest billets have been allocated as follows :-

    Headquarters .   Q.9.b.9.7.
    1st Durham Battery .   Q.15.c.5.8. and
                                    Q.15.a.3.8.
    2nd   "   "   Q.15.d.0.5.
    3rd   "   "   Q.15.b.4.4.
    "D"   "   "   Q.4.c.3.5.
    B.A.C.   Q.9.c.8.8. and
                                      Q.10.c.1.4.

(16) Other billets will be as undernoted :-

    50th D.A.   EECKE.
    D.A.C. 3rd Section.   Q.16.a.8.4.Q.17.b.6.9.
    50th Divn H.Q.)
    C.R.E.   )   FLETRE.
    D.A.D.O.S.   )
    Signal Co R.E.)
    M.V.S.   R.34.a.3.5.

(17) From 12 Noon on 3 May the Brigade will hold itself in readiness to entrain at 8 hours notice.

(18) Completion of each stage of relief to be reported by orderly to H.Q.

(19) Acknowledge.

                                   Franklin Pickersgill.
                                                 Lieut Col.
    Commanding 3rd Northumbrian Brigade., R.F.A.

Copy No 1 .   H.Q.
 "   " 2   1st Battery.
 "   " 3   2nd   "
 "   " 4   3rd   "
 "   " 5   "D"   "
 "   " 6   B.A.C.
 "   " 7   War Diary.

COPY NO. 7.

OPERATION ORDER NO. BY LIEUT COL F. WRIGHTSON, R.F.A.(T)
COMMANDING 53rd(Northumbrian) Brigade., R.F.A.

Reference Sheets 27 N.E. and 28 N.W. 1/20,000 .

(1)   The Brigade will relieve 3rd R.F.A. Brigade on the
        nights of May 29/30 and 30/31st .

(2)   Units will move via FLÊTRE - METEREN - BAILLEUL .
        Attention is called to 50th D.R.O. No 1.5. as follows :-
        ROAD CONTROL. The road from B.G.C.O.R. to R.C.R.S.O. will
        be closed for repair to all traffic, except to that of units
        billeted on it, from Monday 22nd May inclusive .
        This road is likely to be reopened from the north end to
        R.O.C.R.S. in about a week; the remainder will probably be
        closed for about three weeks .
        Traffic from BAILLEUL to WESTOUTRE will be through LOCRE;
        traffic from WESTOUTRE to BAILLEUL will be through LOCRE
        or SCHAEXKEN .

(3)   Guns will not be exchanged except by mutual arrangement
        in special cases .

(4)   One section per Battery will move on 29th. Headquarters
        and remaining sections on 30th .

(5)   Sections will go into action as soon as possible after
        dark .

(6)   Advanced parties (Battery Commanders and Telephonists)
        will proceed on the morning of the 30th .

(7)   Log Books, Maps, Defence Schemes, photographs and all
        available information relating to 3rd Division Area will
        be taken over .

(8)   Command will pass to C.R.A. 50th Division and Brigade
        Commanders 50th D.A. at 12 noon on 30th May after which
        Headquarters of the Division and Brigade will be at
        WESTOUTRE and LA CLYTTE respectively .

(9)   50th D.A. will be responsible for ammunition supply after
        12.5 p.m. on 30th May .

(10)   Officers Commanding Groups or Batteries of 3rd D.A. will
        be responsible for the return of ammunition expended by guns
        of either Division up to and including the noon 30th May .

(11) Gun Positions and Wagon Lines are as follows:-
    Gun Position.   Wagon Lines.
A Battery. H.16.c.6.6.   ...c.u.o.(with H.Qs)
B   "   H.16.a.6.1.
C   "   H.16.a.3.1.   I.1...6.
D   "   H.11.A.4.4.   ..1..6.4.7.

(12) Position of 1.& 2 Section D.A.C. is ..21.c.3.7.

(13) Attached maps Belgium and France Sheet 36 S.W. Edition
      2.B 1/2,... Herwith.

(14) Acknowledge.

K M Richardson
(Lt) Adjt

for
                                              Lt. Col.,
        Commanding 322nd (Westmoreland) Brigade., R.F.A.

27th May, 1916.

Copy No.1.   Headquarters.
  "   " 2.   A Battery.
  "   " 3.   B   "
  "   " 4.   C   "
  "   " 5.   D   "
  "   " 6.   50th D.A.C.
  "   " 7.   War Diary.

WAR DIARY

Sheet 33

252 (NBN) RFA

Vol 14

Army Form C. 2118.

Place	Date	Hour	Summary of Events and Information	Remarks and references to Appendices
La Clytte	1/6/16		Amm Expend. 116 A 18 AX 12 BX	JWP
	2/6		do 1 B 24 BX	JWP
	3		do 45 A 41 AX 6 BX	JWP
			O.O. No 3 A attached	
			No 1287 Cor. Sadler Potter S A Bty killed in action	JWP
			1033 M/B<u>om</u> Appleby J " wounded	
			1438 Am Denman TH " do	
			1568 " Freeman T " do	
			2696 " Wilkinson GE " do	
			Demonstration on own front — O.O. attached — D/Wilkins JWP 4A	
	4		do 157 A 377 AX 166 BX	digging wounds JWP
	5		15 10 1	JWP
	6		6 61 42	JWP
	7		34 123 23	JWP
	8		41 41 85	JWP
	9		197 28 9	JWP
	10		18 279 22	JWP
	11		100 28 6	JWP
	12		174 134 74	JWP
	13		89 279 33 8 B	JWP
	14		41 159 48 3 B	JWP
	15		78 132 69 10 B	JWP
	16		27 50 17	JWP
	17		52 78 43	JWP
	18		46 38 49	Bt. Atkinson joined D Battery from 250 Bde RFA JWP
	19		13	Frank Hickersgill Bt JWP

Army Form C. 2118.

SHEET 34.

WAR DIARY
or
INTELLIGENCE SUMMARY. 252 (HBH) R.F.A.

(Erase heading not required.)

Instructions regarding War Diaries and Intelligence Summaries are contained in F. S. Regs., Part II. and the Staff Manual respectively. Title pages will be prepared in manuscript.

Place	Date	Hour	Summary of Events and Information				Remarks and references to Appendices
			Am expended	A	Ax	Bx	B
La Clytte	20			~~115~~	~~137~~	~~15~~	—	8/P
	2D		"	112	102	23	—	8/P
	21		"	117	88	47	—	8/P
	22		"	7	27	3		8/P
	23		"	71	44	10		8/P
	24		"	102	24	75		8/P
	25		"	608	906	182		8/P
	26		"	140	140	30		O.D. attacks
	27		"	1440	731	312		8/P
	28		"	463	453	145		8/P
	29		"	1561	381	238		8/P 30th July
	30		"	1046	662	3	Demonstration started on our Front. Demonstration finished on the night of 30th/31st July. Francis Pickersgill	

COPY NO ...1... SECRET

OPERATION ORDERS NO 4 A

BY

LIEUT COLONEL F.L. PICKERSGILL., R.F.A.(T).,

COMMANDING 252ND (NORTHUMBRIAN) BRIGADE., R.F.A.

---

1. A minor enterprise will take place on the 24th Division front on the night 3/4 June. The hour of zero time will be notified later.

2. The Brigade will co-operate and demonstrate as per time table.

3. At 0.15' Strombos Horns will be sounded somewhere on the 24th Division front as a signal for the withdrawal of a raiding party. Care must be taken not to mistake this for a gas signal.

4. At 0.3' our aeroplanes will drop signals behind enemy lines. These signals will be answered from our line by red and green Very lights.

5. The utmost care will be taken to ensure that the enemy are kept in ignorance of the enterprise, and only the necessary information issued beforehand to those concerned.

6. -

Time.		Objective.	
1ST PHASE.	A Battery.	N.18.b.1¾.5½. to N.18.b.1½.7.	
0-0' to 0.15'	B "	N.18.b.1½.7. to N.18.b.1½.8.	Bombardment Front line
	C "	N.18.b.1½.8. to N.18.b.2.9.	

(1)

6.
| Time. | Objective. |

1ST PHASE. D Battery. 1 How. on N.18.b.1¾.5½ ⎫ Bombardment
　　　　　　　　　　　1　"　" N.18.b.1½.7.　⎬ Front line
　　　　　　　　　　　1　"　" N.18.b.1½.8.　⎭
　　　　　　　　　　　1　"　" N.18.b.2.9.

2ND PHASE.

　　　　　A Battery.　1 Gun.　N.18.b.2¾.5½.
　　　　　　　　　　　1　"　　N.18.b.3¼.5.
　　　　　　　　　　　1　"　　N.18.b.3½.5½.
　　　　　　　　　　　1　"　　N.18.b.4.6.

0h.15'　　B Battery.　1 Gun　N.18.b.4.6¼.
to　　　　　　　　　　1　"　　N.18.b.4¼.7.
0h.20'　　　　　　　　1　"　　N.18.b.4½.7½.
　　　　　　　　　　　1　"　　N.18.b.4¾.8.
Barrage
　　　　　C Battery.　1 Gun.　N.18.b.5.8½.
　　　　　　　　　　　1　"　　N.18.b.5½.9.
　　　　　　　　　　　1　"　　N.18.b.6.9½.
　　　　　　　　　　　1　"　　N.12.d.5½.0.

　　　　　D Battery. 2 How. on farm. N.18.b.4.9.
　　　　　　　　　　　2　"　"　"　　N.18.b.4.6.

3RD PHASE.

0h.20'　　AS IN 1ST PHASE.
to
0h.30'

7.　AMMUNITION ALLOTTED.

　　　　4.5 Howrs.　　　160 per battery.
　　　　18-pdrs.　　　　200　"　　"

AVERAGE RATE OF FIRE :-

　　2 rounds per gun per minute for 1st Phase.

7. AVERAGE RATE OF FIRE :-

   1 Round per gun per minute for 2nd Phase.
   2 "   "   "   "   "   " 3rd   "

   Howitzers rather slower rate for all phases.

   BOMBARDMENT :- 18-pdrs fire 75 % AX.
   BARRAGE :-   18-pdrs "   75 % A.

8. Please acknowledge receipt per bearer.

Copy No 1.   War Diary.
 "   " 2.   A Battery.
 "   " 3.   B   "
 "   " 4.   C   "
 "   " 5.   D   "

K M Macdonald
Lt M Adjt

                                        Lieut Colonel.
Commanding 252nd (Northumbrian) Brigade., R.F.A.

3/6/16.

COPY NO. 7.   SECRET 15.

OPERATION ORDER NO 5A BY LIEUT COL F.L.PICKERSGILL., R.F.A.(T) COMMANDING 252ND (NORTHUMBRIAN) BRIGADE., R.F.A.

1. A demonstration will be made for five days by this Brigade on dates and times which will be communicated to units later.

2. <u>'A' DAY</u>.

'A' Battery unassisted will cut wire from N.18.b.2.9. - N.12.d.3½.1. and with assistance of Trench Mortar Battery the wire from O.7.c.4.5. - O.7.c.3½.7½.

'B' Battery with assistance of T.M. to cut wire at a point between O.7.b.2.2. and O.7.b.6½.5.

'C' Battery to cut wire at a point between O.7.c.4.8. and O.7.a.8.1.

'D' Battery. By day fire on craters ~~and surrounding wire~~ at :-

    O.7.c.4.3.
    N.12.d.4.1.
    N.18.b.1½.7.

and at night on dugouts and works at O.13.a.7.3.

'A', 'B' and 'C' Batteries will fire on lanes made during the night to prevent all repairs, also occasional rounds on O.13.a.7.3.

TOTAL EXPENDITURE :- 18-Pdrs 560 Rounds per Battery.
                     4.5" How 250   "   "   "

<u>'B' DAY</u>.

<u>DAYTIME</u>. 'A', 'B' and 'C' Batteries will cut wire next to lanes made on 'A' day and 'D' Battery will fire on craters as on 'A' day.

<u>AT NIGHT</u> at a time which will be notified later 'A', 'B' and 'C' will open rapid fire on hostile front line where wire has been cut - lift to a barrage behind - and then come back to front line again. When fire

is opened on front line a road barrage to be formed as follows :-

    'A' Battery. at points N.18.b.2.6.
                   and   N.18.b.7.8.
    'B' "   between 0.7.b.9.1½. - 0.7.b.8.0.
    'C' "   "   0.7.d.8.9. - 0.7.d.5.6.
    'D' "   2 Guns between N.18.b.2.6. & N.18.b.7.8.
              1 "   on 0.7.d.1.6.
              1 "   " 0.7.c.6.4. to 0.7.d.0.5.

TOTAL EXPENDITURE :-

    18-pdr.   580 Rounds per Battery.
    4.5" How.   250   "   "   "

'C' DAY.

At morning "Stand to" front line barrage and road barrage with Howitzers on junctions and some 18-pdrs on roads will be put up for about 30 minutes. Then "Stand by" for an order for Retaliation "Y" from Headquarters. Barrage on front line will be :-

    'A' Battery. 0.7.c.4.6. - 0.7.c.4.9.
    'B' "   0.7.a.8.0 - 0.7.a.9.2.
    'C' "   0.7.c.4.9. - 0.7.a.8.0
    'D' "   Craters 0.7.c.4.3., 0.7.c.4.9. and
                 building 0.7.d.2½.8.

Road Barrage will be

    'A' Battery. 0.14.a.6.6. to 0.14.a.6.1.
    'B' "   0.14.a.6.1. to 0.14.c.5½.6.
    'C' "   0.14.c.5½.6. to 0.14.c.4.0.
    'D' "   Cross Roads 0.20.a.3.9., Road
                 Junction 0.20.a.3.5½., Road Junctions
                 0.14.a.6.½., 0.14.a.6.6.

TOTAL EXPENDITURE :-

    18-pdrs.   60 Rounds per Battery per Barrage.
    4.5" How.   45   "   "   "   "   "

RETALIATION.

    18-pdr.   40 Rounds per Battery.
    4.5" How.   30   "   "   "

'C' DAY (Continued).

        'A', 'B' and 'C' Batteries continue cutting wire next to lanes already cut.

        'D' Battery on craters and works connecting them with front lines.

        At Night lanes to be kept open by 18-pdrs who will also fire occasional rounds on O.20.a.1½.6. which will be bombarded by 'D' Battery.

TOTAL EXPENDITURE :-

    18-pdrs.   400 Rounds per Battery.
    4.5" How.   130   "   "   "

'D' DAY.

        'A', 'B' and 'C' continue wire cutting next to lanes already made.

        'D' on strong points N.18.b.8.2. to N.18.b.9½.5. and at O.13.c.3.9.

        At Night. 'A'. 'B' and 'C' keep lanes open and fire occasionally on O.20.b.1½.2¾. which will be bombarded by 'D' Battery

TOTAL EXPENDITURE :-

    18-pdrs.   560 Rounds per Battery.
    4.5" How.   250   "   "   "

'E' DAY.

        'A', 'B', 'C' and 'D'. As in 'D' Day, but more intense than any previous day and to last longer during day -- to lead enemy to expect attack that night.

At night 'D' Battery to fire on :-

        O.13.a.7.3.
        O.20.a.1½.6.
    and O.20.b.1½.2¾.

TOTAL EXPENDITURE :-

    18-pdrs.   560 Rounds per Battery.
    4.5" How.   250   "   "   "

Combination of T.M's and 18-pdrs must be arranged to obtain the best effect and to get useful information and guidance for the future.

Stray rounds to be fired at night on roads, and communication trenches.

The object of the Demonstration is :-

    (a) To make enemy think we are going to attack.

    (b) To worry & fatigue him as much as possible.

TOTAL EXPENDITURE FOR FIVE DAYS.

18-Pdr Battery.	2840 Rounds.
4.5" How do,	1250 "

Lieut Col,
Commanding 252nd (Northumbrian) Brigade., R.F.A.

Copy No	1.	Headquarters.
"	" 2.	A Battery.
"	" 3.	B "
"	" 4.	C "
"	" 5.	D "
"	" 6.	50th D.A.
"	" 7.	War Diary.

SECRET.

Copy No ...7...

OPERATION ORDER NO 6A BY LIEUT COL F.L.PICKERSGILL., R.F.A. COMMANDING 252ND (NORTHUMBRIAN) BRIGADE., R.F.A.

(1) In addition to Minor Operations now in progress the following will be carried out by 'A', 'B' and 'C' Batteries.

(2) ON 28 JUNE.

On the order from H.Q. "Scatter boys."

Shrapnel barrages will be put up as follows :-

'A' Battery on C.T. from :-
   N.18.b.8.8. to Q.13.a.1.8.

'B' Battery on C.T. from
   N.18.b.8.7. to N.18.b.10.4¾.

'C' Battery along road from
   N.18.b.2.5¾. to N.18.b.7.8¾.

ALLOTMENT 150 ROUNDS A PER BATTERY.

(3) ON 28, 29, 30 JUNE and 1ST JULY.

Parapets to be breached as follows :-

'A' Battery   N.18.b.6.8. to N.18.b.6.7.
'B'   "   N.18.b.6.7. to N.18.b.7.8.
'C'   "   N.18.b.8.8½. to N.18.b.10.4½.

ALLOTMENT PER BATTERY FOR FOUR DAYS :-

   1670 AX.
   250 A.

(4) The object of this being to damage works in HOLLANDSCHESCHUUR Salient and in rear and especially to prevent him tapping to our mine head.

(5) To meet this expenditure of ammunition a special issue will be made of which batteries will be informed later.

(6) Acknowledge.

Frank L Pickersgill Lieut Col.
Commanding 252nd (Northumbrian) Bde, R.F.A.

Copy No 1.   H.Q.   Copy No 2.   'A' Battery.
" " 3.   'B' Bty.   " " 4.   'C' "
" " 5.   'D' "   " " 6.   151 I.B.
" " 7.   War Diary.

VOL 16

WAR DIARY
or
INTELLIGENCE SUMMARY.
(Erase heading not required.)

Army Form C. 2118.

SHEET 25
252ND (HBM) RFA

Vol 15

Place	Date	Hour	A	Ax	B	Bx	Summary of Events and Information	Remarks and references to Appendices
La Clytte	July 1916		(Amm. expended)					
	1		690	654	0	209	17941 6/ Armstrong wounded 1st July	JLP
	2		9	0	33	128		JLP
	3		69	133	19	33		JLP
	4		68	21		21		JLP
	5		161	143		18		JLP
	6		578	31		52		JLP
	7		486	308		124		JLP
	8		208	48		43	Pte W.J. Johnson Lt G.B. Semeston joined A Bty 4-7-16 Bty (horses)	JLP
	9		305	228		60	Lt Burke rejoined 251 Bde	JLP
	10		186	50		52		JLP
	11		226	108		92	Carried on minor operation were to be carried out tonight. Lt Wm JLP	JLP
	12		210	273		38	Lt Burke joined C Bty from 251 Bde (horses)	was unfavourable 0.5 JLP
	13		172	69		58		7A attacked JLP
	14		312	48		99		JLP
	15		266	224		118		JLP
	16		197	99	7	107	6/ Springer killed attached 2/50 TM Bty J. Flynn joined D Bty R.S.M. Moloney awarded M.C.	JLP

WAR DIARY
or
INTELLIGENCE SUMMARY.

Army Form C. 2118.

SHEET. 36

252ND (NBH) RFA

Place	Date	Hour	Summary of Events and Information				Remarks and references to Appendices
				A	AX	BX	
La Clytte	July 17	Amm expended		166	176	112	JHP
	18	"		473	40	82	JHP
	19			668	81	370	JHP
	20			221	90	290	JHP
	21			69	33	67	JHP
	22			59	64	95	JHP
	23			41	14	49	JHP
	24			124	18	25	JHP
	25			59	98	86	JHP
	26		Lt. Wright Joined B Bty from 50 TM	339	224	104	JHP
	27		Right Section Relieved by RFA Shoreham	169	425	64	JHP
	28		Right Section Relieved by 2nd RFA Operation orders/OA	44	125	5	JHP
	29		Left Sections Relieved & R. Section took over new	180	170		JHP
	30		Left Sections took over new Position RFA	162	11		JHP
	31		position from 172 Bde RFA				JHP

Frank Pickering Lt.

SECRET.   COPY NO 5

OPERATION ORDER NO 7A BY LIEUT COL F.L.PICKERSGILL,
COMMANDING 252ND (NORTHUMBRIAN) BRIGADE., R.F.A.

1. The 2ND CANADIAN DIVISION carry on a Minor Operation to-night (wind permitting) with Gas and Smoke.

   Point of attack between where DEEPENDALL BECK crosses (O.7.B.9.7)   (O.8.A.3.9.) enemy front line and PICCADILLY Farm.

2. The 252ND (NORTHUMBRIAN) BRIGADE., R.F.A. will assist as follows :-

   A/252.   Barrage enemy communication trench from
                    O.7.b.8.3.
                       to
                    O.7.b.6.5.
            BATTERY FIRE 20 Seconds.
   D/252   Maintain a fire on enemy Machine Gun
                    Emplacements at O.7.a.9.2.
                        and   O.7.b.4½.4½.
            1 GUN on each.

   C/252   1 SECTION on the same Machine Gun
                    Emplacements.
            1 GUN on each.

   Remaining Batteries will be on their 'S.O.S.' lines as under normal circumstances.

3. Raiding Party leaves our trenches at 1-0 a.m., 12/7/16, and fire will be maintained until raiding party returns, of which the two batteries concerned will be advised from Brigade Headquarters.

4. Should Gas Expert decide to postpone Operation, Batteries will be advised about 12.45 a.m. 12/7/16

                              Franklin Pickersgill
                                            Lieut Col.
          Commanding 252nd (Northumbrian) Brigade., R.F.A.

11/7/16

SECRET .   Copy No 10

OPERATION ORDER NO 10A   BY LIEUT COL F.L. PICKERSGILL., R.F.A.
COMMANDING 252ND (NORTHUMBRIAN) BRIGADE., R.F.A.

1. The Brigade will be relieved by 2nd C.F.A. on nights of 29th/30th and 30th/31st .

2. Right Sections will move out 29/30 and left 30/31 and proceed to wagon lines .

3. Relieving Batteries as follows :-

   A/252 . by 20th C.F.A.
   B/252   " 18th C.F.A.
   D/252   " 23rd C.F.A.
   C/252)
   B/253) positions will remain unoccupied .

4. A/252 and D/252 will hand over all ammunition at Gun Positions except that carried in gun limbers, which should be full, to relieving units of 2nd C.F.A.

   B/252, C/252 and B/253 will move out on relief with echelons full and will hand over remainder of ammunition at gun positions to 250th F.A.B. Group .

5. Batteries will go into the new positions with echelons full with the exception of A/252 and D/252 who will move in with gun limbers only full taking over from units they are relieving all ammunition at gun positions .

6. Amounts of ammunition handed over and received to be reported to H.Q. immediately reliefs are completed .

7. Maps, registrations etc to be handed over on relief and receipts in duplicate taken .

8. Completion of relief to be reported by telephone to H.Q.

9. Command will pass on completion of relief .

10. Wagon Lines will not be changed .

11. Instructions regarding handing over of ammunition to 250 F.A.B. Group will be issued later .

                                  Frank Pickersgill
                                                Lieut Col.
              Commanding 252nd (Northumbrian) Brigade., R.F.A.

Copy No 1.   Office .   Copy No 3.   B/252 .
 "   " 3.   A/252 .   "   " 4.   C/252 .
 "   " 5.   D/252 .   "   " 6.   B/253 .
 "   " 7.   2X C.F.A.   "   " 8.   C.I.B.
 "   " 9.   50th D.A.   "   " 10.   War Dairy .

29/7/16 .

August 1916 VOL XVI SHEET No. 36. Army Form C. 2118.

WAR DIARY
INTELLIGENCE SUMMARY.

262ND (HBN) BDE., R.F.A.   Vol 16

Place	Date	Hour	Summary of Events and Information					Remarks and references to Appendices
			Amm Expended					
	August			A	AX	BX	B	
Dramoutz	1		Operation orders IIA for defence scheme attached	101	1		42	ZW
	2			95	1		99	ZW
	3			253	283		5	ZW
	4			175	116	73	4	ZW
	5		Right Section of A252 Relieved also of A253 (attached) to group) O.O. 12A attached	181	78	—	—	
	6		Left Section of A252 Relieved also of A253	1054	749			ZW
	7			—	—		Ky	ZW
	8		Right Section of B.C.D 252. Bde relieved by 19.D.A. O.O.13A Attached Section proceeded to Rest Area	160	110	17		ZW
	9		Left Sections relieved + proceeded to Rest area in Egypt	141	—	34		ZW
Feke.	10							ZW
	11		At 23.15 A Battery entrained for Candas					ZW
	12		HQ B, C, D Batteries entrained for Candas. All Batteries					ZW
	13		detailed from Candas to Billets at LE MEILLARD					ZW

VOL XVII SHEET No 37.   Army Form C. 2118.

WAR DIARY
INTELLIGENCE SUMMARY.
252ND (HBM) BDE., RFA

Place	Date	Hour	Summary of Events and Information	Remarks and references to Appendices
	AUGUST			
Le Meillard	13			J/J
	14			A/J
	15		Trecked from Le to Meillard	A/J
Behencourt	16		Left Boudon at 12 midnight and arrived at Behencourt 10-30 AM	J/J
	17		C.O. & D.O. visit 1st C.o.F.A.B. re taking over	S/J
	18		Right Sections of A B C D Btys relieving right section of A B C D Btys	A/J
			of 176 Bde. Sections arrived at Albert at 10-30 AM. D.O. attached	J/J
Albert	19		Left Sections move to Albert with HQ & Take over from	A/J
			176 Bde R.F.A	A/J
	20		A/13 B/13	J/J
			1917 684 729	A/J
	21		1233 809 22 280 Cpl. Sedgwick C Bty wounded (No 1228)	A/J
	22		308 96 168	A/J
	23		44 499 944 142 4 Elliot C Bty & Cp. H. Hutchins D Bty wounded (Nos 15919 & 629)	A/J
	24		642 301 813 395	S/J
	25		684 1056 261	A/J
	26		525 1457 30 B	A/J

VOL XVII

WAR DIARY
~~INTELLIGENCE SUMMARY~~
(Erase heading not required.)

SHEET N° 38. Army Form C. 2118.

252ND (NBN) BDE., R.F.A.

Place	Date	Hour	A	AX	Smoke	BX	Summary of Events and Information	Remarks and references to Appendices
Albert	AUGUST 27							
	28		1472	889		86	97818 L/ Smith 16 E Y. Dodds D Bty wounded + 6 horses killed	DHP
	29		876, 1272	46,	160	2nd Lieut W.D. Ronney joined.	DHP
	30		1011	826	—	247		DHP
	31		1106, 715	—	49		DHP
			1405, 786	—	298		DHP

Frank Pickering
Lt. Col.
252 F.A.B.

S E C R E T .   Copy No .....

OPERATION ORDER NO 13A BY LIEUT COL F.L.PICKERSGILL., R.F.A. COMMANDING 252ND (NORTHUMBRIAN) BRIGADE., R.F.A.

1. The Brigade will be relieved by 19th D.A. by sections and as soon after dark as possible on nights 8/9 and 9/10 August. Sections will march on relief to V Corps Rest Area No 4, E E C K E .

2. Guns will not be exchanged .

    B/252 will be relieved by B/86 .
    C/252   "   "   "   C/86 .
    D/252   "   "   "   D/86 .

3. A/252 will march from wagon lines to Rest Area on afternoon of 8th August .

4. All will march via WESTOUTRE - MT KOKEREELE - BOESCHEPE - Road junction R.1.d.2.4. - GODWAERSVELDE .

5. Units will move out with all echelons full to establishment with ammunition . Surplus ammunition to be handed over to relieving units and amount handed over reported by wire to H.Q. by 11 a.m. on 9th .

6. Battery Commanders will march with their second sections .

7. Command of Groups passes at noon on 9th when responsibility for supply of ammunition also passes also command of Divisional Artillery .

8. Log Books, defence schemes, orders, maps, photographs and all useful information will be handed over. (Refer to previous instructions regarding handing over of stores).

9. Completion of each stage of relief to be reported by wire.

10. Location of Units in Rest Area will be as follows :-
    Headquarters .   Q.9.b.0.7.
    A/252 .   (Q.15.a.3.8.
                              (Q.15.c.5.8.
    B/252 .   Q.15.d.5.0.
    C/252 .   Q.15.b.4.4.
    D/252 .   (Q.9.c.8.8.
                              (Q.10.c.1½.4.

11. The Brigade will hold itself in readiness to entrain at short notice.

12. ACKNOWLEDGE.

                                        Lieut Col.
    Commanding 252nd (Northumbrian) Brigade., R.F.A.

7/8/16 .

Copy No 1.   Office .
"   " 2.   A/252 .
"   " 3.   B/252 .
"   " 4.   C/252 .
"   " 5.   D/252 .
"   " 6.   War Diary .

Copy No 1 A/252   4. Office
       2 A/253
       3 War Diary   4/8/16

Operation Order No 12 A
       252nd (Nm) RFA Brigade

1. A/252 and A/253 batteries will be relieved by sections on nights 5/6 and 6/7 August by batteries of 36th Division and will proceed to wagon lines.

2. Command of these two batteries will pass to OC 172 Brigade RFA on completion of Infantry relief on night 5/6th August. Sections will march out with gun limbers full. Remaining ammnt. at gun positions to be handed over to relieving batteries. Ammts. handed over to be wired at once to H.Q. and receipts taken.

3. Relief will take place after dark.
4. Completion of each relief to be wired to HQ
5. Completion of Infantry relief will be wired to Batteries

K M MacDonald
Lt & Adjt for CO 252 RFA

SECRET. Copy No 4.

OPERATION ORDER NO 11A BY LIEUT COL F.L. PICKERSGILL, R.F.A.(T) COMMANDING 252ND (NORTHUMBRIAN) BRIGADE., R.F.A.

AUGUST, 1916.

-o-o-o-o-o-o-o-o-o-o-o-o-o-o-o-o-

Reference Map :- 1:10,000.   28 S.W. WYTSCHAETE-WARNETON.

1. **GENERAL.** The Brigade will from this date be in support of the 149 Infantry Brigade, whose H.Q. are at DRANOUTRE. The front is divided into sectors, the right sector holding trenches C3, C4, D1, D2, having their H.Q. in ST. QUENTIN - the left sector holding trenches D3, D4 D5 and D6, having their H.Q. in COOKERS FARM.

    Infantry reserves will be in farms at T.4.c.6.6., T.10.c.9½.9. and along road just South of DAYLIGHT CORNER.

2. **BATTERY TASKS :-**

	Position.	Zone(trenches)	O.P.	Zero Point	Maximum Switch Right	Left.
A/252	T.36.6.6.	D1, D2.		O.32.b.2½.0.	15°	7°.
B/252	H.26.d.7½.½.	D5 D6.		O.32.b.3.0.	20°	20°
C/252	H.33.a.8.0.	D3 D4.		O.32.b.2¼.¾.	13°	5°
				over 3500x	13°	14°
D/252	H.24.a.½.2½.	C3 to D6 (inclusive).		O.32.a.8.9. (4 HUNS FARM).	25°	25°
A/253	H.33.a.8.8½.	C3 C4.		H.30.c.2.8. (SPANBROECK MOLEN).	30°	7°

BRIGADE H.Q.   DRANOUTRE.

3. **COMMUNICATIONS :-** Each Battery will be connected by phone to Btn H.Q. of sector it covers & with Coy H.Q. of trenches in zone. Batteries will arrange their own wires to O.Ps. indenting on Brigade H.Q. for requisite wire.

    Lamp signals will be carried on with front line as before - batteries will arrange position of these with Company Commanders but Code will be a brigade arrangement.

4. **BRIGADE F.O.O. :-** A/252 and A/253 will in turn supply F.O.O. to be with Infantry in right sector who will report at night to Btn H.Q. in ST QUENTIN and billet there. B/252 and C/252 will in turn supply F.O.O. to be with Infantry in left sector who will report on relief to

Btn H.Q. at COOKER FARM and billet there. A report will be furnished by these Brigade F.O.Os. to arrive at Brigade H.Q. at 4.15 p.m. daily.

O.C, D/253 will arrange for direct communication from his O.P. in use so as to get direct and immediate call on any of the 18-pdr batteries for suitable targets that are invisible from either the trenches or battery O.Ps. A Brigade post will be found on HILL 63 for a similar object but occupied under brigade arrangements.

5. Visual signalling will be revised and brought into efficient working - at present routes are :-

C/252. Lamp from front line to KEMMEL HILL and from there a line to battery.

B/252. " " Infantry to KEMMEL HILL and from thence to battery.

A/252 " " D2 to a house 200X to flank of battery.

Every possible attempt must be made to get direct signals from front line (or support) to battery or at least to O.Ps. and from there back to battery.

6. S.O.S. Lines with and without GAS.

A/252. N.36.d.1½.9¾., N.36.d.2.8., N.36.d.4½.6½., N.36.d.5½.5.
B/252 N.36.a.5½.8., N.36.a.6.6., N.36.a.6½.5., N.36.a.6.3½.
C/252 N.36.a.7.2¾., N.36.a.8½.2½., N.36.a.9½.1¾., N.36.b.x.x.
D/252 N.36.a.9.5., N.36.b.3.3., O.34.c.2½.6., N.36.b.7.9¼.
A/253 N.36.d.6.3., N.36.d.6½.1¾., N.36.d.7.½., U.1.a.½.8.

7. ARTILLERY Look-out will watch for S.O.S. rockets from the following points :-

Trench.	Bay No.	Map Reference.
C3.	7.	T.6.b.3½.4½.
C4.	17.	N.36.d.2.0.
D2.	9.	N.36.c.9½.6.
D3.	2.	N.36.c.8½.7.
D5.	Coy H.Q.	N.36.a.¾.4½.
D6.	6.	N.36.a.3.4½.
R.E.Farm.		N.36.d.2.7.
ST QUENTINS CABARET.		T.6.d.3.3.

On receipt of S.O.S., batteries will fire 2 rounds of gun fire, and then go to section fire 30 seconds until information as to situation is received.

On receipt of order "TEST S.O.S." battery receiving this will immediately fire <u>one round</u> only over the S.O.S. Line.

All lines between Batteries and Infantry must be tested every 45 minutes by dayand every 30 minutes by night .

8. <u>RETALIATION</u> Will be carried on at in LA CLYTTE section with following combined shoots :-

<u>Code Name</u>.	<u>Trenches.</u>	<u>Battery</u> .	<u>Task</u>.
KRUISTRAAT .	D5 D6	A/253 & A/252.	Where C.T. joins front line at N.36.a.6.6.
		C/252.	Junction S.T. & C.T. from N.36.a.6½.6½. to
		B/252.	Junction C.T. & S.T. at N.36.a.8.7.
		D/252.	Front line N.36.a.6½.5¾.
FACTORY .	C3 C4 D1 D2.	A/252 & A/253	N.36.d.5½.5. junction C.T. and front line .
		C/252	C.T. from N.36.d.5½.5. to N.36.d.7.5.
		B/252.	Junction C.T. & S.T. at N.36.d.7.5.
		D/252.	Ruins N.36.d.7.3.
CROSS ROADS .	D3 D4	A/252	N.36.~~a.7.8.~~ a. 8.4½.
		A/253	N.36.a.9.5.
		B/252	N.36.b.1½.7.
		C/252.	N.36.b.1.6¾.
		D/252.	One X N.36.~~a~~ b.8½.7¼. One X N.36.~~a~~ b.3.6.
HELL.	D6.	All 18-pdrs.	Front line N.36.a.5½.8.
		D/252.	One X Support Line N.36.a.9½.~~8~~ 9 One X Support Line N.36.a.7¾.8.
JUMP.	D5.	All 18-pdrs.	Front line N.36.a.6½.5¼.
		D/252.	One X + trench S.T. & C.T N.36.a.7.6½. One X N.36.a.8.7.
QUICK.	D4.	All 18-pdrs	Junction C.T. & S.T. at N.36.a.8¾.3¾.

Code Word.	Trenches.	Battery.	Task .
QUICK.	D4.	D/252.	Loop Trench N.36.a.9¾.4¼.
HUNT.	D3.	All 18-pdrs.	Front Line N.36.b.1.1½.
		D/252.	N.36.b.2.½.
CIRCUS.	D2.	All 18-pdrs.	Front Line N.36.d.2.8.
		D/252.	One gun on each corner of square trench on line ~~N.36.b.6¾.10. to N.36.b.8.10.~~ N.30.d.6¾.0 to N.30.d.8.0. above and below .
KICK .	D1.	All 18-pdrs .	N.36.d.4.6½.
		D/252.	One X at N.36.d.4¾.6¼. One X at N.36.d.7.7.
DROP.	C4.	All 18-pdrs.	Front line N.36.d.6¾.1¼.
		D/252.	One X O.31.c.2.7. One X O.31.c.3.6.
ALL IN.	C3.	All 18-pdrs.	Front Line T.6.b.9.8. 9 9
		D/252.	One X U.1.a.4½.9¼. One X ONTARIO FARM .

Order will be from Brigade Office and will be "Retaliation.........at.....o'clock for....minutes"

Rate of fire will be 3 rounds per gun per minute .

Should heavy retaliation be required a "PRIORITY" message will be sent through to this Brigade H.Q.

9. POSITIONS. Alternative and for Switch. (Zone N.33.b.2.6. to T.5.d.8.5.) G.H.Q.2 (Zone N.33.b.2.6. to T.3.b.6.1.) G.H.Q.3 (Zone N.32.b.0.8. to T.1.d.5.8.)

Baty.	Alternative. Switch. Zone	G.H.Q.2. Zone.	G.H.Q.3. Zone.
A/252.	T.1.a.1.8½.	T.1.a.1.8½.	S.6.b.0.4½.
A/253.	N.31.a.2.3.	N.31.a.2.3.	(M) M.35.a.4¼.5¾.
B/252.	M.35.a.4¼.3¾.	M.35.a.4¼.3¾.	M.35.a.4¼.3¾
C/252.	T.1.a.1.6½.	T.1.a.1.6½.	M.35.d.2.1.
D/252.	N.31.c.4.4.	N.31.c.4.4.	M.35.c.6.1.
	N.33.b.2.6 to T.5.d.8.5.	N.33.b.2.6. to T.3.b.6.1.	N.32.b.0.8. to T.1.d.5.8

B/252 will not move from present position until other batteries are in their positions for "SWITCH".

10. Wagon Lines will remain at SEAHAM HOUSE. Brigade H.Q. have theirs at DRANOUTRE .

11. **MUTUAL SUPPORT.**

In event of Brigade on our left being attacked and ours not, a barrage will be put up as follows :-

"B"/252 left ½ }   Left half of
"C"/252 right ½ } 4-18-pdrs. on support line from H.30.c.9½.2 to }
                   Ditto. right half ditto. do H.30 central }
                                                        ditto.

D/252:   One gun on H.30.d.2.9.
           One gun on KRUISSTRAAT CABT. + Roads.

Order being "BARRAGE LEFT"

For that on our right the barrage will be

"A/252" 4 guns. R. ⅔ of line
"A/253" 2 -   L. ⅓ five 18 pdrs on line from T.6.b.9.9. to U.1.a.3.7

D/252.   One gun on   U.1.a.4½.9½.
          One gun on   T.6.b.9½.9½.

order being "HELP RIGHT"

If our front is attacked and that on our left not the 251 F.A.B. Group will put up barrage :-

4 18 pdrs on trenches from H.30.c.7½.0 to H.36.a.9.5
4 "   "   road . 100x N. of KRUISSTRAAT CABT + roads.
             to 100x S. "   "   "   "

One 4.5" on   H.36.b.7.9.
    4.5 "   H.36.b.6.6.

call being "BARRAGE RIGHT"

Similarly the 153 F.A.B. from our right
will put up barrage.

Four 18-pdrs on trenches from T.6.b.9.9 to H.36.d.6.3.
One 4.5" on H.36.d.9.1.
    4.5" - O.31.c.1½.½.

             call being "HELP LEFT"

12.   Aeroplane squares and balloon targets will be allotted at earliest opportunity.

D.252	O.19	O.20
A.253	O.21	O.26
A.252	O.33	O.34
B.252	O.31	O.32
C.252	O.27	O.25

Balloon targets will be allotted as soon as possible.

Lieut. Colonel.
Commanding 252nd (Northumbrian) Brigade, R.F.A.

Copy No 1. Brigade Office.
"   " 2. A/252 Battery.
"   " 3. B/252   "
"   " 4. C/252   "
"   " 5. D/252   "
"   " 6. A/253   "
"   " 7. 149 I.B.
"   " 8. War Diary.
"   " 9. Spare.
"   " 10. M.D.A
"   " 11. 153 R.F.A

S E C R E T. Copy No. 6

OPERATION ORDER NO. 14A BY LIEUT. COL. F.L.PICKERSGILL, R.F.A.
COMMANDING 252ND (NORTHUMBRIAN) BRIGADE, R.F.A.
- - - - - - - - - - -

Reference:- Sheet 11. 1:100.000 LENS Map

1. The Brigade will march to BOURDON on 15th instant.

2. Starting Point, as shewn on tracing attached.

3. Head of column will pass Starting Point at 4.0 a.m.

4. An officer from each Battery to report at 3.45 a.m. to Starting Point that Battery is ready. He with 6 cyclists will comprise a battery watering party with as many canvas buckets as they can carry.

5. Watering parties will reconnoitre watering facilities from RIBEAUCOURT to DOMART. O.C. each party will send report back to meet head of column and on these reports detailed orders for watering will be issued.

6. Nosebags to be carried full and unexpended forage will be carried on vehicles.

7. Water carts to travel full. Each officer, N.C.O., and man will carry unexpended portion of days ration and water bottles full.

8. Tracing shewing route to be followed herewith.

9. All reports to be sent to Head of Column.

10. A C K N O W L E D G E.

H M Macdonald
Lt/Adjt
for Lieut.Col.
Commanding 252(North'bn)Brigade, RFA.

14th August 1916.

Copy No. 1. Officer
"   "   2. A/252 Battery.
"   "   3. B/252   "
"   "   4. C/252   "
"   "   5. D/252   "
"   "   6. War Diary.

OPERATION ORDER NO 16A.
252ND R.F.A. BRIGADE.
17/8/16-

1. The Brigade will relieve 176 Brigade 34th D.A. on the nights 18/19 and 19/20 August.

2. On completion of relief Left Group D.A. III Corps consist of 47th D.A. and 50th D.A. commanded by Brig-Genl Spedding, C.M.G., R.A.

3. 50th D.A. will march via BAIZIEUX-HENINCOURT-MILLENCOURT.

4. All telephone wires, maps etc will be taken over from 176 Brigade.

5. All ammunition left to be taken over and ammunition reported to H.Q.

6. B.Cs., 1 Officer and 3 telephonists per battery will proceed by motor bus on morning of 18th to 34th D.A. area. B.C. and telephonists will remain in 34th D.A. area and the other officer in each case will return to 34th D.A. wagon lines to bring in first sections.

7. Command of batteries, brigades and D.A. will pass at 6 p.m. on 19th.

8. Sections will leave present area at 6.30 a.m. on 18th August 19th

9. C.R.A. 34th Division will decide as to hour of relief of sections 176 R.F.A.

10. Acknowledge.

Kinmarshall
Lt/Adjt 252 RFA
17/8/16

Copy No. 1

OPERATION ORDER No. 15 A by Lieut Col. F.L. Pickersgill RFA, Comdg. 252 (Nth) Bde RFA

1. The Brigade will march to BEHENCOURT via :- S of BOIS du GARD.
  VIGNA COURT.
  OLINCOURT CHAU.
  FLESSELLES.
  VILLARS BOCAGE.
  MOLLIENS au BOIS.

2. STARTING POINT 400 yards past BOURDEN church on VIGNA COURT Road.

3. Officers from each Battery to report to Head of Column at 1.30 AM, 16/8/16.

4. Head of Column will pass starting point at 1.45 AM, 16/8/16.

5. Order of march :- HQrs.
  D Bty
  C "
  B "
  A "

2.

6. Length of march 20 miles.
7. Acknowledge on envelope.

Frank H Pickersgill.
Lieut Col.
Comdg. 252 (Nth) Bde RFA

15/8/16.

Copy No. 1   War Diary
 "   " 2   A/Bty
 "   " 3   B "
 "   " 4   C "
 "   " 5   D "
 "   " 6. Office.

50th. DIVISIONAL ARTILLERY

252nd. BRIGADE R. F. A.

50th. DIVISIONAL ARTILLERY

SEPTEMBER 1916.

VOLUME XVII
SHEET No 34
252 (N&N) Bde RFA

WAR DIARY
or
INTELLIGENCE SUMMARY

Army Form C. 2118.

(Erase heading not required.)

VDC 17

Place	Date	Hour	Ammunition Expended				Summary of Events and Information	Remarks and references to Appendices
		Shell	A	AX	BX	B&F		
ALBERT	1/9/16		70	1245	1227	856	Fourth Army renewed the attack 00174 attached also 18A ØLP	ØLP
	2			2174	601	286 90	Guillemont & Guinchy captured by British. Bty captured by French	ØLP
	3			2386	391	386		ØLP
	4			2193	287	237		ØLP
	5			1411	360	164		ØLP
	6			1631	391	209		ØLP
	7			1633	363	205 3	B/D Willis & 18th Willis of B Bty awarded M.M.	ØLP
	8			1658	349	124 1	Cpl 1276 Sherils A Bty wounded.	ØLP
	9			1856	1218	447	A Bty Ammunition dump blown up by 5.9 Shell. 4th Army renew attack at C.019 A ØLP	
	10			2149	937	5-77	Wagon lines moved up to Recruit wood	ØLP
	11			1145	391	75	Relieved 73 Bde RFA. Capt Squire admitted to hospital sick (Battock) 108	ØLP
	12			885	373	732 SK	PS	ØLP
	13		St	878	776	494 139 26	C/252 attached to Bde and go into action	ØLP
	14		Shell 737	1315	225	776	¾ All A.B.C. Btys shelled Casualties killed B.P. Bogen 1234 J. Horn 1924 A. Tut 3057 ØLP	
	15		7388	1667	504 B 120	506	18X wounded	Kohn JW 1316 Tompkin R 1941	ØLP
							McGeehan W 1316 Tompkin R 1941	
							Armstrong J 2742	

WAR DIARY or INTELLIGENCE SUMMARY.

SHEET No 42 Army Form C. 2118.

252 (NBN) RFA

Place	Date	Hour	Summary of Events and Information	Remarks and references to Appendices
ALBERT	24.		A/252 D/252 C/250 all move into forward position H.Q starts relay Station at Infantry Bele H.Q at Cemetry. Ammunition A647 AX 415 BX NIL	OUP
	25.		The Division on our Right attacked but were apparently unsuccessful 2 ft. Scouson and Hole fori Bele and are jutted to D 252 Ammunition A 706 AX151 BX84 PS90	OUP
	"		II Corps capture Thiepval about 1500 prisoners captured. Gomcules Taken by French. Sergt Watt Bar Nixon awarded Military Medal for gallantry when A/252 Ammunition Dump was blown up. Gunners + Br Juff awarded M.M.	OUP
	26.		Ammunition A 625 AX 253 BX673 PS 100	OUP
	27.		50 Div Patrols went forward and established points in the Flers Line. Apparently the Enemy have evacuated Flers line. Sergt 1561 Seib ennett wounded C 145 Hayes Cmg Ammunition A 511 AX 157 BX 585 Infantry 114	OUP
	28		Germans re-establish themselves in Flers Line Ammunition A859 AX100 88 BX	OUP

WAR DIARY or INTELLIGENCE SUMMARY.

Army Form C. 2118.

SHEET No 4
252 (N Bn) RFA

Place	Date	Hour	Summary of Events and Information	Remarks and references to Appendices
ALBERT	29		Ammunition A1112 AX1758x51	Inf
	30		Durham Light Infantry made a bombing attack on Flers Line it was unsuccessful. Ammunition A391 AX 256 BX284 SK52 PS3	Inf

Branich Pickerigill
Lieut. Col.
252nd (Nbn) Bde RFA (TF)

Opuaha Order No 18 a (continued)

page 2

3. (d) All batteries 12·5 pm – 12·7 pm
      Lift 200 yards
      Rate as in (c)

   (e) All batteries 12·7 pm
      objective as in (c)
      One Salvo from each Battery and
         stop firing; then return to
         normal barrage and daily
         programme.

   K M macdonald
   Lt Adjt 9.45 am.

252 M.G.C. A.
Operation Order No 17A   4-9-16

1. 4th Army is renewing the attack on ... and in conjunction with the French XX Corps is attacking GINCHY 7th Divn will attack WOOD LANE + HIGH WOOD

2. At 2 pm on Z Sept and 10 am on 3 Sept 7th Divn will discharge smoke from trenches facing Western edge of High Wood + the 15 Bde will discharge Smoke along their whole front – both for 20 minutes.

3. At 2 pm Z Sept + 10 am 3 Sept the Brigade will open fire with machine guns, all available guns so that of the German front line opposite its own position and on
   A MG M31 d 5 0 – S16 c 9 5
   B   S16 c 9 5 – S16 d 7 9 3
   C   S16 d 7 9 3 – S16 d 8 9
   D   M31 d 5 0 – S16 d 8 9

252 RFA
Operation Order No 17A continued

4. Zero hour on 2nd — 2 p.m.
   " 3rd — 5.45 a.m.

(a) Zero to plus 3
    18 pdrs & 4 pr. 50 yds short of German
    4.5 Hows on German front line.

(b) Plus 3 to plus 5
    18 pdrs lift on to front line. Hows
    remain on front line

(c) Plus 5 to plus 10
    all lift 150 yards

(d) Plus 10 to plus 12
    Jump back to front line

(e) Plus 12 to plus 15
    lift 150 yards

(f) Plus 15 to plus 20
    burst of fire on front line

(g) Plus 20 stop firing

262 RFA

Operation Order No 17A

5. Rate of fire
   (a) 18 hours 3 rounds per gun per minute
       yellow 1

   (b) As in (a)

   (c) 18 [hours] 1 round per gun per minute
       yellow 1

   (d) As in (c)

   (e) As in (c)

   K M Macdonald
   (?) RGF
   9.15 A.M.
   2/7/16

252 Brigade R.F.A.
ALTERATIONS AND ADDITIONS TO OPERATION ORDERS
NO. 17 A.

A.4

Para. 2 for 10 read 5.
  " 3   " 10 " 5.
  " 4   " 10 " 5.

    Sub para. f delete "bursts of fire"
     "   "   g read as follows:-
    "+20 to +25 lift 150 yards".

New sub para. h.
    +25 to +30 bursts of fire on front line.

New sub para. i.
    +30 stop firing.

Para. 5.
    Sub para. a. for 3 read 2.
     "   "   d " 2 " 1.

New sub para. f.
    18pr. 3 rds. per gun per min.
    4.5How. 2 "   "   " How "   "

New sub para. g.
    as in f.

                                  Lieut.Co
            Commanding 252(North'bn)Bde. R.F.A.

2nd September 1918.

2 RFA
O.O. No 20 B

1. 10th Bty RFA will relieve 73 RFA during afternoon of 10th and evening 11th inst. Relief to be completed by 12 noon 11th inst.

2. Relieving sections will march from their positions at 3 pm on 10th and 9.30 am on 11th.

3. Guns will remain in position and not moved. They will be handed over as in use.

4. Ammunition at gun positions to be handed over. Amounts handed over and taken over to be reported to HQ as soon the relief is completed. Responsibility for supply of Ammunition will change with completion of relief sections, in from 1 at 12 noon on 11th.

5. Liaison Officer will hand over and take over from 73rd Brigade

O.O. No 20 page 2

Liaison Officer at 12 noon on 11th inst.

6. All maps, photographs etc will be handed over.

7. 253 Brigade guns are now to be handed over. They will be taken to Battery wagon lines.

8. Completion of the jobs to be reported to H.Q. by wire.

9. A/252 relieves A/73 at S20 d 7 8
　B　　　　　　　B/70　　S20 d 4 7½
　C　　　　　　　C/73　　S20 b 0 3
　D　　　　　　　D/70　　S20 a 2½ ½

H.Q.S. at F 6 a 7 3

K.M. MacDonald
L/Adjt

5.15 pm
9-9-16

252 RFA

A1
9-9-16

O.O. No 19 A

1. 4th Army is renewing attack today.
   XV Corps, Canadian Corps & 1st Division are attacking.

2. The assault will be immediately preceded by the explosion of a mine at S4d 2.0 6.5 at ½ minute before Zero. Flammenwerfer will be fired 10 seconds before Zero.

3. From Zero to plus 15, if wind is favourable, 15 Division will liberate smoke along its whole front.

4. Zero hour is 4.45 pm September 9th.

5. The Brigade will bombard as follows:-

① 4.45 pm to 4.47 pm   S 1 6 8 9 to M 31 d 20 25
② 4.47 - - 4.48 -   Lift 150 yards
③ 4.48 pm   as in ①

Rate of fire ① and ② 18 pdrs 3 rds per gun per minute 4.5 How 2 rds per gun per minute ③ Fire 1 salvo and return to daily programme

252 RFA

O.O. No 19 A cont°

6. Battery Zones as follows:-

A M 31 d 20 25 – M 31 d 40 13
B M 31 d 40 13 – M 31 d 60 30
C M 31 d 60 30 – S 1 b 8 9
D M 31 d 20 25 – S 1 b 8 9

H M MacDonald
Lt & Adjt
12.25 pm
9-9-16

Operation Order No 18A   3/9/16
252 RFA Brigade

1. With reference to 1st Division operation
mentioned in O.O No 17A para 1

2. Zero hour will be 12 noon on 3rd September
1916 at which hour infantry will assault.

3. The Brigade will bombard hostile trenches
as follow:-
   (A) D Bty   10.25 am to 11.20 am
       Trenches S2a 75 60 to S2b 0 8
       1 round per gun per 1½ minutes
   (B) D Bty   11.20 am to 12 noon
       Trenches S2a 75 60 to S2b 0 8
       1½ rounds per gun per 1 minute
   (C) All Batteries, as under, 12 noon to 12.5 pm
       A Bty   M31 d 5 0 - S16 b 95
       B .   S16 b 95 - S16 b 7 43
       C .   S16 b 7 43 - S16 b 8 9
       D .   M31 d 5 0 - S16 b 8 9
       18 pdrs 50 yds short of trenches as above
       4.5 How on trenches
       18 pdrs 3 rds per gun per minute
       4.5 How 2 " "

Army Form C. 2118.

October 1916
Volume XIX

WAR DIARY or INTELLIGENCE SUMMARY

262ND BRIGADE RFA
SHEET NO 144
Vol 18

Instructions regarding War Diaries and Intelligence Summaries are contained in F.S. Regs., Part II. and the Staff Manual respectively. Title pages will be prepared in manuscript.

(Erase heading not required.)

Place	Date	Hour	Summary of Events and Information	Remarks and references to Appendices
ALBERT	October 1		50 Division attacked Flers line and took their objective. 8/Thornton attached	0021A
	2		" attacked on our Right & 47 Divsn on our Left. C/262 wounded also by Richardson 359 Ammunition A2773 AX520 BX566	Rab
	3		Further operations hindered by weather. St Martin went to Hospital Sick. Ammunition A2928 AX297 BX291 50 Division Infantry relieved by 23 Divsn. 23 Div CRA takes over. Tactical command of 50 Div ARty Ammunition A812 AX851 BX392	Rab
	4		Brigade H.Q. move forward to the Quarries. Trig Bde moves to Martin puick. Pt S in Milburn regains Bde from 50 DA Ammunition A556 AX1173 BX46	Rab
	5		Pt S in Milburn posted to D/252. 1545 L/ Dickinson C/252 wounded. Ammunition A1655 AX16-2 BX99	Rab
	6		Ammunition A697 AX 826 BX 430	Rab
	7		23 Div attack the Tangle & LeSars O.C. 22A attached BX816	Rab

252ND BRIGADE, RFA(T)

Army Form C. 2118.

SHEET. N° 46

WAR DIARY
or
INTELLIGENCE SUMMARY.

(Erase heading not required.)

Instructions regarding War Diaries and Intelligence Summaries are contained in F.S. Regs., Part II. and the Staff Manual respectively. Title pages will be prepared in manuscript.

Place	Date	Hour	Summary of Events and Information	Remarks and references to Appendices
ALBERT	8		D/252. Move formed to Martinpuich Brigade come under 15 DA. Ammunition 1908 A 1144 AX 963	Rab.
	9.		No 4664 Gr Robinson D/263 wounded Gr Thornton died of wounds	Rab.
			Ammunition 755A 517 AX 1084 BX	Rab.
	10		592 A 463 AX 80 BX	Rab.
	11		2178 A 980 AX 260 BX	Rab. OO 23A attached Rab.
	12		2/Lt Hornsby awarded M.C. Butler-de-Warlencourt attacked e.g. 9 Div objective not gained	Rab.
	13		A 2088 AX 684 RX 77 Ammunition	Rab.
	14		Lt. A.R. West of awarded M.C. Am.n	Rab.
	15		Sergt L.A. Morelli D/252 killed and Gr Lewis wounded Am.n	Rab.
	16		Gr Sanders C/252 killed Gr Dimmock & Gr Fleet Wounded Am.n	Rab.
	17		Bde pulled out of action at 5AM and proceeded to Frechencourt in action	OO 24A attached Rab.

WAR DIARY 252ND BRIGADE, R.F.A. (Army Form C. 2118.)
or
INTELLIGENCE SUMMARY. SHEET No 46

(Erase heading not required.)

Hour, Date, Place	Summary of Events and Information	Remarks and references to Appendices
18th Frettencourt	Regt. Brigade Clean up	Rae.
19	Rest Brigade Clean up. Sgt. Walker 1495	Rae
20	" (awarded meritorious Service Medal)	Rae
21	Gnrs Sanger, Vickerson, Young, Thornton (ac) Murphy, Wilson, Steel awarded M.M. 2/Lt Hurst Jones Bde.	Rae. Rae
22		Rae
23		Rae
24	Gr Fleet 1342 died of wounds (1 General Hospital Rouen)	Rae
25	2/Lt Atkinson wounded B" Davis awarded M.M.	Rae
26		Rae
27		Rae
28		Rae
29		Rae
30		Rae
31		Rae

Rabouineau Major

Cmdg. 252nd (Non.) Bde R.F.A.

SECRET   COPY NO 5

OPERATION ORDER NO 23 A BY LIEUT COL F.L.PICKERSGILL.,
R.F.A.(T)., COMMANDING 253ND (NORTHUMBRIAN) BDE. "R.F.A."
----

1. The 9th Division are carrying out their attack on WARLENCOURT LINE and the BUTTE DE WARLENCOURT on October 12th. There will be no period of intense fire prior to Zero. The Infantry Advance at Zero, the first objective being the German Trenches in M.17.c. and d. At Zero plus 23 the advance from the first to the final objective is to commence. The final objective is the GIRD TRENCH both front and support from the Corps Boundary to M.17.a.4.7½. and the BUTTE DE WARLENCOURT.

2. The 44th Infantry Brigade will work in close communication with the 1st S.A. Brigade, advancing on the left of the 9th Division. The advance will commence at ½ 30 minutes and will be continued to the line M.16.b.9.9. to M.16.b.3.5.

3. If the wind is favourable a smoke barrage commencing at Zero will be placed to assist the Division on our right and to cover the front of the 15th Division.

4. Artillery Programme is attached.

5. Zero Time will be 2.5 p.m.

ZERO is 2.5 p.m.

Previous to this A/252 will search ground from our trenches to the GIRD LINE MEthodically in its allotted zone.

	K.T.	H.J.	H.L. (Rover)
Zero to +5.	M.17.d.0.5. to M.17.c.7½.4½.	M.17.c.7½.4½. to M.17.c.5.4.	M.17.d.0.5. to M.17.c.5.4½.
+5 to +23	M.17.b.0.4. to M.17.a.7½.3.	M.17.a.7½.3. to M.17.a.5.0.	M.17.b.0.4. to M.17.a.5.0.
+23 to +28.	M.17.b.0.5½. to M.17.a.7.6½.	M.17.a.7.6½. to M.17.a.4.7.	M.17.b.0.5½. to M.17.a.4.7.
+28 to +34	M.17.b.0.8. to M.17.a.7½.9.	M.17.a.7½.9. to M.11.c.5.0.	M.17.b.0.8. to M.11.c.5.0.

At +5 lift.
 " +23 " 100 yards due North on to GIRD FRONT LINE.
 " +28 " due North to GIRD SUPPORT LINE.
 " +34 " 200 yards due North and remain on that line until further orders.

RATES from Zero to +6.   3 rounds per gun per minute.
  "   "   +6 "+23.   1   "   "   "   "   "
  "   " +23 "+28   3   "   "   "   "   "
  "   " +28 "+33   2   "   "   "   "   "
  "   +34 onwards .   1   "   "   "   "   "

D/252 Battery.

Zero to +40.   M.10.c.6.6. to M.10.c.2.6.

At plus 40, the Battery will resume normal work.

It should however be prepared to open on the above barrage at a moment's notice in case of a counter-attack.

Zero to plus 6.   2 rounds per gun per minute.
Plus 6 to plus 23. 1 " "   "   "   "
Plus 23 to plus 33. 2 " "   "   "   "
Plus 33 to plus 37. 1 " "   "   "   "
Plus 37 to plus 40. 1 " "   "   "   "

Frank H. Pickersgill

SECRET.   COPY NO ..16.

OPERATION ORDER NO 24A BY LIEUT COL F.L.PICKERSGILL.,
COMMANDING 252ND (NORTHUMBRIAN) BRIGADE., R.F.A.

1.   The Brigade will move into Rest Billets at FRECHENCOURT on 17/10/16.

2.   Batteries will march with full echelons of ammunition, B/252 and C/252 leaving residue at positions for use of 250 F.A.B. and A/252 for 253 F.A.B. Amounts handed over to be reported on joining H.Q.

3.   D/252 will come under command of 253 F.A.B. from 5 a.m. 17/10/16 and will remain in action.

4.   Batteries will pull out their guns at 5 a.m. 17/10/16. O.C.s. making their own arrangements for picking up their wagon line personnel etc.

5.   Batteries will move independently but all must be clear of ALBERT before 10 a.m. 17/10/16.

6.   Route will be via BECOURT - ALBERT - to a point on ALBERT-AMIENS Road as far as LAHOUSSOYE. Orderlies from H.Q. will report forming-up point to O.Cs. as picked up on ALBERT-AMIENS Road.

7.   Present Headquarters will close at 5 a.m. 17/10/16.

8.   All wagon lines will be left clean and latrines properly filled in.

9.   2nd Lieut G.B. JAMESON and one N.C.O. proceed on the 16/10/16 as a billetting party.

                                      Frank L Pickersgill.
                                                Lieut Col.
                         Commanding 252nd. (North'bn) Bde., R.F.A.

Copy No 1.   War Diary.
"   "   2.   A/252.
"   "   3.   B/252.
"   "   4.   C/252.
"   "   5.   D/252.
        6   Capt Wood.

16/10/16

SECRET   Copy No. 7

352 (NORTH'BN) BRIGADE RFA.

OPERATION ORDER NO. 21 A.

1. On 1st October 50th Division will capture and hold the two lines of hostile trenches between R.31.b.3.4. and H.31.b.8.4. 47th Division and 23rd Division will attack on right and left respectively. *Objectives shown on attached map*

2. Artillery will begin a deliberate bombardment of the objectives at 7.0am. on 1st October. Infantry will attack at Zero at which time artillery barrage will begin. The various lifts are shewn on attached programme.

3. At plus 30 minutes 50th Division will push forward to the work at H.31.b.3.6. and 23rd Division will push forward strong patrols into LE SARS and to the Quarry at H.18.d.7.8.

4. At plus 1 hour and 30 minutes 50th and 23rd Divisions will push patrols due North and form an outpost line in the line H.13.c.3.5. - H.19.a.5.1. - round LE SARS - Quarry in H.18.d.7.8.

5. A C K N O W L E D G E .

        K M MacAnder
                Lieut. RFA.
        Adjutant, 352 (North'bn) Brigade. RFA.

30th September 1916.

Copy No. 1. - War Diary.
  "   " 2. - A/352.
  "   " 3. - B/352.
  "   " 4. - C/352.
  "   " 5. - D/352.
  "   " 6. - Liaison Officer.
  "   " 7. - Office.

PROGRAMME OF BOMBARDMENT FOR 18-PDRS.
252ND (NORTHUMBRIAN) BRIGADE, R.F.A.

Serial No.	Unit.	Time.	Objective.

1.   0.00.   All 18-pdrs batteries 50 yards short of German front line as below :-

A/252.   0.02.   Rake back onto German kxx front line.
M.22.b.30.40. to M.22.b.35.60.

B/252.   M.22.b.30.40. to M.22.b.10.40.

C/252.   M.22.b.10.40. to M.22.a.55.60.

Rate of Fire. 3 Rounds per gun per minute till 0.04.

This should be a deep barrage guns being laid to give a depth of 50 yards.

2.   0.04.   Lift to

A/252   M.22.b.50.60. to M.22.b.40.40.

B/252   M.22.b.55.40. to M.22.b.30.40.

C/252.   M.22.b.30.20. to M.22.b.10.40.

Rate of Fire. Decrease to 1 round per gun per minute.

Lift at rate of 50 yards a minute.

3.   0.30.   Lift to

A/252   M.16.d.70.40. to M.16.d.30.30.

B/252.   M.16.d.70.10. to M.16.d.50.20.

C/252.   M.16.d.50.20. to M.16.d.30.30.

Rate of Fire. One round per gun per minute till 1.30.

Lift at rate of 50 yards a minute.

4.   1.30   Lift to

A/252   M.17.a.40.40. to M.11.c.20.40.

B/252   M.17.a.40.40. to M.17.a.30.20.

C/252   M.17.a.30.20. to M.11.c.20.40.

Rate of Fire.

Decrease to 1 round per gun per 3 minutes.

Lift at rate of 50 yards a minute.

PROGRAMME OF BOMBARDMENT
FOR D/252.

| Serial No. | Time. | Objective. |

A.   7 a.m. to 2 p.m.   C.Ts. in zone H.46.b.3.4. to H.22.c.95.60. and work at H.34.a.5.6.

    Rate of Fire. Slow bombardment.

    Allotment. 100 BK.

B.   2 p.m. to C.52.   Front line H.22.b.30.40. to H.22.a.80..w.

    Rate of Fire. 1 round per gun per 4½ minutes.

C.   C.52 to C.54   Support line behind above points.

    Rate of Fire. 1 round per gun per 2 minutes.

D.   C.54 to C.30   Lift 50 yards a minute along roads and C.Ts. to a line
        H.22.b.60.50. to H.16.c.40.40.

    Rate of Fire. 1 round per gun per 2 minutes.

E.   C.30   Jump to N.E. end of LE SARS about H.16.central and road junction H.16.b.9.4.

    Rate of Fire. Slow bombardment.

    Allotment. 40 BK.

                                    Lieut.
                        Adjutant 252nd (North'bn) Bde., R.F.A.

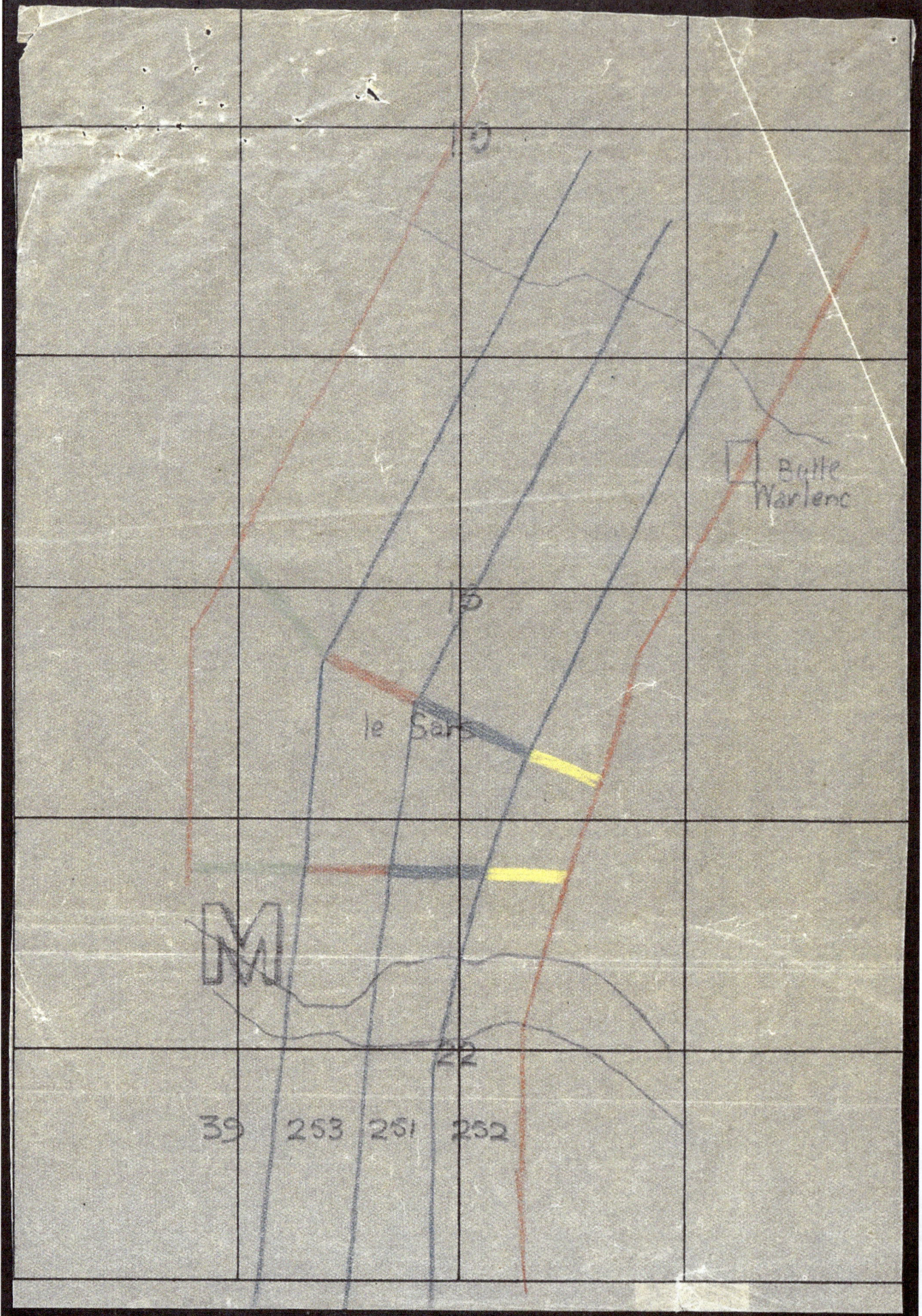

Secret.   Copy No. 1...

ADDENDUM TO OPERATION NO 21 A, 252ND BRIGADE., R.F.A.
----

1. From 10.0 a.m. to 10.10. a.m. 4.5" Howitzers will fire at rapid rate on their objectives.

    10.10 a.m. to 10.14 a.m. -- Pause.

    10.14 a.m., re-commence normal rate of fire with a salvo from the battery.

2. All 18-pdr Batteries, 10.7 a.m. to 10.10 a.m. bursts of fire on front trenches.

    10.10 a.m. to 10.14. a.m.   Lift 300 yards.

    10.14 a.m., 2 rounds gun fire on front line trenches

3. Acknowledge by wire

K M Mainwaring
Lieut.
Adjutant 252nd (North'bn) Brigade., R.F.A.

Copy No 1.   War Diary.
 "   " 2.   A/252.
 "   " 3.   B/252.
 "   " 4.   C/252.
 "   " 5.   D/252.
 "   " 6.   Liaison Officer.

1/10/16j

SECRET COPY NO. I

OPERATION ORDERS NO 22 A, BY LIEUT Col F.L.PICKERSGILL.,
COMMANDING 252ND (NORTHUMBRIAN) BRIGADE., R.F.A.

7th October, 1916.

1. (A) At Zero hour to-day the 23rd Division are attacking LE SARS - 68th I.B. on the Right, 69th on the Left. Dividing Line between Brigades M.21.b.8.5. through X Roads M.16.c.1.4. Northwards.

   (B) 47th Division on our Right are attacking BUTTE DE WARLENCOURT and a line E. and W. of it at approximately the same hour. Dividing Line between 23rd and 47th Divisions is MARTINPUICH - WARLENCOURT Road inclusive to 47th Division.

2. (A) F I R S T   O B J E C T I V E of 23rd Division is the Sunken Road at M.22.b.5.8. to X Roads in LE SARS M.16.c.1.4. and thence to M.15.c.7.5. As much ground as possible will be gained towards M.15.a.5.4. and posts established on this line.
   The attack on the left against the 2nd FLERS LINE N.W. of the BAPAUME Road and the trenches within the general line M.15.d.6.8. to M.15.d.8.6. will not take place until + 20 minutes.

   (B) F I N A L   O B J E C T I V E is a line through M.16.b.0.8. to M.16.a.7.4. to M.15.a.7.10. Strong posts will be established on this line.

3. A Tank if present will cross the trenches at M.22.a.9.4. at zero and clear the TANGLE and SUNKEN Road behind.

(4)

GIRDLESTANE

4. LIEUT. ━━━━ with instrument, telephonist and wire to
extend the existing line; will report at Right Battalion
H.Q., 68th I.B. four hours before Zero and be prepared
to move forward as required to keep in close touch with
Battalion Commander. All information to be telephoned
through Battalion and Brigade Liaison Officer back to
R.A. Headquarters.

5. At + 1 Hour Infantry are showing flares.

6. Zero hour is 4.45 p.m. to-day.

7. ACKNOWLEDGE.

K M MacDonald

Lieut.
Adjutant 252nd (Northumbrian) Brigade, R.F.A.

Copy No 1. War Diary.
"   " 2. Office.
"   " 3. A/252.
"   " 4. B/252.
"   " 5. C/252.
"   " 6. D/252.

252ND (NORTHUMBRIAN) BRIGADE., R.F.A.

PROGRAMME OF BOMBARDMENT.

D/252.   **mid-night to 7.45 a.m. 7th October.**

Search LE SARS Village at 1 round per Howr Gun per 4 minutes.

Zero to 0.1.

SUNKEN ROAD M.16.c.5.1. - M.16.c.2½.2. Fire as fast as possible.

0.1. to 0.30.

S.E. Side of LE SARS. Fire to be North of a line M.16.c.5.7. to M.16.d.0.7.

Two rounds per gun per minute.

0.30. to 1.30.

Area of Railway Station bounded by WARLENCOURT ROAD on East BAPAUME ROAD on West and bottom of square M.16.b. on the South.

One round per gun per two minutes.

1.30 onwards.

LITTLE WOOD M.10.c.0.8.

One round per gun per three minutes.

A. B. and C. Batteries will barrage Road as follows :-

Zero to 0.40.

A.   M.16.d.6½.2½. to M.16.b.9.9.
B.   M.16.d.6½.2½. to M.16.d.9.1.
C.   M.16.b.9.1.   to M.16.b.9.9.

0.40 to 2 Hours.

A.   M.16.d.7½.7. to M.16.b.9.9.
B.   M.16.d.7½.7. to M.16.b.9.3.
C.   M.16.b.9.3.   to M.16.b.9.9.

No fire to be south of M.16.d.7½.7. after 0.40.

Rate of fire as follows :-

0. to 0.10. 4 rounds per gun per minute.

0.10 to 0.20. 3 " " " " "

0.20. to 0.30. 2 " " " " "

0.30 to 1.30. 1 " " " " "

1.30 to 2 Hours 1 round per gun per 2 minutes.

K M MacDonald

Lieut.
Adjutant 252nd (Northumbrian) Brigade., R.F.A.

7/10/16.

WAR DIARY

INTELLIGENCE SUMMARY

SHEET No. 47.
Army Form C. 2118.
Vol. XX November 1916
252ND BRIGADE. R.F.A.(T)
Vol 19

Place	Date	Hour	Summary of Events and Information	Remarks and references to Appendices
FRECHENCOURT	Nov 1.		2nd Lieut. G. STEPHENSON A/252 transferred to Z.50 T.M.B	Ref.
			" E.S. HURST B/252 " Y.50. T.M.B	
			" T. NICHOLSON. Y.50 T.M.B " B/252	
			" E.C. JONES 50TH DAC " "	
	2.			
	3.		1495 Sgt J.R. Walker, 46 Cpl J. Birbeck, 1159 Pte R. Johnson, 972 a/Sdr J.W. Gallagher, 1490 a/Sdr J. Duggan, 1303 Gunner R. Blake 4358 Gun J. Poole awarded Military Medal	Ref.
	4.			Ref.
	5.			Ref.
	6.			Ref.
	7.			Ref.
	8.			Ref.
	9.			Ref.
	10.			Ref.
	11.			Ref.
	12.		Lieut E.H. JOHNSON joined A/252 from 50th D.A.	
	13.		D/252 move into rest area at MOULLIENS AU BOIS. 1268 Gdr. J. Jones awarded MSM 478 Gunner R. Allcott awarded Military Medal. (RAMC)	Ref.
	14.			

SHEET No. 48 Army Form C. 2118.

WAR DIARY

Instructions regarding War Diaries and Intelligence Summaries are contained in F.S. Regs., Part II. and the Staff Manual respectively. Title pages will be prepared in manuscript.

INTELLIGENCE SUMMARY. 252ND BRIGADE, R.F.A.

(Erase heading not required.)

Place	Date	Hour	Summary of Events and Information	Remarks and references to Appendices
FRECHENCOURT	Nov 15.			Ref
MOULLIENS AU BOIS	16		Headquarters and Batteries move to MOULLIENS AU BOIS. A.B. + C. Batteries reorganized into two 6-gun 18 pdr batteries 'C' Battery transferred to 'B' and Right section 'B' Battery transferred to A/252.	Ref
	17.			Ref
	18.			Ref
	19.			Ref Ref
	20.		Headquarters ones	Ref
	21.	11.0 am	Headquarters and ½ of each battery move up and put up in wagon lines near MONTAUBAN	Ref
MONTAUBAN	22.	6.30 am	Remainder of Batteries move up.	Ref Ref
FLERS	23	7.0 am	62nd Brigade command is taken over by this Brigade	Ref
	24		Ammunition expended 126 A Lieut U.M. LINKLATER joined from D/253rd Bde.	Ref
	25		Ammunition expended 203 A 153 A X 30 Bx.	Ref
			" 76 A 134 A X 91 Bx.	
	26		" 245 A 115 A X 100 Bx.	Ref

WAR DIARY

SHEET No 49. Army Form C. 2118.

INTELLIGENCE SUMMARY. 252ND (NORTH'BN) BDE. RFA

Place	Date	Hour	Summary of Events and Information	Remarks and references to Appendices
FLERS.	Nov. 27.		341 Driver Bruce W wounded.	Ref.
			Ammunition Expended. 49A 483 Ax 85 Bx	
	28		Capt RL West proceeded to England under W.O. instructions.	Ref.
			Ammunition Expended. 60 A 441 Ax 147 Bx.	
	29.		Ammunition Expended. 366 Ax	Ref.
	30.		Ammunition Expended. 420 Ax. 30 Bx.	Ref.

R.H.Browne Major
OC 252 (Northumbry) Bde RFA

Army Form C. 2118   252ND (NBN) BDE RFA

SHEET No 50

WAR DIARY
or
INTELLIGENCE SUMMARY.
(Erase heading not required.)

VOLUME No XX   DECEMBER 1916   Vol 20

Place	Date	Hour	Summary of Events and Information	Remarks and references to Appendices
FLERS	1/12/16		Amm expended 379 AX 15 BX	
	2		390 AX	
	3		300 A 62 AX 24 BX	
	4		205 A 40 AX 43 BX	
	5		118 A 150 AX 24 BX	
	6		Brigade goes under Tactical command of 1st Div C R A	
	7		Cp. Hollywood - J. 60 17 B/252 died of wounds received on 6th	
	8		—	
	9		D/252 relieved by D/261. D/252 move to wagon lines	
	10		D/252 move into rest Billets at Bavelincourt	
	11		—	
	12		—	

PROGRAMME OF BOMBARDMENT FOR 18-PDRS.
252ND (NORTHUMBRIAN) BRIGADE., R.F.A.

| Serial. No. | Unit. | Time. | Objective. |

1.   0.00.   All 18-pdrs batteries 50 yards short of German front line as below :-

A/252. 0.00.   Rake back onto German front line. M.22.b.30.40. to M.22.a.05.00.

B/252.   M.22.b.30.40. to M.22.b.40.40.

C/252.   M.22.b.40.40. to M.22.a.25.00.

Rate of Fire. 3 Rounds per gun per minute till 0.04.

This should be a deep barrage guns being laid to give a depth of 50 yards.

2.   0.04.   Lift to

A/252   M.22.b.50.40. to M.22.b.40.40.

B/252   M.22.b.50.40. to M.22.b.30.40.

C/252.   M.22.b.30.40. to M.22.b.4.40.

Rate of Fire. Decrease to 1 round per gun per minute.

Lift at rate of 50 yards a minute.

3.   0.30.   Lift to

A/252   M.16.d.70.40. to M.16.d.30.30.

B/252.   M.16.d.70.40. to M.16.d.50.30.

C/252.   M.16.d.50.30. to M.16.d.30.30.

Rate of Fire. One round per gun per minute till 1.30.

Lift at rate of 50 yards a minute.

4.   1.30   Lift to

A/252   M.17.a.40.90. to M.11.c.90.40.

B/252   M.17.a.40.90. to M.17.a.30.90.

C/252   M.17.a.30.90. to M.11.c.20.10.

Rate of Fire.

Decrease to 1 round per gun per 3 minutes.

Lift at rate of 50 yards a minute.

WAR DIARY
or
INTELLIGENCE SUMMARY.

Army Form C. 2118.

252ND (NBM) BDE RFA
SHEET No 52

Place	Date	Hour	Summary of Events and Information	Remarks and references to Appendices
Behencourt	27/12/16		D/252 fired a series with aeroplane observation on Montigny range	B/252 Centin. & Wisdom 9/2 all Batteries refitting &c &c
	28		A/252 took over new Billets in Bavelincourt from the Cavalry	
	29			
	30			

J S Hanson
Lt Col 252 Bde RFA

SECRET.   COPY NO. 5.

OPERATION ORDER NO 27a by MAJOR L.A.COLSON, R.F.A.(T).
COMMANDING 452ND (NORTH'BN) BRIGADE., R.F.A.

1.   B/271 will relieve D/252 R.F.A. personnel only, by
     sections on nights 8/9 and 9/10 December.

2.   A/350 and C/069 R.F.A. will relieve A/252 and B/252
     personnel only; first sections on night 12/13 December,
     remaining sections on night 13/14 December.

3.   H.Q. 350 R.F.A. will relieve H.Q. 252 R.F.A. on 14th
     December.

4.   On relief units will occupy billets in PAULARD HUT
     and BRESNCOURT vacated by the respective relieving units.

5.   Outgoing units will travel by route – ALBERT, and
     ALBERT Road, LAHOUSSOYE.   Tail of column to be clear
     of ALBERT by 12 noon. on 9th, 10th, 13th and 14th
     December.

6.   Completion of each stage of relief to be reported to
     this H.Q.

7.   Any necessary orders regarding order of march on
     13th and 14th December will be issued later.

8. Acknowledge

                              Norman Small
                                         Lieut.
                              Adjutant 452nd (North'bn) Bde., R.F.A.

6/12/18.

Copy No. 1.   Office.
  "   " 2.   A/350.
  "   " 3.   B/252.
  "   " 4.   D/252.
  "   " 5.   War Diary.

SECRET. Copy No 6

OPERATION ORDERS NO 28A BY LIEUT COL H.A. HANSON., D.S.O.,
COMMANDING 252ND (NORTHUMBRIAN) BRIGADE., R.F.A.

26/12/16.

1. The 50th Division (less Artillery) will relieve the 1st Division (less artillery) in the Right Sector of the 3rd Corps – relief to be complete by Jan 1st.

2. Batteries of 50th D.A. will carry out reliefs by sections as per attached table.

3. Batteries of 50th D.A. will occupy billets in BAVLINCOURT and HENENCOURT, respectively vacated by relieving batteries.

4. Routes will be :-
 (a) Relieving Units – BAIZIEUX – HENENCOURT – MILLENCOURT – ALBERT
  Head of Column to reach ALBERT at 12 noon each day.
 (b) Relieved units – ALBERT – main AMIENS ROAD – LAHOUSSOYE.
  Tail of column to be clear of ALBERT before 10 a.m. each day.

5. Details to be arranged between Brigade Commanders.

6. Completion of each stage of relief to be reported to this office by wire.
 Instructions on this point will be issued later.

7. 50th D.A.H.Q. will relieve 1st D.A.H.Q. at 12 noon on Jan 2nd at which hour command of Right Group D.A. (3rd Corps) will pass to G.R.A. 50th D.A.

8. H.Q. 50th D.A. will close at 8.30 a.m. at BAVLINCOURT on Jan 2nd and open at FRICOURT FARM at 10 a.m. the same day.

9. Acknowledge.

 (signature)

 Lieut.
 Adjutant 252nd (North'bn) Bde., R.F.A.

Issued at 5.30 p.m.

Copy No 1.   Office.
 " " 2.   A/252.
 " " 3.   B/252.
 " " 4.   D/252.
 " " 5.   R/252.
 " " 6.   War Diary.

RELIEF OF BATTERIES OF 50TH D.A. AND OF 115TH
BATTERY R.F.A. BY BATTERIES OF 50TH D.A.

Relieving Unit					Units to be Relieved
Unit	Rest Area Position.	Unit	Position	Wagon Lines	Time of Relief
B/250	BEHENCOURT	115 Bty. R.F.A.	~~S.3.c.84.~~ ~~X.30a.~~ S3c84 X30A		Night of 30/31 Dec and 31 Dec/ 1 Jan.
A/252	BAVELINCOURT	A/251	~~S.5.c.42.~~ ~~X.29.a.41.~~ S5c42 X29a41		1/2 Jan and 2/3 Jan.
B/252	BEHENCOURT	B/251	~~S.4.d.63.~~ ~~X.29.a.33.~~ S4d63 X29a33		3/4 Jan and 4/5 Jan.
D/252	BAVELINCOURT	D/250	~~S.11.b.15.~~ ~~X.29.a.45.~~ S11B15 X29A45		5/6 Jan and 6/7 Jan

x Centre Bde Group R.F.A.
Ø Right Bde Group R.F.A.

REMARKS.
1. Commands of Batteries will pass on completion of reliefs.
2. Guns and ammunition will be taken over in situ.
3. All wagons and limbers will move out empty.

WAR DIARY
or
INTELLIGENCE SUMMARY.
(Erase heading not required.)

Army Form C. 2118.

No 53 Vol 2[?]
252ND BRIGADE. R.F.A.
Volume VIII
JANUARY 1917

Place	Date	Hour	Summary of Events and Information	Remarks and references to Appendices
Béhencourt	1/1/17		Right Section A/252 Relieve R. Section A/252 in action near High Wood	Lt. H.N.W. Martin transferred to England
	2/1/17		Left Section - Centre Section A/252 Relieve remainder of A/257	
	3/1/17		Right Section B/252 Relieve R. Section B/257 in action near High Wood	
	4/1/17		Remainder of B/252 Relieve remainder of B/257. HQ relieve HQ 257 Bde	
	5/1/17		near Longueval C/252 attached to this Brigade. Right Section D/252 relieve Right Section D/250. A suspected enemy's relief refused 80.A 576.AX 106 BX. Am'n expended	
	6/1/17		Left Section D/252 relieve Left Section D/250. German relief continued Am'n expended 432 A 237 AX 200 BX	
	7/1/17		Battery's fire again all night. Am'n Expended 372 A 340 AX 200 BX 150 Fd Bde relieve 149 Fd Brigade on our Sector. Am'n Expended	
	8/1/17		Am'n Expended 210.A 216 AX 100 BX. Five casualties caused by a shell landing in A/252 position. Bd'r Carling S. gnr Goldrich T. Riley P. Brown Dr L. Niehoe (wounded)	
	9/1/17		Am'n Expended 195.A 271 AX 125 BX. A bombardment of enemies trenches started Today D/252 Taking part	
	10/1/17		Am'n Expended 180 A 434 AX 128 BX. Bombardment of enemies trenches Continued by A & D/252 9/251 all taking part	
	11/1/17		D/252 Continues bombardment of enemies trenches Am'n expended. 190 A 551 AX 139 BX	

Army Form C. 2118.

No 54

252nd BRIGADE RFA

WAR DIARY
or
INTELLIGENCE SUMMARY.
(Erase heading not required.)

Place	Date	Hour	Summary of Events and Information	Remarks and references to Appendices
Longueval	12/1/17		All Battery's bombard enemies trenches in conjunction with the Heavies. Amm expended 103 A 550 AX 140 BX	
	13/1/17.		Amm expended. 99A 540 AX 130 BX A/252 Start to clear an old German dugout for an O.P.	
	14/1/17.		Work continued on O.P. Amm expended 103A 528 AX 128 BX	
	15/1/17.		" " " " 108A 550 AX 119 BX	
	16/1/17		R. Section D/252 relieved by R Section D/251. D/252 proceed 0.0 29 a star to rest Billets in Bertincourt. Amm expended 103A 500AX 130 BX	
	#/17		D/252 receives orders to shift up. Right Section goes to Dbro with 2/Lt. Severson & 2/Lt. Goodall. Left Section to D/251 with Major Knolles. Lt. Gibson & 2/Lt Rennie.	
	17/1/17		Amm expended 200A 490 AX 150 BX	
	18/1/17.		" " " 148A 528 AX 125 BX	
	19/1/17.		" " " 120A 543 AX 128 BX	

Army Form C. 2118.

WAR DIARY
or
INTELLIGENCE SUMMARY.

No 55

252ND BRIGADE R.F.A.

(Erase heading not required.)

Place	Date	Hour	Summary of Events and Information	Remarks and references to Appendices
Longueval	22/1/17		H.Q. relieved by HQ 251 Bde. A & B/252 relieved by A & B/251	
	22		A/252 proceeded to rest billets in Behencourt	
	23		" " " " " " A Elert	
	24		H.Q. attached to 50 DAC at Fricourt.	
	25		The Batteries of 252 Brigade are acceded into Army Troops	
	26		A/262 becomes C/242 Army Artillery Brigade 30A	
	27		B/252 " " C/72 " " O.O attached	
	28		Lt. Col. Hanson in Reg'r in Temporary Command of 251 Bde.	
Fricourt	29/1/17		H Q rept at Fricourt.	
	30		H.Q. move back to Mirvaux	
	31		The following appeared in the New Years honours list:- Major Knowles awarded D.S.O., Lt Col. F.L. Pickersgill, Br Col H. Hanson, Lt. S. Dickenson B.S.M. Johnstone B/252. B.S.M. B. Boyds C/262 were also mentioned R.S.M. Battle the M.M.	

SECRET.   Copy No ..1....

OPERATION ORDER NO 29a BY LIEUT COL H.E. HANSON, D.S.O.,
       COMMANDING 252ND (NORTHBN) BRIGADE., R.F.A..

                                              13th January, 1917.

1.   D/252 and D/251 will carry out relief by Sections,
     personnel only, as per table given below.

2.   On relief, Sections D/252 will proceed straight to
     BAVLINCOURT and take over billets vacated by D/250, and
     on Jan. 17th D/252 will be broken up on re-organization
     and become Sections of D/251 and D/250.

3.   Reference Para. 2., instructions as to disposal of
     surplus personnel, stores etc., will be issued separately.

4.   Routes will be :-

     (a) Relieving units :- BAZIEUX - HENENCOURT - MILLENCOURT -
         ALBERT.

     (b) Relieved Units :- ALBERT - main AMIENS ROAD -
         LAHOUSSOYE.

5.   Details to be arranged between Brigade Commanders,
     but O.C. D/252 will at once take steps to close his
     Imprest Account at the proper date, and have all
     information, nominal rolls etc of his two sections ready
     for the use of Os. C. 250 and 251 R.F.A.

6.   Completion of each stage of relief to be reported to
     this office by wire.

7.   On completion of the reliefs D/251 (less 1 section
     at BAVELINCOURT) will come under the tactical command
     of O.C. Right Sub-group.

8.   When D/252 Battery R.F.A. is broken up on 14th Jan.,
     its right section will remain in its present position,
     under the tactical command of O.C., Left Sub-Group.

9.   ACKNOWLEDGE.
                                     K M Macdonald
                                              Lieut.
                              Adjutant 252nd Brigade., R.F.A.

Issued at

Copy No 1.   War Diary.
  " " 2.   D/252.
  " " 3.   War Diary Office.

RELIEF OF BATTERIES OF 50th D.A.

Relieving Unit.		Unit to be relieved.		Wagon Lines. Relief	Time of Relief	Remarks.
Unit.	Position.	Unit.	Position.			
D/251	S.6.d.3.7.	D/252	S.11.b.1.5.	X29.a.45	Jan 16th & 17th	Command will pass on Jan 17th.

Guns and ammunition will be taken over in situ.
All wagons and limbers will move out empty.

SECRET   Copy No. 1

Operation Order No.30A by Lieut.Col.H.S.Hanson, D.S.O., Comdg.
252nd Brigade R.F.A., 17th January 1917.
----

1. Batteries of 50th D.A. will carry out reliefs by Sections, personnel only, as per attached table.

2. On relief, Sects. A/252 will proceed to BEHENCOURT and take over Billets vacated by B/251 and, on 30th Jan, will become on re-organisation, C Bty, 242 Army Bde. R.F.A.

3. On relief, Sects. B/252 will proceed to a site near ALBERT which will be notified later, and become, on re-organisation, C Bty., 72 Army Bde. R.F.A.

4. On 30th Hd.Qrs. 251 Bde.R.F.A. will relieve Hd.Qrs. 252 Bde.R.F.A. which will, on re-organisation, be attached to 50 D.A.C. until further orders.

5. Sects of D/250 and D/251 now at BAVLINCOURT will move on 31st to Wagon Lines at E.5.d., which will be vacated on that day by D/240.

6. Routes will be:-
   (a) <u>Units moving up</u>:-
   BEHENCOURT - HENENCOURT - MILENCOURT - ALBERT.
   (b) <u>Units moving back</u>:-
   ALBERT - Main AMIENS Road - LABOUSSOYE - BEHENCOURT - ~~HENENCOURT~~ PIERREPONT.

7. Details will be arranged by Brigade Commanders but O.C. A/252 & B/252 will at once take steps to close their respective Imprest A/cs. at the proper date and to have complete nominal rolls ready in triplicate, also returns shewing in detail transfers of personnel, horses and equipment to their respective new Bdes.

10. Completion of each stage of relief to be reported to this office by wire.

11. ACKNOWLEDGE.

RELIEF of BATTERIES of 50th D.A.

Relieving Unit.		Unit to be relieved.			
Unit.	Position.	Unit.	Position	Wagon lines.	Time of relief.
A/251	BAVLINCOURT.	A/252	S.5.c.49.	X.30.a.	Jan.10th & 30th
B/251	BEHENCOURT	B/252	S.4.d.65.		

Guns and ammunition will be taken over in situ.
All wagons and limbers will move out empty.
Command will pass on 30th Jan.

Kinmacdonald
Lieut.
Adjutant, 252nd Brigade R.F.A.

Copy No.1 - A/252.
     2 - B/252.
     3 - D/252.
     4 - Office.
     5 - War Diary.

50TH DIVISION

1ST DURHAM BATTERY R.F.A.
JUN-SEP 1915

50TH DIVISION

121/5842

50th Division

1st Durham Battery (3rd Northern Bde) R.F.A.

Vol I. 5.8.14. — 23.6.15

Army Form C. 2118.

WAR DIARY
INTELLIGENCE SUMMARY.
(Erase heading not required.)

Instructions regarding War Diaries and Intelligence Summaries are contained in F.S. Regs., Part II. and the Staff Manual respectively. Title pages will be prepared in manuscript.

Hour, Date, Place			Summary of Events and Information	Remarks and references to Appendices
9 a.m.	5/8/14	DURHAM.	Mobilized.	
12-1 p.m.	14/8/14	do.	Marched to NEWCASTLE	
10 a.m.	20/8/14	NEWCASTLE.	Marched to RAVENSWORTH PARK, GATESHEAD, arrived 4 p.m. & went under canvas	
11 a.m.	15/11/14	RAVENSWORTH	Marched to LOW FELL. Billeted men in WILSON LANE Schools Horses in Government Stables	
10 p.m.	17/11/14	LOW FELL.	Ordered to SUNDERLAND to defend coast against raids.	
4.30 a.m.	18/11/14	SUNDERLAND.	Halted 150ˣ S. of SOUTHWICK CHURCH.	
6 a.m.	do.	do.	Received orders to park guns at & stable horses under ROKER FOOTBALL GROUND GRANDSTAND & billet men in REDBY SCHOOLS – FULWELL LANE. Came under command of M.Genl. PINK	
	19/11/14	do.	Reconnoitred positions at ROKER	
10 a.m.	20/11/14	do.	Ordered to prepare a position for one X about 100ˣ N of TRAM TERMINUS at SEASIDE LANE & 100ˣ from SEA FRONT & commenced work on epaulements. Billeted few gunners	
4 a.m.	21/11/14	do.	(in noyell at NEWLANDS HOUSE, SEASIDE LANE). Occupied position with Rt.X & billeted gunners at NEWLANDS HOUSE.	
9 a.m.	do.	do.	Capt. WARHAM ordered to prepare position 100ˣ N of E of MERE KNOLLS CEMETERY & proceeded hither with Lft X & billeted gunners at WHITBURN	
11 a.m.	22/11/14	do.	Horses remained at ROKER FOOTBALL GROUND. Moved Lft X on SEA FRONT. Chose position for Lft X on SEA BANKS 250ˣ N of CAFÉ. Moved Lft X into position ready to occupy & sent horses to ROKER FOOTBALL GROUND	
6 p.m.	do.	do.	Lft X occupied position. Gunners billeted at NEWLANDS HOUSE	
	28/12/14	do.	Received orders to vacate positions & hand over to 2ND E LANCS RFA (T) on 29/12/14 & march to LOW FELL.	
4 p.m.	29/12/14	do.	M-General PINK personally complimented me on the work of the Battery whilst under him & on the arrangements made for same, & referred in flagworks to & the excellent discipline displayed & charged me to convey his confidence to the majority of LOW FELL the Battery & to express his regret at parting with it.	
4.20 p.m.	do.	do.	Marched to LOW FELL.	

Army Form C. 2118.

WAR DIARY
INTELLIGENCE SUMMARY
(Erase heading not required.)

Instructions regarding War Diaries and Intelligence Summaries are contained in F.S. Regs., Part II. and the Staff Manual respectively. Title pages will be prepared in manuscript.

Hour, Date, Place			Summary of Events and Information	Remarks and references to Appendices
1 a.m.	30/12/14	LOW FELL.	Arrived. Billetted men at WILSON LANE Schools, stabled horses in Government stables.	
9 p.m.	15/4/15	do.	Commenced drawing kit for adopting a gun as ANTI-AIRCRAFT gun in conjunction with 2nd Bty on receipt of news of Zeppelin in neighbourhood.	
9.30 p.m.	do.	do.	Completed kit & gun mounted.	
11 a.m.	17/4/15	do.	Lft X entrained for SOUTHAMPTON from NEWCASTLE	
1 p.m.	do.	do.	Rt X do. do. do.	
4.0 a.m.	19/4/15	SOUTHAMPTON	Arrived SOUTHAMPTON. Embarked Lft X & all horses & vehicles on "CITY of DUNKIRK" & Rt X on "LYDIA".	
5.30 a.m.	19/4/15	HAVRE.	"LYDIA" arrived & Rt X disembarked.	
1 p.m.	do.	do.	"CITY of DUNKIRK" arrived. Disembarked Lft X guns, horses & wagons.	
midnight 19.20/4/15.	do.	do.	Entrained & left HAVRE.	
8 p.m.	20/4/15	HAZEBROUCK	Arrived & detrained & marched to billets at ROUGE CROIX.	
11 p.m.	20/4/15	ROUGE CROIX	Arrived. Picketted horses, billetted men at ROUGE CROIX.	
4 p.m.	23/4/15	ROUGE CROIX	Marched to BERTHEN 2½ miles Mt DES CATS in readiness to support. Billetted at farm, picketted horses in farmyard & fastening horses thereto at 11.7 p.m.	
2 p.m.	24/4/15	BERTHEN.	Marched back to old billets at ROUGE CROIX.	
3.30 p.m.	do	ROUGE CROIX	Arrived.	
2.30 a.m.	25/4/15.	do	Marched to CAMIL LOONE'S farm near TRAPPIST MONASTERY at RATTEKOT.	
8 a.m.	do.	RATTEKOT.	Arrived & billetted - picketing horses.	
3 p.m.	26/4/15	do.	Received orders to march to ST LAURENT at 3.30 p.m.	
3.30 p.m.	do.	do.	Enemy aeroplane regarded by mistake fell over (farm moved all men & vehicles)	
4. p.m.	do.	do.	Left farm.	
5 p.m.	do.	ST LAURENT.	Arrived. Billetted men at BRUNEEL'S Farm & Bomb dropped at farm (reported by hens party) - no casualties Farm & picketted horses	

Army Form C. 2118.

WAR DIARY

INTELLIGENCE SUMMARY

(Erase heading not required.)

Instructions regarding War Diaries and Intelligence
Summaries are contained in F. S. Regs., Part II.
and the Staff Manual respectively. Title pages
will be prepared in manuscript.

Hour, Date, Place		Summary of Events and Information	Remarks and references to Appendices
4 p.m.	29/4/15. ST. LAURENT.	Marched to LE TEMPLE.	
5 p.m.	do. LE TEMPLE	Arrived. Billeted near De NEVE'S farm - Picketted horses.	
4 p.m.	4/5/15. do.	Moved to WINNEZEELE.	
6.30 p.m.	do. WINNEZEELE.	Arrived. Billeted at CODDEVILLE'S farm - Picketted horses.	
9 a.m.	10/5/15. do.	On receipt of orders marched to WATOU.	
	do. WATOU.	Arrived. Billeted at E. VANDEPUTTE'S farm - Picketted horses.	
5.30 a.m.	19/5/15 do.	On receipt of orders proceeded to Bde. H.Q. ready to move at 6 a.m. to reconnoitre positions. Marched via POPERINGHE & VLAMERTINGHE to YPRES & reconnoitred country N & S. of MENIN ROAD as far as E. of HALTE. under Col EMMERY C.R.A. 27th DIV. Only one position could be found, which he felt, was awarded to 3rd BHy. Returned to WATOU. (Ref. HAZEBROUCK 5A. BELGIUM)	
6 a.m.	25/5/15 do.	Received orders to move by 3rd Bty. Wagon Lines at BRANDHOEK G 7.8.3.9/Ref 20000 BELGIUM (SH 28 NW) & billet there.	
4 p.m.	do.	Marched.	
10 p.m.	do. BRANDHOEK	Arrived & bivouacked. (Position was H.7 6.3.9)	
11 p.m.	do.	Received orders to report to Bde H.Q. at KRUISSTRAAT - YPRES & for Battery to	
1.30 a.m.	26/5/15 KRUISSTRAAT	Reported to H.Q. 42nd Bde. for guide at H 18 C 9.0.	
		Received orders to relieve one x of a Bty. at I 15 d. 8.6.9 another x of a Bty. at I 20.a.4.0	
2.45 a.m.	26/5/15 BELGIUM	(ref 20000 28 NW) Relieved former with RJX & Latter with 2/4X.	
		Relief completed.	
		Sent two subalterns to trenches as forward Obs. Officers	
		Registered RJX Zone with 2/4X & Centre Zone with RJX.	
		Received orders to evacuate I 15 d. 8 6. after dark on being relieved by a	
10.30 p.m.	do.	x of 3 Bty. J for RJX to join 2/4X at I 20.a.4.0.	
		Relief arrived & evacuation completed.	
11.45 p.m	do.	Arrived I 20.a.4.0. being heavily shelled along LILLE ROAD. No casualties	

Army Form C. 2118.

WAR DIARY

INTELLIGENCE SUMMARY.

(Erase heading not required.)

Hour, Date, Place	Summary of Events and Information	Remarks and references to Appendices
10 pm. 31/5/15. YPRES.	Received orders to evacuate one X which would be replaced by one X of 43rd Bty. R/X relieved by L/X 4th Bty. & proceeded to wagon lines	
10 pm. 1/6/15 do.	In accordance with orders R/X relieved by R/X of 41st Bty & proceeded to DETBOUCH REMY'S farm at ABEELE	
3 am 2/6/15 ABEELE	Horse picketting lines arrived.	
4 pm. 4/6/15 do.	In accordance with orders moved to JULIEN VANCAYSEELE'S farm	
5.30 pm. 5/6/15 do.	Received orders for R/X to relieve on X of 41st Bty in old position I.20.a.6.0 between 8.30 & 9.30 pm. & for L/X to retire remaining X at same time 6/6/15 (L/X above wagon lines near H.21.6.3.3 Ref 20000 28NW)	
9.45 pm 5/6/15 YPRES.	Relief completed	
9.45 pm 6/6/15 do.	Relief completed & position taken over. Registered Zone for R/X. Armistice 8/12.	
7/6/15 do.	Registered whole Bty. on Sft Zone. Armistice 8/12.	
8/6/15 do.	Zone allowed to cover Armistice 1/5. Partly registered same	
9/6/15 do.	Completed registering Zone	
10/6/15 do.	Commenced stiffening Reserve Trench from H24 & 3.6. had stopped on being advised Trench not in our area & referred to Bde H.Q. for decision	

H. W. White Major
O.C. Austrn Battery R.F.A.

Army Form C. 2118.

WAR DIARY
INTELLIGENCE SUMMARY.
(Erase heading not required.)

Instructions regarding War Diaries and Intelligence Summaries are contained in F.S. Regs., Part II and the Staff Manual respectively. Title pages will be prepared in manuscript.

Hour, Date, Place		Summary of Events and Information	Remarks and references to Appendices
20/6/15	Ypres	No 796 Dr Lamb H sent to Casualty Clearing Station, having been wounded by Shrapnel & in which gas attained the strength 15 Ky & 3rd Bridge Mole	
9 pm 21/6/15	Ypres	2/1X & 4 Staff 15 hy relieved R.X. which proceeded to wagon Lines & bivouacked	
6.45 am 22/6/15	"	R/X left for new position via BEVECOTEN & LOORE & arrived & relieved R1 X of 3rd Bty 1st N Midld Bde 2 Bde 9 pm	
9 pm do	"	L/1 X relieved by R1 X 4 Staff Bty 3rd N Midland Bde & proceeded to wagon Lines & bivouacked	
6.45 am 23/6/15	"	L/1 X left for new position & relieved L/1 X 3rd Bty 1st N MIDLAND Bde. Same route as R/1 X & same hours. Bty new position T.9 B 5 7 ref Sheet 28 S.W. 1/20000	

H. Buckle Major R.H.A.T
C.O. ? Division

WAR DIARY

INTELLIGENCE SUMMARY.

(Erase heading not required.)

Army Form C. 2118.

Instructions regarding War Diaries and Intelligence Summaries are contained in F.S. Regs., Part II. and the Staff Manual respectively. Title pages will be prepared in manuscript.

Hour, Date, Place			Summary of Events and Information	Remarks and references to Appendices
6/6 a.m.	24.6.15	WULVERGHEM	Registered 9pm. Obs. Station STAMKOTMOLEN – NEUVE EGLISE.	
9.20 a.m.	26.6.15	do	Registration of guns continued	
	27.6.15	do	Altered Observation Station to HOSPICE, N.EGLISE. This day & onwards no hill observation engaged in constructing position.	
	3.7.15	do	Pte BARRY no 1221 sent to casualty clearing station with compound fracture of right arm caused by lorrie slipping on the Pavé.	
11 a.m.	4.7.15	do	Hon. Col. Lord LONDONDERRY visited.	
8.15 p.m.	5.7.15	do	Salvo of HV's towards of trenches of Shrapnel fired at NEUVE EGLISE. One struck battery.	
	6.7.15	do	9.Gun Division established at Stn CN 157.8 Gr DOUGHTY & others on telephone duty.	
	7.7.15	do	Prepared gun position at Hill 63 Ref Sheet 28 SW U.13.c.10.½ 4000	
	8.7.15	do	do new'd ditto ditto	
	9.7.15	do	Sandbagging Observation Station at Hill 63 Ref Sheet 28 SW U.13.c.0.9 4000 completed Hill 63	
	13.7.15	do	ditto	
	14.7.15	do	Ordered to abandon Obs. Station & Hill 63. Reopened Obs. Station at HOSPICE. Preparing Reserve Position Ref Sheet 26 SW T.18.9.2. 4000	
9.30 a.m.	16.7.15	do	R/X relieved by R/X 45 H Bty, 146 H Bde. & proceeded to wagon lines.	
9.30 p.m.	17.7.15	do	2/X do , 2/X ditto ditto	
9.30 p.m.	18.7.15	do	Marched via NEUVE EGLISE – Road junction on the BAILLEUL–ARMENTIERES road – NIEPPE – went into Bivouac Ref Sheet 5A NIEPPE ⟨...⟩	
12.30 a.m.	19.7.15	ARMENTIÈRES	Arrived & Bivouacked at B14.c.2.3. Ref Sheet 36 NW.	

Mᶜᴵⁿᴅʀⁱe Major
O.C. Y Bn 4.A. Bty T.F.

121/6529

ap 296

50th Division

1st Durham Battery (5 howitzer Bde) RFA.

Vol III

From 1st to 30th August 1915

Army Form C. 2118.

WAR DIARY
INTELLIGENCE SUMMARY.
(Erase heading not required.)

Instructions regarding War Diaries and Intelligence Summaries are contained in F. S. Regs., Part II. and the Staff Manual respectively. Title pages will be prepared in manuscript.

Hour, Date, Place		Summary of Events and Information	Remarks and references to Appendices
1/8/15	ARMENTIERES.	Gr. Kelly No.1150 H/L sent to Hospital - Armentieres - Amoebic dysentery	
2/8/15	do.	Dr. Tulip - No.1107 ditto.	
5/8/15	do.	Gr. Kelly - No.1150 - Returned to duty.	
5/8/15	do.	Br. Barry - No.1221 - Struck off strength having been invalided to England.	
6/8/15	do.	Gr. Beck J. - No.1093 - Sent to Hospital.	
6/8/15	do.	Gr. Brown W D - No.1695 - ditto.	
6/8/15	do.	Dr. Geehan W - No.1316 - Returned to duty from Hospital.	
7/8/15	PONT DE NIEPPE	Brigade moved entrance to B'g'd's Hq. 36 N N 20000	
7/9/15	do.	Gr. Kelly - No.1154 H/L Sent to Hospital.	
9/8/15	do.	S.S. Mitchley - No.1001 - Sent to Hospital.	
9/8/15	do.	Sgt. Far. Garget - No.2987 - Sent to Hospital.	
12/8/15	do.	Bugler Howe - No.1527 - R.A.M.C. Sent to Hospital.	
13/8/15	do.	Gr. Hindmarch E. - No.1141 - Sent to Hospital.	
15/8/15	do.	Rt X relieved Rt X of 1st East Riding Bty 2nd Nbn Bde F.A. in action at Houplines Cyclist Rec'd	36 NW 2000
16/8/15	do.	do. do. do.	do.
16/8/15	do.	Gr. Beck - No.1096 - Returned from Hospital. 8th in action supporting 149 K.M.F. Bde on Section of Trenches I5a71/C29c32. Ref 36 NW, 2000 employed registering targets, retaliating from hostile fire & engaging working parties.	
19/8/15	HOUPLINES.	Gr. Hindmarche No.1141 - Returned from Hospital.	
19/8/15	do.	Gr. Plowman. E - No.1437 - Sent to Hospital - face injured by recoil of gun.	
19/8/15	do.	L/. Reid - Lowthian Bdr F.A.T. - Marched for instruction	
22/8/15	do.	Gr. Boggan - No.1442 - Sent to Hospital.	
23/8/15	do.	Reid - Lowthian Bdr F.A.T. - Left on completion of course.	
23/8/15	do.	Gr. Garrigan J. No.2249 - Gr. Johnson J. No.2091 - Gr. Knappe W. No.1299 - Gr. McDade A. No.1877 - Gr. Scollan T. No.1098 - Gr. Madge P. No.1730 - Posted to Bty from Reinforcements. I5a72.	
26/8/15	do.	Bdr changed to I/ Gun 2	
29/8/15	do.	Br. Withinshaw. T. No.2126 transferred full Bombardier with effect from 5/9/15	
29/8/15	do.	Gr. Brunning Ref. Gr. Appointed Acting Bombardier with effect from this day.	
30/8/15	do.	Gr. Waugh No.1315 - do do	
		Sgt. Wheeler Smith D No.583 Promoted Staff Sgt Wheeler from this bty at Pont de Nieppe B3170L 8.8	

Hagan ...... continue to be at Pont de Nieppe

W Chas Mr Jagger
O.C. 1st John P.by 3rd N.N. 4A.B.D.T.F.

137/6496

a2
a96

50th Division

1/1st Durham F.A. R.F.A.
Vol II
24-6-19-7-15

121/6923

a/6

50th Division

1/1 Durham Batty R.F.A.
Vol IV
Sept. 15.

WAR DIARY

INTELLIGENCE SUMMARY

(Erase heading not required.)

Army Form C. 2118.

Hour, Date, Place	Summary of Events and Information	Remarks and references to Appendices
4/9/15 HOUPLINES	Gr Harrison R No 15114 - Struck off strength having returned to England	All references are to Sheets 36 N.W & 36 N.E
do do	L⁄C Mitchell R No 1001 - do	1/20,000 FRANCE
5/9/15 do	Br Kennedy A, No 891 - Promoted above, with effect from 5/8/15.	
17/9/15 do	Cpl MacDonald J - Posted to 2nd Durham Bty R.F.A.T. from this date	
do do	E.R. Bushell - Posted to 1st Durham Bty R.F.A.T. from this date	
18/9/15 do	Gr Bogan C No 1742 - Struck off strength having returned to England	
do.	Completed rebuilding gun pits, roofing same with balks (bags, June 3) layers of broken bricks, & layers of sandbags on corrugated iron supported by 3 ft props. Y can girders 9" deep, also built avenue dugouts for men & officers in gun position.	
4 p.m. 20/9/15 do	Noted on same day. Opening the bombardment. Took part in attack by rifle fire from trench 74 & 2 machine guns 9 & 4/15 R.Dinn How B↑ in 3rd Dhm Bty R.F.A.T & 1st & 2nd Bys J.B↑ JM & Bn. 4 A Bde on "Black Redoubt"	
	I.5.C.4.1. opposite trench 74 to dominate parapet Asking fire lasted for 10 min. - action fire lasted for 10 min. Heavy fire on trenches 74, 74¹, 7¹6 - retaliated with 12 rounds - 5.15 from How B↑	
5.30 a.m. 22/9/15 do	B²nd Dhm B↑ R.F.A.T cooperated. General attack on whole front ordered. According to orders Infantry of 50 H/D & 13th Bde	
4.50 a.m. 25/9/15 do	-- to attack at this hour. At 5 a.m. the artillery attacked opened fire for — on their trenches (latter on Sabbath). At 5.30 a.m. the Infantry cannot communicate trench owing from 16 Cothl. 16 & 4/N. all slew and opening white flag. A.b.a.t. the 6th am. find refugees one support Trench Retallation. Attacked small bangs & trench as personnel - fires gradually slowed down 9 a.m. Apart this month M.B.Y Section by been firing at enemy trenches between buried for dayship & amount of to cover & strengthening & rebuilding fire. This truncation with gunfire for now on position & supported by trench fire.	

H. Cradha Gmm. R.F.A.T.
O.C. 1st Durham Bty R.F.A.T.

Army Form C. 2118.

WAR DIARY

INTELLIGENCE SUMMARY.

(Erase heading not required.)

Instructions regarding War Diaries and Intelligence Summaries are contained in F.S. Regs., Part II. and the Staff Manual respectively. Title pages will be prepared in manuscript.

Hour, Date, Place	Summary of Events and Information	Remarks and references to Appendices
25/9/15 HOUPLINES.	Gr McDade A - No 1597 - Sent to Hospital sick.	W.R.
do. do.	Gr Gildea F - No 1000 - do.	W.R.
do. do.	Dr Haller R - No 992 - do.	W.R.
27/9/15 do.	Gr Squires A - No 1647 - do.	W.R.
2/9/15 do.	Gr Plowman E - No 1437 - Returned to duty from Hospital	W.R.

M Parker Major
OC Durham Bhy R.F.A.T.

O.C. Durham Bhy R.F.A.T.

50TH DIVISION

2ND DURHAM BATTERY R.F.A.
JUN - SEP 1915

50TH DIVISION

121/6073

50th Division

2nd Durham Battery RFA.

Vol I 4 — 30.6.15

Army Form C. 2118.

WAR DIARY
or
INTELLIGENCE SUMMARY.
(Erase heading not required.)

Instructions regarding War Diaries and Intelligence Summaries are contained in F.S. Regs., Part II. and the Staff Manual respectively. Title pages will be prepared in manuscript.

Place	Date	Hour	Summary of Events and Information	Remarks and references to Appendices
ABEELE	4-6-15	10 pm	Ordered to new billets one mile nearer POPERINGHE (H. Quaghebeur - Schragh) arrived at 11-30 p.m.	SK/
POPERINGHE	5-6-15	10 p.m.	Right Section moved into action at old position ETANGS DE ZILLEBEKE	SK/
—	6-6-15	—	Left " " " " " " near KRUISSTRAAT (YPRES) as reserve	SK/
ZILLEBEKE POND	7-6-15	4-5 pm	Registered on (A Target) on left hand of battery zone (Trenches 6, 7, 8).	SK/
YPRES	8-6-15	8 pm	Ordered to prepare new position for Right Section about 500ˣ S of TROIS ROIS.	SK/
SALIENT	9-6-15	all day	Consolidated & improved protection of both positions.	SK/
	10-6-15	—	Finished digging in "protecting rear section (Right). Rain all day. Repaired all wires, laid direct line to RA Battery. Visited Trenches infantry commander.	SK/
—	11-6-15	10-30a	Registered Right section on Target (A). Laid new line to Headquarters from rear section.	SK/
—	12-6-15	5-13pm	Position got ten shells from enemy but no damage done.	SK/
—	13-6-15	6 pm	Registered battery on Target (B) Right of battery zone. Laid direct line to 3rd Battery to assist their communication. Corporal W. Moot & Corporal G. Moore B.D. Stanton Bainbridge did excellent work as wire men over fire zone. It is vital for batteries to have private wires resolutely look out to prevent tapping by others in same area.	SK/
—	14-6-15	5-11 pm	Registered battery on Target (B) centre of battery zone.	SK/
—	16-6-15	All night	The telephonist again did splendid work, in addition to those mentioned on the 13th were Gunners J.W. Callaghan & J. Willis, during shell fire.	SK/
—	19-6-15	4-35 pm to 10-30 pm	In conjunction with 1st Durham Battery shelled transport all road by LOWER STAR POST as arranged with Infantry Commander (20 rounds).	SK/
—	21-6-15	10-5 pm	Registered transition	SK/
—	21-6-15	10 pm	Withdrew forward section to wagon lines.	SK/
—	22-6-15	6-45 a	Moved to new position, halted at LOCRE during day, at NEUVE ÉGLISE occupied same at 10-30 pm	SK/

1577 Wt.W10791/1773 500,000 1/15 D. D. & L. A.D.S.S./Forms/C. 2118.

Army Form C. 2118.

WAR DIARY
or
INTELLIGENCE SUMMARY.
(Erase heading not required.)

Instructions regarding War Diaries and Intelligence Summaries are contained in F.S. Regs., Part II. and the Staff Manual respectively. Title pages will be prepared in manuscript.

Place	Date "1915 JUNE	Hour	Summary of Events and Information	Remarks and references to Appendices
YPRES	22	9.30 p.m.	Withdrew near section to wagon lines. 3HP	
VLAMERTINGHE	23	6-45 a.m.	Left wagon lines with rear section, halting at LOCRE during day, at NEUVE ÉGLISE - occupied lane at	
NEUVE-ÉGLISE	24		9.p.m. 3HP.	
"	24	10-55 a.m.	Registered forward section on N.36.D. farm (left of battery zone) 16 rounds 3HP. very foggy, 3HP	
"		3.45 p.m.	" " " " " (" ") 4 rounds for correction to rounds 3HP	
"	25	10-55 a.m.	Registered forward section on N.36.D. farm (left of battery zone) 8 rounds 3HP. very dull 3HP	
"	25	10-0 a.m.	Conferred with infantry commander Lt.Col. Spain (6th N.F.(T)) at Infantry HQ. (ST QUENTIN'S FARM)	
"			& signals stretched C, C₂, C₃ which compose battery zone. 3HP.	
"	26	—	Corrected maps, corrected lines & traced telephone wires 3HP	
"	27	—	Visited infantry trenches & infantry commander, 6th N.F.(T), 3HP	
"	28	—	Improved dug-outs & prepared corrected maps 3HP.	
"	29	6 a.m.	Battery zone 4 rounds which had been loaded on night lines overnight for comparison	
"		11-30	Target (1) O 31. B. 5. 6. repulsed 16 rounds	
"		12-1 p.m.	" (2) O. 31. 10. " 24 "	
"			Surge very inconsistent 3HP	
"	30	7 a.m.	Battery zone 4 rounds for comparison when loaded overnight 3HP	
"		10 "	Visited Battery Infantry commander, 10 signals ie 5" N.F.(T) 3HP	
"		12.20 p.m.	Target (3) O. 31. B. registered 35 rounds. Surge very inconsistent. Also trail foundation let to be altered 2HP	
"			This period taught us the value of working for overhead cover in dug-outs in preference to pretty internal curry roofs or incessant predecessors left leaked like sieves would hardly have stopped rifle fire. It rains sandbags on sandays-throw stood stop 5.9 high explosives. Telephones wires had been installed in fir circles zones on altering this by hair about an unit of wire cut next for repairs was reduced to almost nil. 3HP 2nd Battery	
			Francis Pickering Major, 2nd Battery.	

121/6344

50th Division

2nd Durham Battery (3rd Northern Bde) RFA

Vol II

10-7-41 - 8-1-15

Army Form C. 2118.

WAR DIARY
or
INTELLIGENCE SUMMARY.
(Erase heading not required.)

Instructions regarding War Diaries and Intelligence Summaries are contained in F. S. Regs., Part II. and the Staff Manual respectively. Title pages will be prepared in manuscript.

Place	Date 1915 JULY	Hour	Summary of Events and Information	Remarks and references to Appendices
NEUVE EGLISE	10	8.10am to 8.20am	Joined with heavy battery – objective W.1.2 farm – supported dug-outs magazine hidden behind ruins – fired 12 rounds – result satisfactory. From July 1st to 15th most of our work was perfecting cover of position. Constructing Brigade dug-out for telephonists at St QUENTIN's. Preparing a 2nd position to cover WULVERGHEM Switch in case of a retirement. Reconnoitred position for a forward gun in front of Hill 63. HAUBAURDIN at 2 a.m. on the 15th but found same impossible. The wires were kept in excellent order by our telephonists. Bde. visited infantry trenches commanders at every change of battalion in C₁, C₂ trenches; communication was maintained with them in a very satisfactory manner. On four occasions test were tried on the battery from trenches over the last occasion the shot was fired within 15 seconds of the telephonist receiving the message. Staff Sergt Saddler Dowler who has now had charge of the wagon line for nearly 3 weeks has proved himself an excellent disciplinarian the lines are a credit to any battery. JHP.	
	15	5.50pm 6 pm	NEUVE EGLISE church shelled "" on fire.	
		9.30pm	Bty had to take cover in dug-outs owing to rifle fire meant for cross road for. JHP	
	16	5pm	Withdrew guns to wagon lines. JHP	
	18	9pm	Left wagon line for PONT DE NIEPPE. JHP	
PONT DE NIEPPE	19	12.10am	Arrived unmolested. JHP Rested here while guns were overhauled. Bde. kept reconnoitres exactly fly positions new position. JHP Bde. reconnoitred for possible new positions.	

1577 Wt.W10791/1773 500,000 1/15 D. D. & L. A.D.S.S./Forms/C. 2118.

Army Form C. 2118.

WAR DIARY
or
INTELLIGENCE SUMMARY.

(Erase heading not required.)

Instructions regarding War Diaries and Intelligence Summaries are contained in F. S. Regs., Part II. and the Staff Manual respectively. Title pages will be prepared in manuscript.

Place	Date	Hour	Summary of Events and Information	Remarks and references to Appendices
FORT DE NIEPPE	30/7/15	3-30 p.m.	Brig-General Henshaw inspected wagon lines. EHP	
—	4/8/15	7-0 a.m.	Commenced work on position at C.20.c.3.1. Sheet 36 N.W. France&Belgium 1/20,000. EHP	

FrankPickering Major.

1577 Wt.W10791/1773 500,000 1/15 D. D. & L. A.D.S.S./Forms/C. 2118.

50th Division

12/0567

or
a56

2nd Durham Battery (3rd Northn'b Bde) R.F.A.

Vol III

from 5th to 31. 5. 15

Army Form C. 2118.

WAR DIARY
or
INTELLIGENCE SUMMARY.
(Erase heading not required.)

Instructions regarding War Diaries and Intelligence Summaries are contained in F.S. Regs., Part II. and the Staff Manual respectively. Title pages will be prepared in manuscript.

Place	Date 1915	Hour	Summary of Events and Information	Remarks and references to Appendices
ARMENTIERES	5.8.	10am	Gun platforms of reserve position completed. F.P.	
PONT DE NIEPPE	7.8.	12-1pm	As ordered took up new wagon lines at B.18.a.1.1. Sheet 36 NW 1/20.000 'B' series. Belgium & France. F.P.	
— —	14.8	10am	Visited 2nd Bty 2nd N.R. Bde. To arrange for taking over his guns in action. F.P.	
— —	15.8	8-15p	Right section relieved 2nd Brigade at C.27. C.3.t. Sheet 36 NW 1/20.000 'B' series Belgium & France. F.P.	
HOUPLINES	16.8	8-19p	Left section relieved 2nd Brigade at C.27. C.3.t. Belgium & France. F.P.	
			On taking over the importance of security in reference to appearances was again impressed on us. The gun protectors &c dug-outs being very flimsey. The telephone service of wires also was insufficient. The protection & multiplication of wires had to be taken in hand at once. F.P.	
HOUPLINES	18.8		Found one gun unreliable this was a gun originally belonging our 1st battery, then lent to 2nd Battery 2nd North. Bde. F.P.	
	20.8		Visited 2nd Infantry trenches.	
			From 17-20. Battery fired on a reported target which was known to be sandbagged. These machine guns are in a whenever enemy fired in our neighbourhood. (It generally had the desired effect.) F.P.	
	21 to 27 August		In support of Northumberland Fusiliers the battery fired on the opposing trenches & support trenches at several times during these days. F.P. The telephone officer Mr MacDonald Corporal S. Moore Bombrs. C.R. Stanton & W Vincent & Ranforth Callaghan, Willis & Stephenson did excellent work relaying the wire Linesmen & & & under timber under fire. F.P.	

Frank Pickersgill, Major.

Army Form C. 2118.

WAR DIARY
or
INTELLIGENCE SUMMARY.

(Erase heading not required.)

Instructions regarding War Diaries and Intelligence Summaries are contained in F.S. Regs., Part II. and the Staff Manual respectively. Title pages will be prepared in manuscript.

Place	Date	Hour	Summary of Events and Information	Remarks and references to Appendices
HOUPLINES	August 1915 28 to 31st		In support of Northumberland Fusiliers (149th Infantry Brigade) 50th Division in trenches T7 & T8. Northern sector of our covering zone T4 to 8D so as to be able to assist any of other brigade battns. A.W.P	

121/6918

50th Division

3rd Durham Battery R.F.A. (1/3 North'n Bde. R.F.A.)

Vol IV
Sept. 15

Army Form C. 2118.

WAR DIARY
or
INTELLIGENCE SUMMARY.
(Erase heading not required.)

Instructions regarding War Diaries and Intelligence Summaries are contained in F. S. Regs., Part II. and the Staff Manual respectively. Title pages will be prepared in manuscript.

Place	Date	Hour	Summary of Events and Information	Remarks and references to Appendices
HOUPLINES	1915 Sept 1st to 11th		150th Infantry Bde occupy trenches in front of us (T4 - 80). Guns daily on various targets at request of Infantry. Guns are now in good working order, having been all freshly laid with old red coiled by 2/Lt. K.M. Macdonald with Cpl. R. Moore, B/S Stanton. 6th Stephenson. S/S Willis. 2/Lt Callaghan did excellent work in laying these, and one to their daily patrolling the communication was maintained at times daily the trade of the wires is under fire from W/egg Longs TM G's. The forward observing officers 2/Lieuts. J.R. Platt, F.R. Bushell have both done splendid work in identifying targets maintaining its good feeling confidence of the Infantry. R.H.I. Infantry came into our trenches on the 15th and are still in	
	12th to 18th		Capt. J. Macdonald posted to our Battery. 2/Lt F.R. Bushell went to 1st Battery. Fired with good effect on M.G. emplacement on 14th + 15th at night (8-30 pm) stopped enfilade on trenches. Day shooting has been useless as enemy withdraws guns by day early but it in position at night. Good line wire cable here by telephone party.	
	20th to 24th		Capt. Gilles Mauspan attached to 64th B'de to learn 18 PR; Gun.	
	25th		Various targets located by F.O.O's C/S MacDonald Platt were fired on daily in retaliation. Bombarded enemy support trenches in company with Divisional Artillery at 5 am. for an hour [?]	
	26th to 30th		149th Infantry B'de was occupying trenches supported by Battery TT-78. Capt. Gilles Mauspan returned. Daily engaged enemy guns targets spotted by F.O.O.s, Infantry with object of keeping enemy occupied on our front from supporting other parts of their line.	

Frank Pickering. Major.

50TH DIVISION

3RD DURHAM BATTERY R.F.A.
MAY - AUG 1915

121/5617

50th Division.

3rd Durham Battery RFA (3rd North'n Bde RFA).

Vol I   9 —— 31.5.15.

Army Form C. 2118.

WAR DIARY
or
INTELLIGENCE SUMMARY.
(Erase heading not required.)

Instructions regarding War Diaries and Intelligence Summaries are contained in F. S. Regs., Part II. and the Staff Manual respectively. Title pages will be prepared in manuscript.

Places	Date	Hour	Summary of Events and Information	Remarks and references to Appendices
Degueaker	May 9/15	8.30 A.M.	left for new billets at WATOU.	
WATOU	May 16	10.30 A.M.	arrived at billets lieust Mondeieur Jonghe	
VLAMERTINGHE	May 19	6.30 A.M.	Battery Commander Capt. K.L. Yeaman went forward to reconnoitre a position for the guns from a position with Right section on South of the Reuleu Rly + Left section on North side of park, Belgium 1.16.A.0.6. from which came be viewed zone from 1.6.B to 1.M.B. The Battery left WATOU under Capt Common + arrived at VLAMERTINGHE at 6 p.m. + bivouacked.	Ref. map 20000 Sheet 28 N.W.
YPRES	19/20 5/15.	11.30 P.M.	The gunners were marched up to the position & parapets were made in the hedge with sand bags + shelters for the detachments.	
	20 5/15		Occupied the day cutting concealment + finishing gun pits, the guns were brought up to places under cover of dark. F.B. Wagons were put in an old barn behind the Battery. 100 rounds were put in each gun pit. Zone allotted J 13 a. 4.5. to J 13 D. 5. v. B.C. observing station Reulway Bridge 1.16a.6.9 from which point could be seen hut 55 + graves in between.	Sheet 28 NE
	21/15	6.0 A.M.	Zone allotted 16a.8.9. the Reulers Railway. I found it necessary to change observing point from one at crossing 1-C.1.7 less were along the Reulway at dusk + got communications with the Battery.	

Army Form C. 2118.

WAR DIARY
or
INTELLIGENCE SUMMARY.
(Erase heading not required.)

Instructions regarding War Diaries and Intelligence Summaries are contained in F. S. Regs., Part II. and the Staff Manual respectively. Title pages will be prepared in manuscript.

Place	Date	Hour	Summary of Events and Information	Remarks and references to Appendices
YPRES.	19/3/15	10.0 AM	Allotted new zone which necessitates a move of observing station, was ordered to co-operate with 11th & 13th no Batteries A.30 1st Brigade new zone T.13.a.7.0 to T.13.a.7.8	
		6 p.m.	Observing station moves back to Railway Bridge 1.16 a 6.9 telephone communication with Buses & HQS establishes also O.P. in L.13.y no Battery	
	22/3/15	3 AM	Germans guess our front trenches from north of ROULERS Railway were offered by it at observation station. I was offered, although using a syphon, which was of the better wood type & got too sudden to breath through, in about ten minutes	
		3.5 AM	Opened fire 3 rounds p.m. fire every 1/5 minutes on zone T.13.a.7.0 & T.13.a.7.8	
		3.25 AM	Reduces rate of fire to section fire one minute. German attack still continuing continues this rate of fire for about 3 hours with occasional stops of 15 minutes	
		5.30 AM	Fire reduced to distinction fire 15 minutes was unopposed to leave my observation station owing to sharp fire the Germans were shelling I frome a fresh station behind the Battery 19 d 5.4 from where I could see HOOGE a whole of ammo 1.16.	
		6.30 AM	Capt. L.A. Brown brought up fresh supply of ammunition.	

WAR DIARY
or
INTELLIGENCE SUMMARY.

Army Form C. 2118.

Place	Date	Hour	Summary of Events and Information	Remarks and references to Appendices
YPRES.	23/5/15	10.0 AM	Receives message from 131 Battery forward observer in trenches in SANCTUARY Wood. that Germans were advancing from WEST front of BELLEWAARDE LAKE. Orders all guns 7 deg more Right. drop 800 3 rounds. Gun fire every 1/2 minute.	
		10.50 AM	Slightly switched back to target A. (original zone) Rate fire 15 minutes.	
		11.30 AM	Receives message to turn on to BELLEWAARDE LAKE again.	
		Noon	Receives orders from Col. EMORY 1st C.R.A. to take the Battery out of action as the Germans has advanced to within 1500 yards of the Battery position.	
		1.0 pm	Retires one gun at a time.	
		1.30 pm	Last gun left Position. No casualties.	
		5.30 pm	Battery reaches wagon lines.	
VLAMERTINGHE	24/5/15		Remains in wagon lines.	
	25/5/15	10 pm	Receives orders to take the Battery into action to relieve 30th + Battery R.J.A.	
	26/5/15	1.30 AM	Took over position 131 d. 5.4 gone altered 1.30 to 7.3 to 1.30 d.o.8. Telephone communication has found it impossible to register till our first and second Batteries hun trenches Infantry trenches of zone north of zone segment. Part of the 2nd Brigade.	

Army Form C. 2118.

WAR DIARY
or
INTELLIGENCE SUMMARY.
(Erase heading not required.)

Instructions regarding War Diaries and Intelligence Summaries are contained in F. S. Regs., Part II. and the Staff Manual respectively. Title pages will be prepared in manuscript.

Place	Date	Hour	Summary of Events and Information	Remarks and references to Appendices
YPRES.	25/5/15	1.30pm	Attempted to form telephone communication forward. Observer in trench S 4 30 a 9.3 unsatisfactory, sent lineman out & repaired line	
	26/5/15	10 pm	Sent communication through to forward observer & registered	
	27/5/15	1.30 pm	Finished registration A 9 30 min E L Cott 16.2 No 1 5550 No 2 5800 No 3 5750	
			No.4 5900	
	28/5/15		Quiet all day	
	29/5/15		Quiet all day	
	30/5/15		Quiet all day. Fired two rounds to verify Concealer 10.30 A.M	
	31/5/15	9 P.M	79th Batt. relieves our left Sector which retires to waggon lines at VLAMMERTINGHE.	

121/6735

50th Division

3rd Durham Battery (3rd Northumbrian Bde) R.F.A.

Vol II — 1 — 30.6.15.

a2
a/6

Army Form C. 2118

WAR DIARY
or
INTELLIGENCE SUMMARY
(Erase heading not required.)

Instructions regarding War Diaries and Intelligence Summaries are contained in F.S. Regs., Part II. and the Staff Manual respectively. Title Pages will be prepared in manuscript.

Place	Date	Hour	Summary of Events and Information	Remarks and references to Appendices
YPRES.	1/6/15	9 P.M.	29th Battery relieves our Right Section which returned to Wagon lines at VLAMMERTINGHE.	
	2/6/15	12 noon	Wagon lines Right Section left for [?] ABEELE	
	3/6/15	9 P.M.	Left Section relieved & [?] Waggon lines at ABEELE	
	4/6/15		at Wagon lines.	
	5/6/15	10 P.M.	Left section under Lt. G.F. JOHNSON relieves one section of 29th Battery at 13d.	
	6/6/15	3:30pm	Left section registeres zone 13d 7.3 to 13od.0.8	
		9:30pm	Right section relieves remaining section of 29th Battery	
	7/6/15	1. P.M.	Right section registers ranges as before on [?]	
	8/6/15		quiet day	
	9/6/15	10 PM	Right Section went forward to new position I.27.a.8.10.	
	10/6/15	10 PM	Left section went forward to new position	
	11/6/15		Strength to position	
	12/6/15	3:30pm	Registered 3 gun zone covers Tigers, to Tige 6.9 Corrects to 3850.	
			[?] 4 No 2 gun had been damaged on Whit Monday & was not reliable reported this gun out of action	

Army Form C. 2118

WAR DIARY
or
INTELLIGENCE SUMMARY
(Erase heading not required.)

Instructions regarding War Diaries and Intelligence Summaries are contained in F.S. Regs., Part II. and the Staff Manual respectively. Title Pages will be prepared in manuscript.

Place	Date	Hour	Summary of Events and Information	Remarks and references to Appendices
YPRES.	13/7/15	7.30pm	Requires No 11 gun. Corrects 160. 3880.	
	14/7/15		No 2 gun taken out & sent to 1.O.M.	
	15/7/15		Quiet	
	16/7/15		"	
	17/7/15	10.30pm	No 2.5 gun returned.	
	18/7/15	7.30am	British attack on HOOGE. 3rd Battery was in reserve but was not called on.	
		4.5pm	Requires No 4 gun Corrt 156 & 3,700.	
	19/7/15	5.45am	Fires 11 rounds to verify requires.	
	20/7/15		Quiet	
	21/7/15	9.P.M.	Right Section relieves by section from 64 Staffordshire Battery.	
LOCRE.	22/7/15	6.45AM.	Left wagon lines to rest camp near LOCRE.	
		9.A.M.	Arrives rest camp.	
		7.P.M.	Left to relieve section 2nd line Battery in action near NEUVE EGLISE.	
NEUVE EGLISE	23/7/15	1AM	Left section in position to replace section of the section in action near Kennedy	

WAR DIARY
or
INTELLIGENCE SUMMARY.
(Erase heading not required.)

Army Form C. 2118.

Instructions regarding War Diaries and Intelligence Summaries are contained in F. S. Regs., Part II. and the Staff Manual respectively. Title pages will be prepared in manuscript.

Place	Date	Hour	Summary of Events and Information	Remarks and references to Appendices
NEUVE EGLISE	23/6/15	12 noon	Right section fired 2 rounds to register line RAB.	
		9 pm	Left section arrived to relieve section 2nd Lines Battery. Major Heanrau ill RAB.	
	24/6/15	3:30 pm	Left section fired 3 rounds to register line RAB. Battery zone N 36 d 2.8 — N 36 d 8.4 RAB. Quiet RAB	
	26/6/15	4 pm	17 rounds fired to register corrector 160 Range R x 4000 Left x 4°30' A.S. 15' elevation RAB.	
	2/7/15		Quiet RAB	
	28/6/15	11:30 am	12 Rounds percussion fired to test effect of direct hits on trenches Rd x 3875 RAB	
	29/6/15	12:45 pm	2 Rounds fired to empty guns. Major Heanrau taken to hospital RAB. Zone altered to N 36 d 5.3 — N 36 d 2.7 covering trenches D1, D2 held by 6th Northumberland Fusiliers. 6 rounds fired to register new zone RAB	
	30/6/15		Quiet. Telephonists engaged in altering wires to new trenches & Battalion Headquarters RAB.	

50th Division

121/6568

3rd Durham Battery (8hoth 4th Bde) RFA.

Vol III

From 1st to 31st July 1915

Army Form C. 2118.

WAR DIARY
or
INTELLIGENCE SUMMARY.
(Erase heading not required.)

Instructions regarding War Diaries and Intelligence Summaries are contained in F. S. Regs., Part II. and the Staff Manual respectively. Title pages will be prepared in manuscript.

Place	Date	Hour	Summary of Events and Information	Remarks and references to Appendices
NEUVE EGLISE	1/7/15	4.40AM	4 rounds fired to test effect on charge of resuming in breech all night. Difference negligible	RAL
	2/7/15	6pm	4 rounds fired covering zone. Proceed fired on ENFER WOOD.	RAL
			8 rounds fired on working party reported at O.25.d.2.4.	RAL
	3/7/15		Quiet. Infantry occupying D1 & D2 trenches. 5th Border Regiment. Arranged alternative communication by means of signalling lamp for trenches.	RAL
		10pm	Tested lamp. Satisfactory.	RAL
	4/7/15	4pm	13 rounds fired on zone.	RAL
	5/7/15	2.30p	Test S.O.S. signal from trenches	RAL
	6/7/15	11.15AM	Working party at O.25.d & 3.04 registered	RAL
		9pm	Fired at working party	RAL
	7/7/15		Quiet	RAL
	8/7/15		Quiet	RAL
	9/7/15		Quiet	RAL
	10/7/15	5.30pm	Registered O.31.B 5.6 Farm	RAL
	11/7/15	11.15AM	Fired a few rounds at O.31.B 5.6	RAL
	12/7/15	1.15PM	S.O.S. Test from D2 trench	RAL

Army Form C. 2118.

WAR DIARY
or
INTELLIGENCE SUMMARY.

(Erase heading not required.)

Instructions regarding War Diaries and Intelligence Summaries are contained in F.S. Regs., Part II. and the Staff Manual respectively. Title pages will be prepared in manuscript.

Place	Date	Hour	Summary of Events and Information	Remarks and references to Appendices
NEUVE EGLISE	12/7/15	2 PM	Commenced digging reserve position. RAB	
	13/7/15	11.15AM	Test S.O.S. D1 trench. Infantry reported communications good. Shell heard 29 seconds after signal.	
		5 PM	Spal gunners working on reserve position. RAB Registered Rifle grenade battery opposite Trench D1. RAB	
	14/7/15		Quiet. RAB	
	15/7/15	11.15AM	Acting on information received from 5th Durham Right Infantry in Trench D1 engaged & silenced grenade battery. RAB	
		7 PM	Again fired at grenade battery. RAB	
	16/7/15	3.30PM	Fired at grenade battery. 5 wished working at reserve position. RAB	
		6.30PM	Fired at Grenade Battery. RAB	
	17/7/15	5.6 PM	Emptied guns	
		9 PM	Withdrew battery to waggon lines. RAB	
	18/7/15		At Waggon lines	
		8 PM	Moved to Waggon lines at PONT DE NIEPPE. RAB	
PONT DE	19/7/15		At Waggon Lines RAB	
NIEPPE	20/7/15		At Waggon Lines RAB	

Army Form C. 2118.

WAR DIARY
or
INTELLIGENCE SUMMARY.
(Erase heading not required.)

Instructions regarding War Diaries and Intelligence Summaries are contained in F. S. Regs., Part II. and the Staff Manual respectively. Title pages will be prepared in manuscript.

Place	Date	Hour	Summary of Events and Information	Remarks and references to Appendices
PONT DE NIEPPE	21/7/15		at waggon lines in reserve Pal	
	22/7/15		at waggon lines Pal	
	23/7/15		at waggon lines Pal	
	24/7/15		at waggon lines Pal	
	25/7/15		at waggon lines Pal	
	26/7/15		at waggon lines Pal	
	27/7/15		at waggon lines Pal	
	28/7/15		at waggon lines Pal	
	29/7/15		at waggon lines Pal	
	30/7/15	7.30 p.m.	at waggon lines to 2nd NORTHUMBERLAND Bty. Pal	
	31/7/15		at waggon lines Pal	

121/6743

50th Division

No 3 Durham Battery RFA.

Vol IV

August 15

Army Form C. 2118.

WAR DIARY
of
INTELLIGENCE SUMMARY.
(Erase heading not required.)

Instructions regarding War Diaries and Intelligence Summaries are contained in F. S. Regs., Part II. and the Staff Manual respectively. Title pages will be prepared in manuscript.

Place	Date	Hour	Summary of Events and Information	Remarks and references to Appendices
PONT DE NIEPPE	1/8/15		At waggon lines. Lt. P.M. Rickslaber attached joined	
	2/8/15		At waggon lines. D Bruer lent to 1st Northumbrian Bde	
	3/8/15		At waggon lines	
	4/8/15		At waggon lines. D Gun returned. C guns sent to Northumbrian Bde	
	5/8/15		At waggon lines. D Gun lent to 1st Northumbrian Bde	
	6/8/15		At waggon lines. Lt. S. Dickinson attached joined. A Gun lent to 2nd Northumbrian Bde	
	7/8/15		Moved waggon lines work of PONT DE NIEPPE	
	8/8/15		At new waggon lines	
	9/8/15		At waggon lines	
	10/8/15		At waggon lines	
	11/8/15		At waggon lines	
	12/8/15		At waggon lines	
	13/8/15		At waggon lines	
	14/8/15		At waggon lines	
ARMENTIERES	15/8/15	8 pm	Right Section relieved section of 3rd NORTH RIDING BTY in action near ARMENTIERES. Personnel only. A gun taken over	
	16/8/15	8 pm	Left Section relieved remaining section of 3rd NORTH RIDING BTY	
	17/8/15	Noon	2nd. Right Section registered BLACK REDOUBT	
	18/8/15	5 PM	Registered zone I 5 c 9.0 to I 5 & 4i.	
	19/8/15		Fired on Enemy trenches. Enemy shelling houses on left rear. Two enemy batteries replied with H.E. from direction of L'AVENTURE & PREMESQUES. They fired 35 rounds. Two	Position C 26 d. 8.50 Ref sheet 36 N.W. Enemy 2 amplitude 2 joined

Army Form C. 2118.

WAR DIARY
or
INTELLIGENCE SUMMARY.

(Erase heading not required.)

Instructions regarding War Diaries and Intelligence Summaries are contained in F.S. Regs., Part II. and the Staff Manual respectively. Title pages will be prepared in manuscript.

Place	Date	Hour	Summary of Events and Information	Remarks and references to Appendices
ARMENTIERES	19/8/15	12 noon	Guns direct Rds on gun emplacements. Nobournalles R&G	
	20/8/15		Quiet R&G	
	21/8/15		Quiet R&G	
	22/8/15	5 pm	R&G Divns assisting 3RD NOTTS RIDING BY to prepare position at CHAPELLE D'ARMENTIERES	
	23/8/15		Retaliated on enemy trenches opposite 75 Trench which was getting too troublesome R&G	
	24/8/15		Quiet R&G Raying wires to new positions R&G	
	25/8/15	6.30AM	Quiet R&G	
			3 Detachments sent to new position at CHAPELLE D'ARMENTIERES to take over 2nd DURHAM BATTERY GUNS placed in position by 2nd Northumbrian Bde the night before. Position I.8.a. 7.9½ R&G Sheet 36 N.W. R&G	
		12.45 PM	Registered guns on trenches opposite 79 § 80 R&G	
		10.45 PM	Fired at B'Gazer 029 9 6 dispersed working party R&G	
	26/8/15		Quiet	
		9 PM	Registering detachment. A gun being relieved came into action R&G Goods over new zone opposite trench 79 § 80 R&G	
	27/8/15	3.15 PM	Registered part of XII DIVISION zone on left opposite trench 81 § 82. A German working party appeared to be at work FOUR HALLOTS FARM C.23.d.37. Who replied trenches 76.77.78.79 on right R&G THREE DECKER FARM C.23.d.81	
	28/8/15	11.2 AM	Fired on 79 Trench	
		3 PM	Registered 74.75.76.	
			A great deal of dust in front of guns owing to the firing across a railway. This was eventually overcome by putting down Willesden canvas in front of R&G	

Army Form C. 2118.

WAR DIARY
or
INTELLIGENCE SUMMARY.
(Erase heading not required.)

Instructions regarding War Diaries and Intelligence Summaries are contained in F. S. Regs., Part II. and the Staff Manual respectively. Title pages will be prepared in manuscript.

Place	Date	Hour	Summary of Events and Information	Remarks and references to Appendices
CHAPELLE D'ARMENTIERES	28/8/15		wangles & covering this with strips of expanded metal which served the double purpose of keeping the canvas in place & also by absorbing much of the heat prevented its being scorched. RAB	
	29/8/15	2.30PM	Quiet. Fired at dugouts behind trenches which appeared to be Battalion Headquarters. RAB	
	30/8/15	8.30PM	Exchanged No 3 & 2nd Bty gun for our own C Gun just back from Ordnance. RAB B Gun returned to wagon lines from Ordnance. RAB	
	31/8/15	11 AM	Retaliated on Trenches opposite 80 which was being intensely sniped. RAB	

R.H. Owens Capt
3rd Bde Batty 1 Fd(?)

www.ingramcontent.com/pod-product-compliance
Lightning Source LLC
Chambersburg PA
CBHW081754220426
43649CB00038BA/3327